DUBAI

The Epicenter of Modern Innovation

A Guide to Implementing Innovation Strategies

T0299145

DUBAI

The Epicenter of Modern Innovation

A Guide to Implementing Innovation Strategies

Dr. William R. "Buzz" Kennedy
Dr. Aaron G. "Sandy" Amacher
Dr. Gregory C. McLaughlin

CRC Press
Taylor & Francis Group
Boca Raton London New York

CRC Press is an imprint of the
Taylor & Francis Group, an **informa** business

A PRODUCTIVITY PRESS BOOK

CRC Press
Taylor & Francis Group
6000 Broken Sound Parkway NW, Suite 300
Boca Raton, FL 33487-2742

First issued in paperback 2021

ISBN-13: 978-1-4987-5809-3 (hbk)
ISBN-13: 978-1-03-217925-4 (pbk)
DOI: 10.1201/9781315367828

Library of Congress Cataloging-in-Publication Data

Names: Kennedy, William R., 1960- author. | Amacher, Aaron G., author. | McLaughlin, Gregory C., author.
Title: Dubai--the epicenter of modern innovation : a guide to implementing innovation strategies / William R. Kennedy, Aaron G. Amacher, and Gregory C. McLaughlin.
Description: Boca Raton, FL : CRC Press, 2017. | Includes bibliographical references and index.
Identifiers: LCCN 2016036663 | ISBN 9781498758093 (hard back : alk. paper)
Subjects: LCSH: Technological innovations--United Arab Emirates--Dubai. | Diffusion of innovations--United Arab Emirates--Dubai. | Dubai (United Arab Emirates)--Economic policy. | Dubai (United Arab Emirates)--Social policy. | Dubai (United Arab Emirates)--History.
Classification: LCC HC415.36.Z7 D8354 2017 | DDC 338/.064095357--dc23
LC record available at https://lccn.loc.gov/2016036663

Visit the Taylor & Francis Web site at
http://www.taylorandfrancis.com

and the CRC Press Web site at
http://www.crcpress.com

Contents

List of Figures

List of Tables

Preface

From the dawn of recorded history, the one element that has distinguished human beings from all other life forms on this planet has been their relentless desire to change things, for whatever reason; you can chalk it up to curiosity, you can say we want to find an easier way, or you can say it is in our DNA. Some might even say it was given to us by some higher power as we seek a path to perfection (and we can let the theologians, anthropologists, and agnostics argue this position until the end of time). However, the fact still remains that we, as a species, have an innate craving and apparent unending desire to make things better, to improve our condition and the condition of others, to find a better way, to find unique solutions to problems, to make things easier, or to simplify our lives. In a single word, we INNOVATE!

Although there are more than 60 internationally accepted definitions of what innovation is, one might contend that a short and succinct definition of innovation is any product, process, or service that is new, changed, or improved. However, innovation is far more complex than just the introduction of new methods and ideas or new gadgets at one particular point in time. It broadens our mind and opens the aperture of thought, exponentially expanding the realm of possibilities. In order to get to this singular point or stage, one must consider the genesis of true innovation. With a complex genealogy of combinations and connections built by the shared ideas and experiences of multiple people expressed over extended periods, the information shared (explicit to tacit) and new knowledge generated (tacit to explicit) across multiple domains has evolved into a robust ecosystem connected by seemingly infinite pathways of learning and information exchange. These ideas and experiences merge to form enclaves of knowledge and information, which can then become the foundation of base data from which individuals can draw stimulus when encountering situations in which they see opportunities or visions to improve.

Innovation is a direct result of curiosity and stimulus. It requires a fertile environment in which there is typically a process of nurturing, a process of thought (thinking), and one of supporting a perceivable vision of a different reality of something better. But these visions of a different reality are not easily or readily recognizable and require fertile ground to be nurtured and wide screens to be projected on, as well as multitudes of inquisitive, creative, and insanely imaginative people to work on them. Methodologies like N²OVATE™ were designed and structured to stimulate the innovation process.

In observations of early world history, it can be seen that the progress and investment in visions of pioneering innovation were limited primarily due to the lack of universal information exchange. It was not until the invention of the Gutenberg press, which unleashed the exchange of information, that the very notion of innovation was revolutionized and the real march toward modern innovation initiated. Now, with the ability to exchange massive amounts of information at the stroke of a key, the world is enjoying unfettered access to a deluge of information and the movement of collective, cooperative massive innovation. The first critical mass of innovation introduced the dawn of the Industrial Revolution and led to the sunset of agrarian society as the defining way of life. In essence, the Industrial Revolution drove a major societal structure transformation whereby a large segment of the world's farming industry was moved by the promise and inspiration of city manufacturing.

The Industrial Revolution subsequently delivered on its promising preamble of expectations, delivering major innovations such as harnessing the power of steam, the production of multiple-loom textile mills, and the development of massive steel mills. These changes brought creative celebration and divergent thinking about the ability to provide for mass-production techniques, new construction methodologies to allow buildings to be built taller and stronger, and the notion and concept of massing human resources in clusters and concentrations never before seen. This convergence of human resources and assemblage of contrasting views became a bountiful pathway for the free exchange of ideas and the acceleration of innovative ideas and products. The resulting outcome was the proliferation of goods and services provided to the masses throughout the world. It also promoted increased standards of living and enjoyment, while further stimulating the formation of visions and the creation of ways of thinking geared toward continuous process improvement.

From the early days of the Industrial Revolution, the advent of change as a norm in our daily lives was a new concept. The thought of innovation as a common word in our lexicon of everyday life kindled the mindset and mechanical ways of thinking that moved us into a graduated realm of more complex issues. We began to think beyond the single dimension and more toward the realm of how components (elements) of a system contribute to the greater whole (i.e., the collective of elements that contribute to a system). This led to innovation within systems and information manipulation. As a logical outgrowth of the systems view and information manipulation, pockets or clusters of communities were direct recipients of the Japanese and Korean quality innovation revolution, Silicon Valley's information age or computer revolution, and now, the innovation revolution. Whether it's worthy of a coined term or simply a result of evolutionary nature, the global community is now witnessing a country and city willing to go "all in" to establish and pronounce itself as the epicenter of modern innovation. Once known for its role as an integral part of the Fertile Crescent, the incredible transformation of the United Arab Emirates, and particularly of Dubai, is truly revolutionary and worthy of the preeminent designation as "The Epicenter of the Modern Innovation Revolution."

This book will attempt to take the reader through the construct of this new innovative revolution, particularly in Dubai, and provide a bird's-eye view of how it came about. Most notably, the discussion will walk the reader through key milestones instrumental to Dubai's success—such as the present and past leadership, culture, strategy, and strategic vision. In addition, the discussion will present an agile and progressive approach to building and leading a successful innovation team through to a successful project outcome and the attributes of good innovation leadership.

The discussion will wrap up with an exordium to a pioneering set of market-sector agnostic and agile tools, techniques, and suggested methodologies that will arm any organization (i.e., profit, nonprofit, or governmental) with the capability to enhance their current enterprise-level innovation culture and environment. The N²OVATE™ methodology is also a dynamic and tailorable innovation project management approach that was designed, proved, and verified through actual application and case studies. Serving as a roadmap and blueprint for achieving sustainable innovation opportunity and project management success, the N²OVATE™ methodology is flexible in its application and adaptable to any organization's existing innovation management processes. It was also designed to function as a first-string or stand-alone approach for leading and managing innovation opportunities to a successful outcome. On a final note, the enhanced tools and techniques offered under the N²OVATE™ umbrella will have a game-changing impact on any organization's collective journey toward paradigm busting and innovation transformation success!

The future belongs to those who innovate, and is lost to those who stagnate!

Dr. Aaron G. "Sandy" Amacher

Acknowledgments

Dr. Kennedy: To my wife (Jannette), for her enduring inspiration, support, love, and understanding throughout our lives together. I am truly blessed. To my family (Darell, Samantha, Will, Shea, Rey, Dialano, Aniya, Michael, Emma, and Sasha) for their steadfast love, support, and encouragement. To my mother, Mary Elizabeth Kennedy, and my father, Paul Edward Kennedy. Without their exemplary courage, unconditional love, and the wisdom they shared throughout my life, I would not have the faith, core values, and beliefs that formed the very basis of who I am today. To my sisters Carol and Susan, for their love, sage advice, and continued support in my writing endeavors.

I would like to thank my very close friend, brother, and business partner, Dr. Greg McLaughlin. His unwavering core values, spiritual beliefs, and sage consult coupled with his visionary thinking on innovation and an integrity-based approach to business are central components of what makes us a great team. To Dr. Sandy Amacher, whose in-depth knowledge, understanding, and exemplary track record for leading and implementing successful innovative solutions across the international community was instrumental in delivering a turn-key approach for public and private industries to succeed in their innovation endeavors. I look forward to working with both of these innovation pioneers in further developing value-added methodologies in the innovation arena!

To Song Amacher and Geraldine Salonoy for their support and contributions in completing this work. To all my friends and business associates over the years who have contributed to my development as a leader and individual and to my work in developing value-added contributions to the innovation body of knowledge. Thank you.

Dr. Amacher: To my loving and supportive wife, Song, who has provided me with lifelong inspiration through her dedication to self-improvement and her innovations in the world of art and literature, and her never-ending pursuit of new ideas in all her endeavors. To my son, Dr. Aaron III, and daughter Liana, who gratefully have taken after their mother and continue their pursuit of excellence and innovation in their chosen fields.

Special thanks to HRH Sheik Mohammed bin Rashid Al Maktoum, for his deft leadership and inspiration to me for his vision and his commitment to innovation and excellence. To Staff Brigadier General Hassan Mohammad Bani Hammad, Commander of the United Arab Emirates (UAE) Land Forces, 5th Brigade, Training Brigade and the Land Forces Institute, for his eternal friendship and brotherhood and his insight into the history, culture, and the proper protocols of the Emirati people. To Staff Major General Saeed Mabkhoot Louteya Al Ameri, UAE Land Forces Chief of Staff and General Officer, General Headquarters (GHQ) UAE Military, for his tutelage and deft advice on my first arriving in the UAE and his dedication to innovation and transformation within the UAE Land Forces. To Staff Brigadier General Mubarak Saeed Al Jabri, Chief of Communications and Information Technology and former Armaments Director at Land Forces, for his personal enduring friendship, his great intellect, and for sharing his deft understanding of state of innovation into the Industrial Base of the UAE. To Staff Lieutenant General Juma Ahmed Al Bawardi Al Falasi, Adviser to Deputy Supreme Commander of the Armed Forces, Commander of the Land Forces, and Commander of the Special Operations Command (SOC), for his example and understanding of the true nature of innovation and transformation within organizations, and his willingness to demonstrate true leadership during change; and in his support of my efforts to support him. To Ashok and Manju Puri, chairman and managing director (respectively) of the MGT Group Dubai, for their friendship and business association, and their many introductions to the elite within the UAE and Dubai world of business and government leaders. For their special insight and input into their corporate innovation initiatives, I especially thank, Mr. Nanab Shaji Ul Mulk, Chairman, Mulk Group and Mr. Paras Shahdaadpuri, Chairman, Nikai Group, both innovative business leaders currently doing business in Dubai. To Buzz and Greg, my coauthors, who helped me understand the true synergies and business power of the correlation and integration of the concepts, methodologies, ideas, and tools that have made this book possible.

To my siblings, Daphne, Grant, Mark, and Alison, for their love, support, and wisdom sharing.

To Geraldine Salonoy, researcher, technical editor, and professional engineer, for her tireless efforts in support of the creation of this book and the materials it contains.

Finally, to all those business associates and friends over the years who have contributed so much to my growth and understanding of how to affect change and introduce innovation within organizations and myself.

Dr. McLaughlin: I, Dr. Gregory C. McLaughlin, would like to especially thank Dr. William (Buzz) Kennedy for all the hard work in assembling and managing this manuscript. Having a business partner such as Buzz makes the experience so rewarding.

In addition, I would like to thank my wife, Dr. Heidi McLaughlin, for her love and support during the writing of this book.

I would also like to thank the students, administration, and instructors of the MBA Healthcare Program at Florida International University for their assistance and help in evaluating the Dubai case study in December 2015. Their response was overwhelmingly positive.

The book cover was designed and created by Chongsoon Song Amacher, BS Art and Visual Technology, George Mason University, VA, USA.

Authors

William R. "Buzz" Kennedy is currently an independent consultant and managing partner at IPS Consulting. He is an internationally renowned author and award-winning organizational leader with over 30 years' experience in the public and private sector. Buzz has an extensive background in leadership and management with a proven track record of success leading world-class business strategy development, organizational culture, and change management efforts across multiple industries. He is considered a subject-matter expert in executive and organizational leadership, government and aerospace program and project management, information technology and aircraft platform management, acquisition, and international procurement. He has led several pioneering strategy and innovation development initiatives in the aircraft, manufacturing and production, and maintenance management disciplines (using Six Sigma, Agile, Lean manufacturing, and Lean supply chain management methodologies).

His educational achievements include a doctorate in business administration (DBA) from Capella University, a master's degree in secondary education from Grand Canyon University, and a bachelor's degree in business management from the University of Maryland. His latest publications are *A Guide to Innovation Processes and Solutions for Government* (2015) and the *Innovation Project Management Handbook* (2016), which he cowrote with his good friend Dr. Greg McLaughlin.

Aaron "Sandy" Amacher brings over 40 years of experience in highly diverse and competitive organizations. Sandy's talents and proficiency in leadership, management, logistics, systems engineering, and information technology as well as in program and project management provides a solid base in support of customer requirements. Dr. Amacher currently resides and works in the city of Dubai and has spent the last six years in the United Arab Emirates completing projects of national interest in the United Arab Emirates and other Middle East and African countries. Throughout his career, Sandy has engineered management and information systems for both business and government. The strategies he developed for these systems incorporated the fielding, conducting, and expanding of his customers' management, business, quality, information technology, and leadership efforts. During his military career, he served in command and staff positions of combat and joint command units, from platoon to division, and with organizations involved with space operations. He led integrated logistics support (ILS) for a $250 million space logistics remote-site contact in support of worldwide space program operations and strategic defense initiatives. Dr. Amacher has received special recognition and numerous awards for his work from many companies and government agencies, such as the White House, United States Postal Service, Office of Secretary of Defense, United States Army and United States Air Force, Aerospace Industries Association, Lockheed Martin, Black and Decker, Rockwell International, Colorado Conference of Quality, Mark Industries, and many others. Dr. Amacher served as adjunct faculty member to Texas A&M University in their Executive Program, teaching Logistics and Quality Management. He is recognized both in *Who's Who Worldwide in Business Leaders* and in *Who's Who in Quality* and is a frequent guest speaker and presenter.

Greg McLaughlin is a managing partner at Innovation Processes and Solutions (IPS), LLC. Greg brings a broad set of technical and practical skills in quality improvement, innovation, and data analysis. Beginning as an analyst, he progressed quickly to the director of research at a Fortune 200 company. Refining his skills in continuous quality improvement, he worked for Dr. W. Edwards Deming as an instructor/consultant. Greg authored a book for research and development in organizations (*Total Quality in Research*

and Development, 1995) committed to quality improvement. He was an early adopter of Six Sigma and worked for many years as a Six Sigma Senior Master Black Belt, saving organizations over $300 million. Many projects resulted in innovative products and services. His most accomplished skill is in interpreting data and finding a practical application. He can look beyond the numbers to find a solution to complex problems. His skill set organically transitioned into developing innovation strategies, deployment, and sustained success as evidenced by the creation of the ENOVALE™ and N²OVATE™ methodologies. He maintains a leadership role in developing training, tools, books, and publications for both practitioners and scholars. His latest publications are *Chance or Choice: Unlocking Innovation Success* (2013) and *Enovale: Unlocking Innovation Project Success* (October 2013), *Leading Latino Talent to Champion Innovation* (2014), *Unlocking Sustained Innovation Success in Healthcare* (2014), *A Guide to Innovation Processes and Solutions in Government* (2015), the *Innovation Project Management Handbook* (2015), and *Innovation Processes and Solutions for Innovation Project Success: A Workbook* (2015).

His educational achievements include a doctorate in business administration (DBA) from Nova Southeastern University, a master of science degree in statistics from Florida State University, and an undergraduate degree in meteorology from Florida State University. Greg was the director of doctoral research at Nova Southeastern University and was instrumental in creating an innovative dissertation process for the DBA degree at Capella University. Since its creation, the DBA program is the largest and most profitable doctoral program in Capella University's history.

Chapter 1

The Pearl of the Arab World: Inspiring a Culture of Transformational and Sustainable Innovation

The best way to predict your future is to create it.

Abraham Lincoln

Innovation is the key that unlocks the future's potential!

Dr. Aaron "Sandy" Amacher

Introduction

For the last three centuries, mankind has been moving at an unprecedented pace in creating the world of the future. Many would agree that this unprecedented rate of change was initiated by the innovation of a simple device called the Gutenberg press. For the first time, this simple device allowed mankind to register, share, and communalize tacit and explicit knowledge while igniting the generation of new knowledge over a wide spectrum of the world's population. The proliferation of books, manuscripts, and other printed material became not only the nexus for sharing and learning at its origin but also for the sharing of knowledge beyond the geographical

1

boundaries that separated diverse populations, cultures, and nations. The introduction of this simple but revolutionary innovation and change in technology also ushered in a new era of learning in which an increasing number of inquisitive minds across the world's populations would not only share their creative ideas but also, more importantly, build on the innovations and creations created by others. This allowed for the breaking of existing paradigms in the movement out of millenniums of imagination and innovation stagnation. In his book titled *The Structure of Scientific Revolution* (1962), Thomas Kuhn introduced the term *paradigm shift*. Kuhn's premise was that paradigms act as patterns, which we use to control the way we view the world and new information coming in. In effect, paradigms create a box in which we are comfortable in thinking, acting, and controlling. However, there is a downside to paradigms in that they also restrict our ability to see new and innovative ways that can improve our lives and change the future. Joel Barker elaborated on Kuhn's work in his 1989 video *The Business of Paradigms*. Barker demonstrated one of Kuhn's examples of how paradigms can physically prevent people seeing new information or innovative ways. He did this by using a simple deck of cards and rapidly showing a series of seven cards to groups of individuals. However, within the set of cards, which contained the normal red diamonds, red hearts, black spades, and black clubs, a few of the cards were changed so that there were red spades and red clubs along with black diamonds and black hearts. As the audience viewed the cards flashed rapidly before their eyes, they were aptly able to discern the legitimate cards (i.e., red hearts and diamonds, black spades and clubs) very rapidly, but those cards that did not match their paradigm of what a normal card deck should look like (i.e., black diamonds and hearts and red clubs and spades) were not readily identifiable by the individuals. These people physically could not see those cards because they didn't match the paradigm that they had in their head. Barker's comment was that in some cases, as Kuhn stated, paradigms block new information and innovation from taking place.

The Gutenberg press and the knowledge transfer that it affected acted as the major catalyst for pushing the world into breaking the agrarian paradigm that has persisted for millenniums. It provided a course for evolutionary decision paradigms, which created revolutions in thinking and inventions and the future changing of decision paradigms key to innovation. Decision-making paradigms have evolved in much the same manner as mankind has evolved. For most of mankind's history, the decision-making paradigm was based on an agrarian society that traditionally based its decisions on nature.

Emblematic of the agricultural age, planting and harvesting were based on the seasons and the weather; most of people's life's decisions were based on what was happening around them on a day-to-day, season-to-season basis. The fundamental ingredient was that man or the beast of burden was the source of work.

The advent of the Industrial Revolution and the building and introduction of complex and modern machinery required a new way of making decisions. The decision-making paradigm changed as new innovations in the form of machines were introduced to replace traditional roles previously performed by humans. This machine or mechanical decision paradigm primarily dealt with the process or the replacement of the human by the machine as the source of work. But work was defined as the transformation of matter from one form to another, or the transformation of matter and energy, or the transformation of energy into one form or another. In other words, work was conceived in physical terms and, therefore, mechanization was about the use of machines to create the energy to perform physical work. Commonly referred to as the Industrial Revolution, the resulting innovative developments, such as the harnessing of steam power, offered an enticing new frontier for many developing nations. Europe and the Americas grasped the opportunity and saw a vast migration of their population from farms to urban areas to populate the factories necessary to implement the innovations of this Industrial Revolution.

As the machine-age society became more sophisticated and machines became more complex, along with the emergence of the need to integrate multiple sets of machines and humans, we gradually started to move from "machine thinking" to "systems." However, the machine decision paradigm failed to provide the necessary methodology to meet new "systems" requirements. The underlying basis for the innovation of systems thinking was totally changing the point of view to one according to which everything belongs to something greater; all elements are part of a larger whole. The result of this type of systems paradigm thinking was the true massing of industrial power in nations such as the United States, Great Britain, Germany, Japan, and Korea in the fields of electronics, shipbuilding, automotive and major manufacturing, and the production of a plethora of consumer products. The result is that the system is an indivisible whole, and it is in the difference between an indivisible part and an indivisible whole that the root of the so-called intellectual revolution, based on the information-age decision paradigm, lies.

The first essential difference is the conversion of our preoccupation with *parts* of which things are made, into the preoccupation with the *whole* and with the wholes of which they are part. This is moving us into information-age thinking and the information-age decision-making paradigm, which can be called *synthesis*. We are currently in the process of again shifting into an even more advanced decision-making paradigm, which is mental manipulation, because mental work is a manipulation of symbols, whereas physical work is a manipulation of matter. Therefore, what we have now consists of the mechanization of mental work, which we have come to call automation or the *information-technology age*. In what is yet another revolution, the information-technology age is fundamentally different from the one that preceded it. It is not merely an extension of it, because it is the mechanization of something entirely different: the mind and how the mind functions. It mechanizes what man does with his head, rather than what he does with his body, and can do it at incredible speeds with incredible accuracy.

We are starting to see a world where very large parts of everyday life and operations will be controlled by computers and the manipulation of the data to provide enterprises with their required goods and services and the ability to conduct enterprise operations. We are seeing innovations in this decision paradigm that allow computers to directly conduct business one with another, thereby removing mankind from the interface. These current innovations in the decision paradigm have found a center of gravity within the United Arab Emirates (UAE), and especially in Dubai. Here, we truly see Dubai becoming the modern epicenter of the innovation revolution.

Background

Dubai is one of seven emirates (the others being Abu Dhabi, Sharjah, Ajman, Umm al-Quwain, Fujairah, and Ras al-Khaimah) that make up the UAE. The acknowledged epicenter of wealth and innovation in the UAE, Dubai is strategically located between the East and West. This favorable geographic position has furnished a panegyric stage and iconic showcase for the enterprising visions by the vice president, prime minister, and ruler of Dubai, His Royal Highness (HRH) Sheikh Mohammed bin Rashid Al Maktoum (2016). Leveraging the pioneering vision of his father, Sheikh Rashid, Sheikh Mohammed envisioned what can best be described as a "develop for survival" approach to supplant the country's reliance on oil revenues, which are estimated to drop significantly over the next 10–30 years. Prior to oil, the central products sold in the ports of Dubai were pearls, gold, and oriental carpets. Central to Sheikh Mohammed's strategic vision (or the "vision of Dubai") is for Dubai to nucleate into the international community's leading financial-services provider, the world's largest international transportation and redistribution hub, and, ultimately, the globe's top medical tourism destination spot.

Dubai has registered many innovation successes to date in pursuit of its ultimate ambition to become the most innovative city since the documented innovative solutions introduced by ancient Rome. One notable but until recently overlooked innovation made by Rome in its early effort to expand its empire was the adjustment to the diverse geographical environments it was trying to influence. As anyone familiar with the challenges of living in an arid and generally desiccate climate will attest, foliage is a welcome site for sore eyes. In an effort to protect the growing communities on the peripheral boundaries of the city from the drifting sand dunes of the Arab Al Khali (Arabian desert), Dubai has developed forest belts made up of eucalyptus trees imported from Australia. Since its precipitation occurs generally in December and January each year, an innovative underground watering system was engineered to sustain the forest belts. In a nation where oil is cheaper than clean, consumable water, Dubai, like its Emirati partners and neighbors (i.e., Qatar, Saudi Arabia, Oman, and Yemen) on the Arabian Peninsula, face a different set of challenges, which they are navigating with incremental success.

While typical Americans and the Western world recognize Sunday as the day of rest, in the Middle East, it is Friday. Thanks to the exemption from duties, commodities such as gold and jewelry are much cheaper than what one would find in the United States or Europe. Alcohol, although shunned in most of the Middle East and North Africa (MENA) region, can be acquired, but it is expensive and requires significant paperwork through government channels and is not a favorite of the host nation's culture.

When drilling for water, they found oil. One innovative idea was born when the Dubai Petroleum Company (2016) faced the daunting dilemma of where to store large quantities of oil cultivated from the shallow waters off the shore of Dubai. The solution was truly innovative and resulted in the building of large portable storage tanks that stored the harvested oil from the offshore oil fields of Fetah, Falah, and Rashid. This was truly a logistics innovation, as it allowed tankers to be filled near the source offshore, reducing time and the potential congestion common to most ports (Figure 1.1).

Figure 1.1   Early offshore oil field storage tank. (From Dubai Petroleum, Early off-shore oil field storage tank. Retrieved from http://www.dubaipetroleum.ae/about.php, 2016.)

Inhabited some centuries before the birth of Christ, areas near the sea-shore were settled and small city-states were formed in the seventh and eighth centuries. Around the sixteenth century, the Portuguese attempted to occupy the area, but the Turks' continued attacks discouraged their effort. A few centuries later, the French, British, and Dutch tried to bring the area under their control to bolster their trade with India, but the venture only bore fruit for the British East India Company, which benefitted handsomely. In 1820, Abu Dhabi (meaning "Father of the Gazelle") came under British control, and in 1903, Dubai followed suit. In 1833, indigenous Bedouins settled in the area we now know as Dubai under the leadership of the Al Maktoum family. In the early 1950s, oil was discovered during the search for water, and the first oil fields broke ground, putting Dubai on a meteoric ride to economic prosperity. In 1968, the British advocated their role as protector-ate and helped the emirates become their own rulers in 1971 (Cities of the World Dubai United Arab Emirates, 2009).

Dubai and Innovation

Much like the term *epic*, the term *innovation* is another one of the most overused and misunderstood words in today's global business lexicon and environment. Innovation often conjures up feelings of life-changing events, visions of hope, and good times. In reality, the diverse perceptions and understandings of innovation across the international landscape make defining innovation an elusive endeavor. As the slide rule of time builds and evolves, communications and knowledge-sharing ties across the globe, cultures and ethnicities in geographically remote locations tend to be less attuned to every incremental improvement or innovation achieved in more densely populated regions like the Western hemisphere. These geographically separated and isolated pockets or communities often find themselves lost in time and marvel at what visitors bring with them on their annual vacation get away to a far-off land. In reality, poor and disadvantaged countries tend to have a less complicated definition and understanding of innovation. Subsequently, these cultures do not make the same parallel interpretations of innovation but can certainly assign the same level of importance to an innovation.

For example, Leatherman's multipurpose pocket-size work tool combines a knife blade, a saw, a file, a can opener, a metric and standard ruler, wire-stripping capability, small scissors, and two screwdrivers (Philips and standard tip), all within the foldable handles of a set of pliers. The tool came with a small compact leather case with a belt-loop capability and was inconspicuous to the human eye, which fit military uniform regulation restrictions limiting accessories and accouterments that could be worn in uniform. Because of its innovative nature and the value technicians placed on its application potential, time-saving benefits, and appealing appearance, this tool was introduced to communication and telephone-equipment maintenance technicians in the United States Air Force in the mid to late 1980s and became a standard-issue item. The tools quickly found their way to military operations sites across the globe.

During one scenario in Khamis Mushayt, Saudi Arabia, in the early 1990s, Dr. Kennedy was deployed in support of military operations and worked closely with the Royal Saudi Air Force (RSAF) under the foreign military sales (FMS) program. He made frequent site survey trips throughout the vast desert expanses of the Kingdom of Saudi Arabia (KoSA) to remote communications sites, often crossing paths with multiple Saudi government personnel and indigenous Bedouins. Although the Leatherman was an everyday tool in Dr. Kennedy's tool kit, he was amazed at the level of interest it garnered among every Bedouin and Saudi military member that saw its capabilities for the first time.

This multipurpose "tool bag" that fit in the palm of one's hand had been adopted and diffused so quickly into the military culture, it was no longer seen in the same light, as several other companies were developing their own versions of the Leatherman. However, every Bedouin and Saudi government member Dr. Kennedy worked with was simply amazed by the tool and was willing to go to great lengths to obtain one. If one is familiar with the life of a desert Bedouin, a multipurpose tool like the Leatherman was very valuable and was a very attractive option and a complement to the typical tools a Bedouin would use in daily life.

Dubai's Modern Makeover

Known for its pearl diving, busy trading ports, magnificent sunsets, and iconic buildings, Dubai is etching a place in world history that is truly remarkable and stunning by anyone's account. From the Burj Al Khalifa (Figure 1.2), a daunting 2717 feet high, which has attracted over 25 million tourist and foreign investment, to the nautically inspired, sail-shaped Burj Al Arab Jumeirah (Figure 1.3), the world's first seven-star hotel, many ongoing innovative projects have become the hallmarks of modern Dubai's legacy.

Once the favorite spot for a villa beside the sea, Jumierah remains the center of the residents' daily regime as demonstrated by the building of the Palm Jumeirah (Figure 1.4), the world's largest man-made island, which can be seen from space. In sum, the Emiratis indigenous to Dubai want to build a city that is unique and extraordinary in the global landscape. Less than

Figure 1.2   Burj Al Khalifa. (Courtesy of Dr. Aaron "Sandy" Amacher.)

Figure 1.3   Burj Al Arab Jumeirah. (Courtesy of Dr. Aaron "Sandy" Amacher.)

Figure 1.4   Palm Jumeirah. (Courtesy of Dr. Aaron "Sandy" Amacher.)

half a century ago, Dubai was a small fishing village at the edge of the center west coast of the UAE. At the nexus of the city are two sections: downtown, with iconic sites and the business side, with the Dubai International Finance Center, an exclusive tax-free enclave or district where art museums, nightlife, fine dining, and international financial institutions coalesce 24/7.

Figure 1.5　Old Dubai district, Deira. (Courtesy of Dr. Aaron "Sandy" Amacher.)

From the largest mall in the world, the Dubai Mall, to the nearby souks (markets) and trade in the Old Dubai district, Deira (Figure 1.5), near the Dubai Creek where all the trade actually started, it is truly a shopper's paradise. If any country in today's international landscape can achieve the virtually impossible in record time, the UAE can, and Dubai is truly making its play to become a leader in the world landscape. Dubai also presents a world-class forum and stage for wildlife conservation.

The seven emirates established a political and economic federation on 2 December 1971. The largest city in the emirates is Abu Dhabi, while Dubai is perhaps the best recognized at the moment. Driven by the vision of HRH Sheikh Mohammed bin Rashid Al Maktoum, Dubai's goal is to achieve long-lasting prosperity for the emirate. Dubai (the most densely populated city within the emirates) and Abu Dhabi (capital of the UAE) are the two commercial and cultural centers of activity within the UAE. It is worthy of note that although Abu Dhabi is the center of political rule in the UAE, and although other members of the UAE (Abu Dhabi, Ajman, Fujairah, Ras al-Khaimah, Sharajah, and Umm al-Quwain) are making concerted efforts to follow Dubai's lead in solidifying their future, none are near the level Dubai's vision, commitment, and maturity. It is not hard to imagine that other emirates within the UAE will soon pick up the pace and journey down a similar path as Dubai (Figures 1.6 through 1.8).

The UAE has a high-income economy, which ranks approximately 19th in the world and gross domestic product (GDP) per capita, and it also enjoys a sizable annual trade surplus. This is truly remarkable, as only approximately 1 percent of the total area is considered habitable. It is not hard to imagine that other emirates within the UAE will soon pick up the pace

Figure 1.6   Old Deira district—Dubai Creek. (Courtesy of Dr. Aaron "Sandy" Amacher.)

Figure 1.7   Dubai Creek and Gold souk. (Courtesy of Dr. Aaron "Sandy" Amacher.)

Figure 1.8   Dubai Creek and Old Port. (Courtesy of Dr. Aaron "Sandy" Amacher.)

and journey down a similar path as Dubai. Dubai's underlying premise and strategy toward innovation appears to be in line with taking something done well and doing it better. How does a population of approximately 800,000 Emiratis in a desert community accomplish so much so quickly? Many believe that it is the oil revenues that have made this incredible journey possible. We contest, however, that it takes much more than natural resources to sustain rapid growth; it takes a strong leader with passion, a vision, and integrity, one with the love and respect of his people and the international community. HRH Sheikh Mohammed bin Rashid Al Maktoum (Figure 1.9) could arguably be one, if not the top, of few national leaders who are the most influential and respected on the international landscape leader board at the time of writing.

In this chapter, we set the stage for the discussion through the remaining chapters on how innovation across key industries (i.e., education, health, energy, environment, space, economy, and services), has contributed to Dubai's overarching vision, strategic goals, and objectives. Something that we'll likely see in a country that elevated its very status on the international scene with its wealth of oil is its adoption of electric vehicles and perhaps even the next-generation non fossil-fuel vehicles and transportation that complements the "Smart City."

Understanding the right processes and tools to achieve your innovation goals is one side of the coin. The other is ferreting out and understanding what processes you currently employ that are holding you back or creating the very barriers that bottleneck, muzzle, or hamstring your innovators;

Figure 1.9   HRH Sheikh Mohammed bin Rashid Al Maktoum. (From Sheikh Mohammed bin Rashid Al Maktoum, United Arab Emirates Protocol Department. Retrieved from http://protocol.dubai.ae/Media-Center/Official-Placement-of-Photos#prettyPhoto, 2016.)

and effectively identifying, assessing, and pursuing innovation opportunities within your organization.

Central to Dubai's current economic growth and sustainment strategy is a three-pronged approach focused on establishing world-class and sustainable tourism, industrial base, and financial systems to offset the drop in oil and natural-gas revenues (ranked the seventh largest reserves in the world), which are estimated to deplete significantly over the next 10–50 years (depending on which estimate one follows). Commercially, Germany and the United Kingdom are the largest export markets for Dubai.

Dubai is already one of the world's top 10 most visited cities and was also awarded the World Expo 2020, which represents an unprecedented achievement for the region. World Expos are known as the key meeting point for the global community to share innovations and make progress on issues of international importance (e.g., the global economy, sustainable development, and improved quality of life for the world's population). The World Expo is also a catalyst for economic, social, and cultural transformation, generating important legacies for the city and nation hosting this event.

Embracing more than 200 nationalities and cultures, the UAE is already an important international tourism destination (with over 95,000 hotel rooms and 11 million tourists recorded in 2012). It is also home to 63 business councils and a financial center for 18 of the world's top 25 international banks, six of the top 10 law firms and six of the top 10 insurance companies. Expo 2020 is also expected to provide some 277,000 new job opportunities, having a positive and comprehensive economic impact on small and medium enterprises (SMEs), which constitute approximately 95 percent of all registered companies in the UAE (Woods, 2014).

Ahead of World Expo 2020, the UAE government has embarked on a journey to upgrade its infrastructure, prompting more interest in the country and encouraging businesses and investments. In sum, many new business development opportunities and projects across all business sectors, to include demands on goods, will be drastically increased over the next 5–10 years, and that will certainly energize the overall trade market overall. World Expo 2020 will also facilitate economic diversification by finding new paths for economic development. According to the latest statistics, in 2015, construction and infrastructure projects announced and underway in the Gulf Cooperation Council (GCC) countries account for $1.9 trillion, while the UAE's shares account for 49 percent of the overall projects. The UAE continues to remain the largest projects market, with around $940 billion worth of projects under execution (Bitar, 2014).

Looking Ahead

In the following chapters, we will present discussions on key points and facets of Dubai's international influence, commitment, and exemplary pursuit of innovation as a cultural norm. The first six chapters will help address the current state of affairs in Dubai and help set the stage for latter three chapters introducing the N²OVATE™ methodology, tools, and processes. The final chapter, which outlines a selected case study relevant to the healthcare industry, is provided so that readers can apply what they have learned in this text to an actual event-driven innovation scenario that is developing in Dubai at the time of writing. With the intent of continuously improving the N²OVATE™ methodology and the combination of new and existing tools offered in this text, we encourage readers to download the electronic versions of our tools and share their experiences in applying the methodology and tools on our website at www.ipsinnovate.com.

In Chapter 2, "Geopolitical Environment of Dubai and the United Arab Emirates," we walk the reader through a brief history of Dubai and the UAE region and take a reflective look at the visions of the founding fathers, Sheikh Zayed bin Sultan Al Nahyan (2016) (Figure 1.10) and Sheikh Rashid bin Saeed Al Maktoum (1962) (Figure 1.11), and go back to the inception of when, why, and how the vision has been created.

We start with the quest to seek a catalyst for all that has been done over the years and the total paradigm shift from a poor and undeveloped land to a vast and luxurious, as well as industrious destination for all nationalities of different lifestyles. Before all of the changes, beautiful structures, breathtaking sceneries, and fun-filled activities, and the incredible emphasis on innovation and business revolution, the UAE and Dubai were just one barren, empty desert land area.

Figure 1.10   HRH Sheikh Zayed bin Sultan Al Nahyan. (From Sheikh Zayed bin Sultan Al Nahyan, United Arab Emirates Protocol Department. Retrieved from http://proto-col.dubai.ae/Media-Center/Official-Placement-of-Photos#prettyPhoto, 2016.)

Figure 1.11 **HRH Sheikh Rashid bin Saeed Al Maktoum. (From Sheikh Mohammed bin Rashid Al Maktoum, United Arab Emirates Protocol Department. Retrieved from http://protocol.dubai.ae/Media-Center/Official-Placement-of-Photos#prettyPhoto, 2016.)**

In Chapter 3, we provide a brief look at Dubai's innovation culture and strategy. Based on the socioeconomic dynamics at play across the international stage, individual and cultural perspectives are strong influences contributing to the value and impact of what might be categorized as an innovative offering. In reality, unless an innovation offers recognizable value or a positive change in our environment, a product, or a process, the populace is less likely to accept that process, product, or new offering.

Dubai's underlying premise and strategy for innovation is rooted in the philosophy of taking something done well, and doing it better. In Chapter 4, "Innovation in Dubai's Private Sector," we assess this acclimation toward innovation as generally incremental in nature but do not rule out the potential pursuit of disruptive innovation or ideas. We also explore just some of the central innovations championed across key industries central to Dubai's Vision 2020, its strategic goals and objectives, and other supporting visions and plans as they relate to those specific industries.

In Chapter 5, "Innovation in Government," we introduce HRH Sheikh Mohammed bin Rashid Al Maktoum's strategy and approach for repeatedly achieving vision excellence. We also demonstrate the importance of having an achievable but challenging vision as well as a methodology to implement that vision and its supporting innovative initiatives, associated goals, objectives, and tasks. Additionally, we briefly introduce two instruments or tools that can be employed across the spectrum of innovation opportunities—the Innovation Team Project Charter (ITPC) and the Innovation Opportunity Profile (IOP) instrument. We described how the IOP instrument is used and how the information can best prepare an organization for innovation project success.

The relationship between innovation and leadership can best be described as covalent and complementary. One without the other simply diminishes the quality and outcome of the other. In Chapter 6, "Innovation and Leadership," we introduce and elaborate on the commonalities and relationships that bind the two terms. We start our discussion with an introduction to general leadership axioms, logics in business and management, and how a leader's vision, commitment, and approach to innovation is essential in setting the tone for an organization's innovation culture. The chapter wraps up our leadership and innovation discussion with an examination of leadership and best practices, dynamic capabilities, and effectively managing risk in an innovative culture.

The material presented in Chapters 7 through 9 will introduce the reader to a cadre of agile, disciplined, and transformational tools and processes for improving innovation opportunity outcomes and achieving sustained innovation project success. The authors introduce new tools and processes developed over their decades of work in the field of innovation, which assist organizations in aligning innovation opportunity decisions with their core competencies, business objectives, and strategic vision. An introductory discussion on how the authors evolved the original ENOVALE™ model into the N²OVATE™ methodology is provided as well as an overview of how to select a project for each type of innovation opportunity, followed by step-by-step instructions on how to implement the desired innovation process type. Based on innovative outcomes, the authors identify seven unique processes, each having its own unique circumstances for the reader's consideration. A more detailed explanation of the N²OVATE™ methodology, tools, and processes can be found in a companion book to this work, the *Innovation Project Management Handbook* (McLaughlin and Kennedy, 2016).

In Appendices I and II, we provide a case study and some additional tools relevant to the discussion and assignments at the end of each of the preceding chapters (Chapters 1 through 9). This case study focuses on one of Dubai's seminal pillars of the Vision 2021 and "Vision of Dubai" innovation strategy, medical tourism.

Summary

Firmly rooted in the Islamic traditions of Arabia, the way in which Dubai's leadership texturizes its vision, strategy, and approach to realizing the dream will certainly be the deciding factors in whether it sustains long-term relevance and the new definition of the cosmopolitan city of the international landscape. In essence, as in every organization, it truly is a favorable trait in a leader of a country to have a visionary spirit that can change the course of a nation's history (one synonymous with terms such as *futurist*, *ideator*, and *disruptive thinker*). They are not easy to find, and some are restricted to a particular domain (industry or subject matter). Others can see things from an enterprise level (economies and markets). They are capable of seeing beyond the horizon and can paint a literal blueprint and vision for those who cannot. From obscure fishing village to the most modern city in the world today and the evolution from camel (ship or cloud of the desert), caravans, and dhows (ships) to supertankers and air transport caravans, the modernization of Dubai's trade and economy is truly like no other. Dubai is also considered the sporting capital of the Middle East (golf, tennis, and camel and horse racing).

The only fear that Dubai has at this point is a global economic downturn much like that of 2006–2007, but much worse. During that period, Dubai found itself on pause, and investors were simply out of money. Sheikh Mohammed's ultimate vision is for Dubai to be number one in the world across every category according to which a country can be measured and evaluated. The sheikh displays all the traits and hallmarks of history's most admired and trusted leaders. He is a man of vision who sincerely believes that what empowers a leader is the trust, respect, and love of the people. He wants a better life for his people now, not some decades in the future. As Dubai continues to weave its way into the hearts and minds of the international community, a truly fascinating story emerges beyond the opulent modern buildings, landscape, and lavish lifestyle, and we hope to share that in the following discussion. In the next chapter, we provide a high-level discussion on the UAE's geopolitical environment and the myriad of changes that have taken place from some 40 years ago to the present, which have transformed this once barren and undeveloped desert oasis into the epicenter of modern innovation.

Discussion Questions

1. In your own words, provide key points in Dubai's history you feel were essential factors in setting the stage for their current economic and political success.
2. Name the three key leaders in the UAE's history who are chiefly credited for building the foundation of the UAE's philosophy and vision on innovation.

3. In your own words, describe the key economic factors Dubai must retain to achieve economic stability over the foreseeable future.
4. Are there any major impacts that a downturn in international economic stability would have on Dubai and the UAE? If so, please explain in your own words.
5. In your personal opinion and words, share in a one-page paper the reasons for Dubai's massive development projects and commitment to a culture of innovation. Prepare a short presentation to share in the course room.

Assignments

1. Doing your own research using information available in the public domain, select one project that was recently completed or is ongoing in Dubai that you feel is innovative in nature. Provide a background explaining the project objectives and goals, its current status as of the date of writing, and why you feel the project is innovative. In your discussion on why you feel the project is innovative, include the potential value-added or competitive advantage the project outcome might bring and discuss whether it is something other countries in the MENA region could adopt. Complete this assignment in a—three- to five-page report and share your work with your classmates.
2. Using the direction provided in the preceding assignment, build a short presentation (i.e., PowerPoint) and deliver your findings to your peers in the course room.

Chapter 2

Geopolitical Environment of Dubai and the United Arab Emirates

Introduction

The vast changes in the United Arab Emirates (UAE), and specifically in Dubai, have left the world awestruck for many years now. Reviewing the old pictures of the country when it was still barren and undeveloped more than 40 years ago will keep you wondering at the bravery of the leaders of this country, Sheikh Zayed bin Sultan Al Nahyan and Sheikh Rashid bin Saeed Al Maktoum, to have taken such an innovative and visionary step and to have totally transformed the land into a technology/tourist/business destination with so many things to offer for those from all cultures and walks of life. Credit has also to be given to the leaders who have upheld and stood up for their beliefs and strongly held on to their vision and all possible ways of making the vision a reality, especially His Royal Highness (HRH) Sheikh Mohammed bin Rashid Al Maktoum.

Before we continue appreciating the complexity of what the UAE has now achieved, it is best to take a reflective look at the founding fathers' vision and go back to when, why, and how the vision has been created. This starts with the quest for a catalyst for all that has been done over the years and the total paradigm shift from a poor and undeveloped land to a vast and luxurious, as well as industrious destination for all nationalities of different lifestyles. Much has been written about the UAE, both bad and good. Before all of the changes, the beautiful structures, the breathtaking views, the fun-filled activities, and the incredible emphasis on innovation and business revolution, the UAE and Dubai were just one barren, empty desert land area.

United Arab Emirates

The UAE is a country on the Arabian Peninsula located on the southeastern coast of the Persian Gulf and the northwestern coast of the Gulf of Oman. The UAE consists of seven *emirates* and was founded on 2 December 1971 as a federation (Figure 2.1). Six of the seven sheikhdoms (Abu Dhabi, Dubai, Sharjah, Ajman, Umm al-Quwain, and Fujairah) combined on that date; the seventh, Ras al-Khaimah, joined the federation on 10 February 1972. The seven sheikhdoms were formerly known as the Trucial States, in reference to the treaty relations established with the British in the nineteenth century.

Artifacts uncovered in the UAE show a long history of human habitation and regional trade, including with Mesopotamia. The area was settled by a number of tribes along both the coast and interior and was Islamized in the seventh century. A number of incursions and bloody battles took place along the coast when the Portuguese, under Albuquerque, invaded the area. Conflicts between the maritime communities of the coast of the Trucial States and the British led to the sacking of Ras al-Khaimah by British forces in 1809 and again in 1819, which resulted in the first of a number of British treaties with the Trucial States rulers in 1820. These treaties, including the Treaty of Perpetual Maritime Peace, signed in 1853, led to peace and prosperity along the coast; this lasted until the 1930s, when the pearl trade collapsed, leading to significant hardship among the coastal communities.

A British decision, taken in early 1968, to withdraw from its involvement in the Trucial States led to the decision to found a federation. This was agreed between two of the most influential Trucial States rulers, Sheikh Zayed bin Sultan Al Nahyan of Abu Dhabi and Sheikh Rashid bin Saeed Al Maktoum of Dubai. The two invited other Trucial States rulers to join the federation. At one stage, it seemed likely that Bahrain and Qatar would also join the union, but both eventually decided on independence. Today, the UAE is a modern, oil-exporting country with a highly diversified economy; Dubai in particular has developed into a global hub for tourism, retail, finance, and innovation, such as being home to the world's tallest building, the largest man-made seaport, and the busiest international airport.

Dubai

Where Is Dubai?

Dubai is one of the seven emirates that make up the Islamic country of the UAE, situated on the Persian Gulf (Figure 2.1). It borders on Abu Dhabi to the south, Sharjah to the northeast, and Oman to the southeast. Dubai is backed by the Arabian Desert and occupies an area of about 4210 square kilometers.

History

It is believed that Dubai existed at least 150 years prior to the establishment of the union in 1972. The earliest record of the history of Dubai is dated 1095 AD, when the geographer Abu Abdullah Al-Bakri first mentioned it in the ancient *Book of Geography*. No records are known between then and the second oldest record as of 1587, in which the author discusses Dubai as a popular place for pearl diving. But the pearl industry collapsed in the 1930s due to the First World War, the Great Depression, the invention of cultured pearl, and the establishment of that industry by the Japanese, among many other factors.

The most important revolutionary event was the discovery of huge amounts of oil and gas in Dubai, the revenue from which has meant that it had the capability to construct some of the most extravagant skyscrapers, hotels, and shopping centers in the world. Dubai is known for some of the most innovative structures in the world, including the Mall of the Emirates

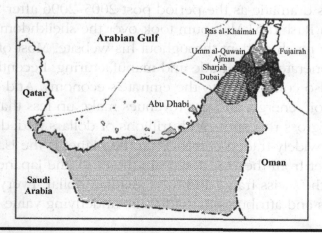

Figure 2.1 Map of the United Arab Emirates (UAE).

indoor ski slope and the Palm Jumeirah, the world's largest man-made island.

In 1999, the Burj Al Arab hotel was completed and at that time was the world's tallest hotel and the only seven-star hotel. Tours of the hotel are available at certain times. Just over a decade later, in 2010, the Burj Khalifa skyscraper was opened. It stands at a breathtaking 828 meters/2717 feet in height, currently the world's tallest building, and it features the world's second-highest observation deck, as well as nine hotels and an impressive fountain system. However, this all came at a cost.

Dubai's ambitious plans were largely built on speculative wealth that far exceeded the country's oil revenues. The assumption that demand for oil would forever push up the price per barrel was rudely brought back down to earth in 2008, when the world recession resulted in a slump in spiraling prices. Overnight, Dubai's governmental and business community woke up and realized it was in financial difficulty. Construction on many buildings ceased and investment confidence fled. The emirate had to consider new and innovative ways to recover and to prevent the same type of financial crisis from happening in the future. One of the key aspects of this rebuild was the focus and emphasis on innovation: innovation in business systems, innovation in governmental systems, innovation in technology, and innovation in education and social services.

Currency

Dubai grew slowly and surely over time, but no period in the history of Dubai was as dramatic as the period post 2005–2006 after Sheikh Mohammed bin Rashid Al Maktoum took over the sheikhdom. Dubai's progress is very much evident throughout his website. Most of Dubai's revenues are generated from trade and manufacturing. Recently, financial services have also contributed to the emirate's economy. And contrary to popular belief, oil, energy, and gas revenues make up less than 10 percent of Dubai's gross revenues. With trillions of dollars traded on a daily basis, the most widely traded currency on the planet is the U.S. dollar. In descending order from the U.S. dollar are the euro, the Japanese yen, the British pound, the Swiss franc, and the Canadian dollar. Every currency has specific features and attributes that affect its underlying value and ultimately its price.

In Dubai, the UAE or Emirati dirham (AED), issued by the Central Bank of the UAE, is the national currency. In 2016, the dirham trades at an exchange rate of 3.67 dirham per U.S. dollar and 5.12 British pounds. The AED is linked to the U.S. dollar, so it is susceptible to the fluctuations (ups and downs) of the U.S. dollar. The AED is printed currency in the denominations of 5, 10, 20, 50, 100, and 500-dirham bills. The currency enjoys a great deal of stability in one measure due to its direct tie to the U.S. dollar. The stability of the currency is also one reason for the great financial business community development that has occurred within the emirate of Dubai. The creation of the Dubai International Financial Center (DIFC) free zone and its innovative structure has marked Dubai as one of the financial centers of the world.

The Seven Emirates

Abu Dhabi

The Al Nahyan family rules Abu Dhabi, by far the largest emirate. It occupies 67,340 square kilometers or 86.7 percent of the total area of the country. The emirate is primarily a vast desert area with about two dozen islands where the city of Abu Dhabi is located, plus six sizable islands further out in the Arabian Gulf. The population of the emirate is concentrated in three areas: the capital city, Abu Dhabi; Al Ain, an oasis city located near the Hajar Mountains; and the villages of the Liwa oases.

Traditionally, the population along the coast relied on fishing and pearling for their livelihood, while those in the hinterland relied on date plantations and camel herding. Through his remarkable leadership and personal commitment, HRH Sheikh Zayed bin Sultan Al Nahyan developed Abu Dhabi into an influential, fully modernized state. Upon Sheikh Zayed's death in November 2004, Sheikh Khalifa Al Nahyan became the UAE president ruler of Abu Dhabi.

In 2008, the Abu Dhabi Councils (Department of Planning and Economy, Abu Dhabi Council for Economic Development, and General Secretariat of the Executive Council) released "The Abu Dhabi Economic Vision 2030" as mandated by HRH Sheikh Mohamed bin Zayed Al Nahyan, Crown Prince of Abu Dhabi and chairman of the Executive Council. This 22-year strategy for Abu Dhabi defines the priorities for public policy in the emirate to achieve its primary goals—a safe and secure society and a dynamic, open economy.

Abu Dhabi Vision 2030

The government has identified nine pillars that will form the architecture of the emirate's social, political, and economic future:

- A large empowered private sector
- A sustainable, knowledge-based economy
- An optimal, transparent regulatory environment
- A continuation of strong and diverse international relationships
- The optimization of the emirate's resources
- Premium education, health care, and infrastructure assets
- Complete international and domestic security
- The maintenance of Abu Dhabi's values, culture, and heritage
- A significant and ongoing contribution to the federation of the UAE

The drive for diversification delivers the great need for Abu Dhabi to focus on its priorities: (1) Abu Dhabi will build a sustainable economy and (2) Abu Dhabi will ensure that social and regional development is balanced to bring the benefits of economic growth and well-being to the entire population.

To achieve a sustainable economy, Abu Dhabi must remain focused diversifying contributors that support progression and advancement of their gross domestic product (GDP). Economic volatility is one main factor that Abu Dhabi's government aims to control; this will surely affect Abu Dhabi's economy, which depends mainly on the oil industry, its primary economic engine since 1960. It is estimated that the oil industry provides more than $90 billion a year in revenue at current prices. This revenue is then invested to develop key areas of the economy and to provide the services required of a modern society. Abu Dhabi Economic Vision 2030 aims to strengthen small and medium-size enterprises (SMEs) and other nonoil sectors while still supporting the oil industry. Abu Dhabi's government established the AED 1 billion Khalifa Fund to encourage the development of SMEs. This fund will provide financial and professional assistance for UAE nationals establishing a business or expanding their business. Developing the SME sector and other nonoil sectors will bring Abu Dhabi in line with its benchmarks and at the same time reduce the economy's exposure to risks, encourage innovation, and create jobs.

This vision/strategy seems to be very aggressive; however, the task force (the Department of Planning and Economy, the Abu Dhabi Council for Economic Development, and the General Secretariat of the Executive Council) has thoroughly and rigorously conducted research studies and analysis of Abu Dhabi's economic performance to ensure that this vision/strategy is not based on false assumptions. They have identified three benchmark countries (Norway, Ireland, and New Zealand) for the key economic characteristics relevant to Abu Dhabi and for their success in establishing successful economic development models. In addition, the task force has sought the advice and opinions of economic development experts in each of the benchmark countries.

Dubai

Dubai, the second largest of the seven emirates, is ruled by the Al Maktoum family. It occupies an area of approximately 3900 square kilometers, which includes a small enclave called Hatta, situated close to Oman, among the Hajar Mountains. Dubai, the capital city, is located near the creek, a natural harbor, which traditionally provided the basis of the trading industry. Pearling and fishing were the main sources of income for the people of Dubai. Under the wise leadership of its rulers, Dubai's focus on trade and industry transformed it into the leading trading port along the southern Gulf. HRH Sheikh Mohammed bin Rashid Al Maktoum is the current ruler of Dubai.

Sharjah

The Al Qasimi family rules Sharjah, which shares its southern border with Dubai. It occupies approximately 2600 square kilometers and is the only emirate to have coastlines on both the Arabian Gulf and the Gulf of Oman. In the nineteenth century, the town of Sharjah was the leading port in the lower Gulf. Produce from the interior of Oman, India, and Persia arrived there. Sharjah's salt mines meant that salt constituted an important part of its export business, along with pearls. In the 1930s, when the pearling industry declined and trade decreased due to the creek silting up, Imperial Airway's flying boats set up a staging post for flights en route to India, which benefited the residents of Sharjah. Today, under the leadership of Sheikh Sultan bin Mohammed Al Qasimi, Sharjah is the cultural and educational center of the UAE and takes pride in preserving the country's cultural heritage as well as promoting Arab culture and traditions.

Ajman

Ajman is the smallest emirate, comprising only 260 square kilometers. It is ruled by the Al Nuami family. Surrounded mostly by the emirate of Sharjah, Ajman also possesses the small enclaves of Manama and Musfut in the Hajar Mountains. Along the creek, dhow building (an Arabian type of ship) was the specialized trade. Fishing and date trees provided the local population with their primary means of sustenance. Ajman benefited greatly from the union of the emirates, a fact that is reflected today in its stately buildings and infrastructure. Sheikh Humaid bin Rashid Al Nuami has been the ruler since 1981.

Umm al-Quwain

Umm al-Quwain is ruled by the Al Mualla family. It is the second smallest emirate, with a total area of around 770 square kilometers. Positioned between the emirates of the Sharjah and Ajman to the south and Ras al-Khaimah to the north, Umm al-Quwain has the smallest population. Fishing is the local population's primary means of income. Date farming also plays significant role in the economy. After the union of the emirates in 1971, Umm al-Quwain developed into a modern state and continues to progress under its present ruler, Sheikh Rashid bin Ahmed Al Mualla.

Ras al-Khaimah

Ras al-Khaimah, the most northerly emirate, is ruled by another branch of the Al Qasimi family. It covers an area of 1700 square kilometers. Thanks to the runoff water from the Hajar Mountains, Ras al-Khaimah has a unique abundance of flora, so it is no surprise that agriculture is important to the local economy. The emirate also benefits from its stone quarries and from fishing, which is plentiful in the rich waters of the Gulf. The city of Ras al-Khaimah, situated on an inlet, has a rich history. It was renowned for its prosperous port and for its exquisite pearls, which were famous as being the whitest and roundest available anywhere. Ras al-Khaimah's current ruler is Sheikh Saqr bin Mohammed Al Qasimi.

Fujairah (Jewel of the Middle East)

The only emirate without a coastline on the Arabian Gulf is Fujairah, which is ruled by the Al Sharqi family. Situated along the coast of the Gulf of

Oman, Fujairah covers about 1300 square kilometers. Unlike other emirates, where the desert forms a large part of the terrain, mountains and plains are the predominant features of Fujairah. Fujairah's economy is based on fishing and agriculture. Because of its coastline on the Gulf of Oman, the emirate sports a large tourist industry, with beachfront hotels and many water-related activities such as scuba diving, deep-sea fishing, and pleasure boating. As in Ras al-Khaimah, the land in Fujairah is irrigated by rainwater from the Hajar Mountains, making it ideal for farming. Sheikh Hamad bin Mohammed Al Sharqi is the present ruler.

United Arab Emirates: The Road Ahead

The UAE will enjoy a budget surplus of between 6.9 percent and 10.5 percent over the next six years (2016–2022). Sound economic planning and stable government policies have ensured that the UAE economy will continue to grow at a steady pace over the next few years, even though many countries in the developed world face the problem of stagnant economies.

The UAE's GDP grew by 4.3 percent in 2014 and edged up to 4.5 percent on average between 2014–2015. That growth is expected to remain consistent in 2016 and 2017 as it inches towards 4.6 percent a year in 2018 and 2019. As Sultan bin Saeed Al Mansouri, the minister of state for the economy, told the UAE Economic Outlook Forum, the country's positive economic outlook has also been confirmed by the International Monetary Fund (IMF) in its 2014 report.

The UAE will enjoy a budget surplus of between 6.9 percent and 10.5 percent over the next six years (2016–2022). The IMF has also reaffirmed the UAE's position as a regional and global hub when it listed the country among the 20 largest exporters in the world. In 2014, exports of goods and services from the UAE exceeded AED1.47 trillion. Next year, this figure is expected to reach AED1.59 trillion and by 2018 breach the AED2 trillion mark. Imports also increased steadily in 2014, to a landmark AED885 billion (as against AED797 billion in 2013). Interestingly, at a time when foreign direct investment (FDI) inflow to several economies has slowed down, the UAE continues to attract substantial FDI, especially in sectors such as tourism, real estate, and construction. In 2014, year, FDI inflows notched AED44 billion, after growing by a hefty 20 percent in the previous year (2013).

Indeed, the UAE economy will witness buoyancy right up to 2020, when the World Expo 2020 will be hosted in Dubai. The minister told the forum that the estimated financial returns from the event would be AED139 billion and Dubai is expected to get more than 25 million visitors, 70 percent from abroad.

Expo 2020 is expected to provide a strong impetus for overall economic activity in Dubai, especially in sectors including tourism, aviation, and infrastructure development, reinforcing the city's reputation as a vibrant, global hub. Al Mansouri noted, Expo 2020 will generate more than 277,000 direct jobs between 2013 and 2020, and that every Expo-related job will lead to 50 additional jobs, boosting the economies of the vast region including the Middle East and Africa and South Asia.

The minister told the forum that the infrastructure and logistics costs of the Expo are projected to be more than $9 billion, drawing international companies from Europe to the projects. Many of these companies have been experiencing sluggish growth, thanks to the recessionary conditions still prevailing in much of the continent.

Of course, the current—and future—buoyancy in the economy does not mean that the authorities are ignoring the impact of the current slowdown in large swathes of the developed world, the sharp fall in commodity prices, and the possible threat of a setback in growth in the United States and China. As Sheikh Ahmed bin Saeed Al Maktoum, president of Dubai Civil Aviation and chairman and chief executive of Emirates Airline and the Emirates Airline Group, told the forum: "Despite the success we have achieved, and our ambitions, we are on alert to face any challenges that may arise on the global economic horizon, or any impact on our finances" (Khaleej Times, 2014).

Thus, for instance, steps have been taken to control government spending to avoid budget deficit. The government is also on alert against volatility in the real-estate market, though it continues to factor in the positive contribution of the sector to economic development in Dubai and in meeting real demand. The government has taken steps to curb speculative practices in the real-estate sector by increasing registration fees from 2 percent to 4 percent of the transaction value and has issued guidelines on adjusting rentals. The UAE Central Bank has also introduced new caps on real-estate mortgages, and the government has also sought to control inflation to ensure that Dubai retains its competitiveness and that households are able to manage their budgets.

Another key aspect of the government's policy is that it is not dependent only on Expo 2020 for future growth. As Sheikh Ahmed pointed out,

"The leadership has developed an integrated strategy, which comprises 100 initiatives and 1000 smart services, to transform Dubai into one of the smartest cities in the world" (*Khaleej Times*, 2014). Economic activities, lifestyles, transportation, and government services will be aligned with smart technologies and environment and human capital development, leading to the realization of the knowledge economy, he observed. A wise leadership, pragmatic policies, and the ability to grasp opportunities and convert them into real benefits for society at large have been the cornerstones of the economic strategy of Dubai and the UAE.

Summary

Today, the UAE is a modern, oil-exporting country with a highly diversified economy; Dubai in particular has developed into a global hub for tourism, retail, finance, and innovation, such as being home to the world's tallest building, the largest man-made seaport, and the busiest international airport. In this chapter, we walked the reader through a brief history of the UAE and its seven emirates, its geography, and the vast and massive changes that have taken place in the UAE and specifically in Dubai. Reviewing the old pictures of the country when it was still barren and undeveloped, more than 40 years ago, leaves the casual observer wondering just how ambitious, far-reaching, and courageous the visions of leaders such as Sheikh Zayed bin Sultan Al Nahyan and Sheikh Rashid bin Saeed Al Maktoum must have appeared at the time they were introduced. One could ponder further how a leader champions such innovative and visionary outcomes, which have literally transformed the land into the world's number one technology, tourist, and business destination in such a short period of time.

As previous critics and naysayers relating Dubai's future to Shelly's Ozymandias change ranks and accept the phenomenon we call "Dubai," the UAE in general will continue to enjoy a budget surplus of between 6.9 percent and 10.5 percent over the next six years (2016–2022). Sound leadership vision, economic planning, and stable government policies have ensured that the UAE's economy will continue to grow at a steady pace over the next few years, even though many countries in the developed world face the problem of stagnant economies. In the next chapter, we narrow our discussion to the "Vision of Dubai," its innovation culture and strategy.

Discussion Questions

1. Identify the seven emirates that make up the UAE. Pick one of the emirates and complete a one-page report on innovative projects in that particular emirate using the information in this book and information in the public domain.
2. In your own words, discuss your thoughts on where you think Dubai will be in a decade (10 years) from the date of this assignment. Complete this discussion in a one-page report and share it with your peers in the course room.
3. Develop a short presentation (six to eight slides) on the state of innovation (in your opinion) of any one of the seven emirates. Use this text and the public domain, and be sure to cite your references. Be prepared to give a 5-min presentation of your work to your peers in the course room. Include an opportunity for your peers to ask questions at the end of your presentation.

Assignments

1. Using the contents of this text and information sources in the public domain, write a three to five-page report comparing and contrasting the innovative cultures of each of the seven emirates that make up the UAE. Present your work in a prioritized manner (from most innovative to least innovative). Give examples to support this prioritization.
2. Pick one industry sector in the emirate of Dubai. Using the contents of this text and any information you can source from the public domain, discuss the following characteristics of that industry in a three to five-page report:
   a. Industry name and description
   b. Business strategy and outlook for the industry
   c. Leading companies and organizations (these can be for profit or nonprofit)
   d. Financial impact on overall GDP
   e. Top three innovation initiatives, objectives, and goals (in your personal opinion)

Chapter 3

Dubai's Innovation Culture and Strategy

Introduction

Based on the socioeconomic dynamics at play across the international stage, individual and cultural perspectives are strong influences contributing to the value and impact we place on what might be categorized as an innovative offering. In reality, unless an innovation offers recognizable value or positive change in our environment, a product, or a process, the populace is less likely to accept that process, product, or new offering. This individual assessment or decision is not only key to the rate of diffusion but also to the acceptance of an innovation opportunity at the personal level. Although the fundamental nature and dynamics of innovation continue to change and provide mixed results across the globe, the introduction of information technology (IT) enablers and forward thinking on structured process reformation (taking what someone does well and doing it better) have provided Dubai with some incredible opportunities that have clearly placed the country at the tip of the innovation spear.

Dubai's dynamic approach in pursuing pioneering innovation opportunities has had a resounding ripple effect across the international landscape. The Dubai Economic Council (DEC) was determined to expedite their National Innovation Strategy, launched by the United Arab Emirates (UAE) in an effort to make it one of the most innovative cities and a global hub for innovation. This commitment to innovation was further materialized with the establishment of a global innovation center (GIC) called the

Mohammed bin Rashid Center for Government Innovation (Issac, 2015). The GIC is the nexus and lynchpin for building partnerships between public and private industry and is chartered to set up the institutional infrastructure framework to evolve the National Innovation Strategy and the "Dubai partners for innovation" initiative (Issac, 2015). Sheikh Mohammed's commitment is not to opulent landmarks but to building a better economic environment, and one that is compliant with corporate social responsibility (CSR), for his people and the world in general. His focus is clearly on increased value and competitive advantage for the host population while setting the stage for public and private organizations from the international community to also benefit handsomely from contributing to Dubai's overall vision.

Innovation and Culture

Leading the international community has its price, and being a trendsetter requires vision, courage, belief, and resolve. Not every innovation opportunity will be accepted with open arms, regardless of the gender, generational, and cultural factors at play. How quickly an innovative process, product, or service is accepted, adopted, or implemented after its introduction is referred to as "diffusion" (Rogers, 2003). According to Rogers' diffusion theory, there are many variables influencing the rate at which a culture accepts or adopts new products, processes, or services. Although every culture has its own special identity or DNA, the following are some variables that can certainly affect the adoption of an innovation opportunity and are generally generic to most, if not all, cultures.

1. Cultural and cognitive norms
2. Cognitive bias
3. Social pressure and independence
4. Compatibility
5. Risk
6. Economic necessity
7. Population diversity

An example of diffusion is shown in Figure 3.1. Drawn from a recent case study on innovation and knowledge management (KM) systems, the chart illustrates how innovators and early adopters to an innovation realize a

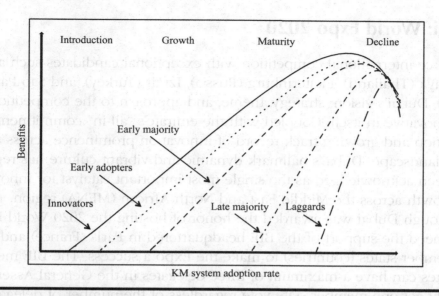

Figure 3.1 Knowledge management system rate of diffusion. (From Kennedy, W. R., Individual [personal] perspectives on innovation: Federal knowledge management working group. ProQuest, UMI Dissertation Publishing, 2014.)

greater gain in competitive value and position in their market sectors versus the late majority or laggards. Based on Dubai's leadership and current approach to innovation, we feel that Dubai's strategic approach to innovation and desire to pursue innovative solutions fits nicely on the "early adopters" to "innovators" curve in the chart.

Sustaining a cycle of continuous innovation in any market sector is a tall order for any company. Sustaining that cycle across a host of market sectors is completely remarkable. Enter Dubai, the small desert nation whose leadership has repeatedly faced austere times throughout its history and has continually risen to the challenge. Driven by the vision and guidance provided by Sheikh Mohammed, Dubai made history yet again when 116 of 169 member nations of the Bureau International des Expositions (BIE) voted for Dubai to host the most prestigious World Expo in 2020. Many are not familiar with just how important that is to Dubai's continued growth and success as an innovative nation, but the theme alone ("Connecting Minds, Creating the Future") is attracting international companies and innovators like a moth to a flame. In support of this discussion, we provide a brief introduction of the BIE's process and a small measure of just how keen the competition is to achieve such a goal.

Dubai: World Expo 2020

In a fierce international competition with exceptional candidates such as Ayutthaya (Thailand), Ekaterinburg (Russia), Izmir (Turkey), and Sao Paulo (Brazil), Dubai's vision, strategy, theme, and approach to the competition was innovative in itself. Coupled with the emirate's "all-in" commitment to innovation and growing track record of innovation prominence across the global landscape, Dubai's hallmark dynamic and vibrant culture has repeatedly been acknowledged as the single most important catalyst for innovation and growth across the Middle East and North African (MENA) region.

Although Dubai was awarded the honor of hosting the 2020 World Expo, it will need the support of the BIE headquartered in Paris (France) and the 169 member states (countries) to make the Expo a success. The BIE member states can have a maximum of three delegates in the General Assembly, but only get one member state vote regardless of the number of delegates. The BIE oversees and organizes four main types of Expos—World Expos, International Specialized Expos, Horticultural Exhibits, and the Design Triennale of Milan (BIE, 2016). The General Assembly has four committees (Executive, Rules, Administration and Budget, and Information and Communication) and a Secretariat that manages the BIE organization. Each committee has a compliment of 9–12 members who handle the internal affairs of the BIE, studies and monitoring of the Expo progress, and oversight and issue proposals for the Expo organization (BIE, 2016). In reality, all member states have some level of responsibility or supporting role in each World Expo even if they are not hosting the Expo.

Selection Criteria

From the first World Fair hosted in London by the United Kingdom in 1851, the history of World Expos over the past 160 years has been founded on helping humanity through the promotion of education, cooperation, and innovation. Needless to say, the selection criteria for hosting an event of this magnitude in the early history of Expos were far less complicated than they are today. That said, determining which member state is positioned to successfully host a specific Expo remains a passionate, daunting, and complex task. For the purposes of this book, we are focused on providing a brief overview of the selection criteria process and highly recommend those interested in greater detail consult the BIE's official website (www.bie-paris.org).

In addition to the requirement of being a member of and in good standing with the BIE, our brief assessment of the two chief selection criteria (basis) the BIE General Assembly employs to evaluate and select the host of a World Expo (also known as "World Fairs") follows. Please note, for more specific criteria, please reference the BIE home page (www.bie-paris.org).

1. Technical infrastructure, such as tourist accommodation (i.e., hotels, food establishments, hospitals, etc.), communications (i.e., telephone, Internet, long-haul communications, etc.), and transportation (i.e., adequate and reliable airport access and capability, public train, bus, taxi services, etc.). Acceptable areas and venues to support exhibition areas are also evaluated.
2. Host nation's vision and theme for the desired Exposition. In essence, the proposed theme and vision is outlined in the proposal documentation and evaluated on its uniqueness and potential for promoting international cooperation and global dialogue in the areas of innovation sharing, educating the public, promoting progress through cooperation.

Dubai certainly met and possibly exceeded expectations in many subcategories of the first criteria. The country's growing reputation for opulence aside, the acknowledged success it has had in building a world-class city and infrastructure and the associated tourist amenities are simply unparalleled. In some corners, Dubai's infrastructure has surpassed many more mature nations in the Western world. Noted for its efficiency, sustainability, environmentally friendly design, and application of the latest technology, Dubai has achieved in a single decade what many countries have labored at for many decades—the model of CSR at the highest level of government.

Regarding the second criteria of "vision" and "theme," Reem Al Hashimy, the UAE's minister of state and managing director of the Higher Committee for Hosting the 2020 World Expo, summarized Dubai's overall Expo 2020 registration document theme ("Connecting Minds, Creating the Future") in the following statement (Al Hashimy, 2012):

> By connecting people, which lies at the heart of our vision as a cosmopolitan nation, we can foster greater cooperation and understanding between peoples and cultures. By connecting minds, we celebrate our common aspirations and work to create a brighter future. That is our vision for the 2020 World Expo in Dubai.

Dubai's World Expo 2020 registration document was officially submitted to the BIE General Assembly in July 2012. The submission also included a site master plan (for Exhibition City, a 400-hectare site located on the southwestern edge of Dubai), a business operations plan, a communications and marketing plan, visitor and participant engagement strategies, event sustainability, and a post-event legacy plan. The Expo is expected to open on 20 October 2020 and is expected to have more than 200 international participants and more than 25 million visitors (70 percent from overseas) over the ensuing six months. Hosting the Expo is expensive, but the direct and indirect benefits have historically been well worth the host nation's upfront investment. In Dubai's case, the organizers plan on investing approximately $2 billion to $4 billion and estimate that the value created for the city will be in the area of $7 billion (Al Hashimy, 2012).

Culture

When the term *culture* is discussed, it often leads to a plethora of diverse thoughts and emotions. From ethnicity to the organizational climate of a company or organization, the relationship between culture and innovation becomes even more complex as more individual opinions and views are added to the calculus. Many scholars and practicing professionals have observed and commented on the "innovation–culture" relationship, but the virtual complexity of decoding or simplifying the relationship effectively is complicated. Every organization faces this dilemma, which only gets more convoluted when considering how fast market and environmental conditions change with the infusion of game-changing innovations from immigration and the application of cross-industry technology, processes, or services. Poškienė (2006, p. 45) observed that

> The relationship between culture and innovation is more complex than the research can reveal. It is characterized by many determinants that are simply too difficult to be expressed, measured or perceived. The impact of culture on creativity and innovation depends on the relationships built and on the nature of agreement.

This may indicate an individual view where the unique qualities and values of employees (determinants or variables) make it very difficult to assess the overall culture of an organization as a single entity. However, we feel that generalizations can be made that characterize the majority of traits (actions, beliefs, values, and behaviors) within an organization or culture, but they are not necessarily absolute. We contend that all agencies and organizations develop one or more predominant cultures that are dynamic and evolutionary in nature. Cultures can shift and change dramatically with age, financial condition, product or service mix, and outside influences (politics, societal priorities, etc.).

The question is not what type of organizational culture is present but rather whether it supports innovation or has the ability to transform itself to become an innovative culture. With an eye on globalization and cross-border integration, industry-leading organizations leverage their culture (i.e., global economic condition, nationality, ethnicity; and political, judicial, business, available freedoms, etc.) to achieve competitive advantage. Cultural influencers (traits) directly impact innovation opportunities since these affect individuals who both innovate and use the innovation to improve efficiency and effectiveness.

In order for any organization to create a sustainable innovation culture, the lion's share of members in the organization must not only understand their organization's core competencies (what they are good at) but also the dynamic capabilities that support those core competencies. This requires a significant effort on the part of leadership and management to foster and sustain a healthy and vibrant open communication environment—up, down, and laterally throughout the organization structure. Further, innovative enterprises require visionary leaders, dedicated resources, and a firm intent to inculcate innovation into everyday operations and daily routines. One recent noteworthy example of a major industry leader realigning his company and culture and resources in one direction—what they're good at—is Satya Nadella at Microsoft. Microsoft's independent product groups were anything but a united consortium of product groups aligned with their dynamic capabilities and core competencies, and, most importantly, innovating with a focus on what the customer wants. Although we discuss dynamic capabilities, core competencies, and organizational culture in more detail in Chapter 6, "Innovation and Leadership," we offer a top-level discussion on innovation culture as it pertains to Dubai. For those seeking additional information on the topic of innovation and culture, we recommend you reference our work in *A Guide to Innovation Processes and Solutions for Government* (McLaughlin and Kennedy, 2015) and the *Innovation Project Management Handbook* (McLaughlin and Kennedy, 2016); or on our website at www.ipsinnovate.com.

Large-Scale Cultural Influences: Individual Perspective

Large-scale cultural influence might begin at the national level with the birth of a person and his or her ancestry, but the mosaic of cultural difference and social identity tends to define national culture. Individuals affiliate with a national identity or culture and see themselves as an extension of that group. Although cultural affiliations may not be that strong, individuals have a natural acclimation to "belong" to a group and will associate with that group, regardless of national identity or heritage. As a case in point, this phenomena is occurring in Dubai as its national identity continues to become more cosmopolitan than many countries in the MENA region. These national groups can exhibit many similar behavior patterns, which is a foundational element in understanding how individuals will evaluate, accept, and act on a particular innovation opportunity. In other words, they can determine whether an individual will purchase, adopt, or use the innovative product service or technology (Poškien, 2006).

National Cultures

National cultures are the attributes of prevailing societies that exist among the citizens of a particular nation or ethnic group. Although not all citizens may follow or agree with the assessment, generalizations can be made based on certain common and accepted attributes (variables) in any national culture. How the generalizations are used may be open to further discussion; the intent is to provide a set of attributes usable for marketing and sales purposes. When discussing national cultures, we offer Hofstede's model of five dimensions to represent the types of cultures found worldwide. These are

1. Power distance—access to and impact on authority
2. Individualism/collectivism—centering on individual needs versus the good of the community
3. Masculinity/femininity—focused, aggressive, or creative
4. Uncertainty avoidance—stability of government, business, and society
5. Long-/short-term orientation—planning process and strategic thinking (de Mooij and Hofstede, 2010)

These dimensions are useful for generalizations but may not apply to a particular individual within a culture. Nonetheless, they provide a

mechanism for evaluating national culture characteristics. As a point of reference, Hofstede's characteristics are helpful in the areas of advertising, sales,
marketing, and market research. Further, we feel that real-time analytics provides instrumental information (data) on individuals and groups worldwide
that will greatly assist companies focused on becoming innovative in nature
to achieve their goals. Analytics is the process of filtering, categorizing, and
classifying a large amount of information generated by individuals. Beyond
pinpointing the individual needs irrespective of national or geographic
boundaries, a common understanding of what innovation is and how it
can be diffused or adopted is of instrumental importance to any nation or
organization.

Ethnicities

As much or more of a contributor to national culture are ethnic influences.
Ethnicities have more to do with natural biological affiliations (language,
skin color, heritage, etc.) than with cultural affiliation. Ethnicity is often associated with uncontrollable traits that can't be easily disguised. It also permits
individuals to make, sometimes falsely, claims about a particular ethnicity
that may not be true for all participants.

Ethnicity has become a major cornerstone of diversity policies. With an
emphasis on CSR, organizations must recognize the unique differences (and
complementary similarities) of ethnic groups. How ethnic groups are recognized and treated are important issues. The concept of "diversity" highlights
the ethnic challenges that countries like Dubai, and organizations operating
in Dubai, must face. The major ethnicity classifications may not be sufficient
for predicting exact behaviors. Therefore, further analysis of ethnic diversity
beyond a simple classification is necessary.

To understand ethnicity requires a familiarity with the culture, history,
geography, and resources. For example, a linkage to innovation is that
certain ethnicities tend to have similar buying behaviors or traits. Some
ethnicities "value" things differently than others; for example, Asians value
the elderly for their wisdom, while Hispanics have strong social and religious ties. Further, innovation adoption or diffusion behaviors are related
to what the individual values. When the value exceeds what is expected,
and a need is satisfied, innovation can occur. Finally, characterizing ethnic traits is essential for understanding how value is created and utilized.
The greater the detail, the better these ethnic characteristics will link to

a successful innovation event and a deeper understanding of consumer behaviors.

Organizational Cultures

According to Berson et al. (2007), there are three major types of organizational cultures:

1. Innovative (entrepreneurial, creative, risk-taking)
2. Bureaucratic (emphasis on rules, regulation, and efficiency)
3. Supportive (employee–customer centric)

From an international organization perspective, these are always considered generalizations of any culture across the globe. Further, the three measurement criteria listed provide (1) a basis on which to judge and determine the influence of an organization's culture on its employees, suppliers, and customers; as well as (2) an accepted measurement criteria for organizations to help evaluate the general state of the organization:

1. Dominance: How frequently does the organization reflect this behavior?
2. Significance: How important (prevalent) is the organizational attribute?
3. History: How long has this attribute been part of the organizational DNA?

In our book titled the *Innovation Project Management Handbook* (McLaughlin and Kennedy, 2016) and on our website (www.ipsinnovate.com), we have developed several agile, interactive, and industry-agnostic tools (i.e., Organizational Culture Assessment) that any organization can incorporate into their existing innovation management process(es) or employ as a stand-alone effort.

Political and Government System Influences

One of the primary influences on innovation in Dubai is access to resources and populace participation. Like many Muslim nations, Dubai's government is based on a monarchy and on a central legal system referred to as the Sharia (meaning "moral or religious") or Islamic law derived from Islam (the Quran and Hadith) and religious prophecy versus human legislation. Further, their system of governance complements Hofstede's characteristics but focuses more on the religious, political, and social realm. Sharia also deals with politics, business, and economics; personal matters; and day-to-day etiquette. As Dubai's resources are limited due to its geographic location and the shortage of raw materials, its dwindling oil supply, which currently makes up approximately 6 percent of its GDP, is a growing concern.

Sheikh Mohammed's vision to create a future for the 800,000 native Emiratis is truly challenging the boundaries of their neighbors and past characteristics of religious intolerance and ideological differences with the West. Dubai prefers a peaceful and mutually beneficial relationship with the international community versus confrontation and isolation. This approach is truly transformational in nature. It has also elevated Sheikh Mohammed to rock-star status on an international scale and Dubai to that of arguably one of, if not the most, elegant, prestigious, and innovative cultures the world has seen for decades.

One might consider Dubai and the UAE's governmental structure as very stable. They have had a relatively short but dynamic history over the past century, culminating in a zenith-style ride to global prominence. Some might attribute that precipitous climb to the country's leadership and ardent commitment to a vision that embraces international investment and an unusual tolerance of Western ideals that differs from its immediate neighbors in the MENA region. In reality, Dubai is carving out its own path toward redefining the traditional concept of the "consumer nation." It has adopted business models with no borders or boundaries and has skillfully targeted the global consumer with precision and decisive action without jeopardizing its national culture and identity. Conversely, unstable governments and regimes can experience a large and dramatic cultural shift.

Some unique cultural characteristics that governments and political systems must consider when developing national and foreign policy follow. This is by no means a complete list of characteristics, but they are germane and often applicable to every nation or nation-state.

1. Availability of resources to basic needs (access to food, water, sanitation, education, medical services)
2. Open communications (press, social media, hospitality, entertainment)
3. Receptiveness to the populace (freedoms/responsibilities, government bureaucracy, trust)

4. Viability of infrastructure (transportation, communications, technology, currency, banking)
5. Policies, procedures, and taxes (licensing, regulations, tax burden, fees)

No government is perfect, and our emphasis in relation to Dubai in this area is on innovation. Thus, for an innovative culture to exist, certain assumptions (criteria) must be met. At a high level, they include but are not limited to

1. Innate creativity encouraged at the individual level
2. Ability to communicate these ideas
3. Receptive management (authorities)
4. Access to resources (technology, information, performance, and experience)

Although Dubai is considered very cosmopolitan and progressive and is certainly not considered a "repressive" nation, its residents do maintain cultural norms and beliefs that other more liberal nations might feel are inhibiting or suppressive. Regardless, we maintain that even the most repressive nations or nation-states can still encourage innovation if the aforementioned criteria are met. That said, for innovation to flow freely, a government must encourage creativity and readily accept those who want to participate. The best approach to understanding (evaluating) the influence of any government's activities on innovation is to evaluate and assess the importance of each attribute or criteria as it relates to the government's situation and its ability to meet the innovative culture criteria. We recommend you consult our book *Innovation Project Management Handbook* (McLaughlin and Kennedy, 2016) if you're interested in learning more about the associated assessments regarding this subject.

Affiliate Cultures

Affiliate groups are best described as individuals joined to a group by a set of shared values (common goals). A typical affiliate group would be members from the same country (i.e., Emiratis) or, for larger countries, regional groups (i.e., Emiratis from the other six emirates). Subpopulaces, such as the expats and third-country nationals (TCN) that make up some 15 million people in Dubai, would also be considered affiliate groups. But it is not just countries or regions that identify these groups—it could be sports teams, religious groups, patient groups, artists, professionals and so on; or, the negative side, gangs or groups who oppose the principles of human dignity and respect.

Affiliate cultures can have a dramatic effect on behaviors, experiences, and information. At this level, trust becomes a major issue. Individuals tend to trust each other when their values are known and similar. Relative to innovation, it is not uncommon for a person to ask an affiliate member about his or her history, experiences, and use of an innovative product, process, or service. Reviewing case studies to date reveals that the amount of influence an affiliate group expends or has on an innovation is unknown, which makes it a ripe candidate for future studies both in business and academia. However, to estimate the affect of affiliate cultures on innovation, we recommend that one consider the affiliations possible and, depending on the product, service, or technology, the impact on the item for starters.

For example, if the product is a sports drink, sports fans' exposure to television advertising makes these individuals aware of the item, thus increasing the perceived benefits of and need for such an item. Research has confirmed time and time again that individuals tend to rely on information and personal experience to judge innovation. Affiliate group members in a circle of perceived trust can provide this information to a member, which subsequently serves as testimony that influences their expectations in a positive or negative manner. As we continue our research, development, and pursuit of new tools to effectively measure the impact that affiliate cultures have on innovation and consumer purchasing behaviors, we feel this area is clearly of paramount interest to both the international business community as well as to academia.

Family

As we have witnessed from our time working and living in the MENA region, the family holds a special place and meaning across the international landscape regardless of race, culture, or religion. Along with many other scholars and business professionals, we feel that family is best categorized as a small-scale influencer, but it often carries more weight and power when it comes to innovation than national, ethnic, or national cultural effects. Parents and family have a tremendous influence as they provide the moral and ethical framework that children eventually adopt and assimilate as they grow to adulthood. We also posit that this relationship, although frequently modified based on the reality that we all continue to grow and change as we age, can certainly persist into adulthood. In our opinion, these influences seem to be location and culture dependent. We maintain that the closer a family is, the greater the tendency to influence others within the family unit. All of us in the past have sometimes used family members to help us with a decision; that is, we have sought out and requested their knowledge and experiences on a matter and combined those with our preferences to form an opinion or make a decision. In sum, families can exert positive or negative pressure on their family members regarding an innovation event, and this pressure to conform (or not) will likely have an impact on the eventual perception of an innovation outcome or decision. Families will always play a role in affecting our behaviors; what that role is can change over our lifetime.

Peers (Friends)

Similar to an affiliate, friendship is best characterized as a personal connection. It is not uncommon for people to seek advice from their peers and friends regarding the use and purchase of a perceived innovation. This is a common characteristic and practice across multiple cultures. Depending on the complexity component and the knowledge and experience with like products, services, or technology, peer advice may be complementary or contradictory when it comes to any type of innovation. Peer pressure is powerful, and companies are keen to exploit the impact it can have on their sales and competitive position in a market sector.

Peer pressure can be consuming and simply unmanageable. It is that innate desire that is triggered within us to be the same, have the same, and appear the same as people we want to fit in with. It is often more powerful than our bond to the family itself, as it signifies a recognition that we have departed from the trust of our inner circle (the family) and are now influenced by those who we admire or want to be like. Peer pressure has no specific affiliations with age, gender, social status, and so on; at its basic level, it is based on the desire to fit in. This is certainly more common in younger individuals, but it can be a lingering challenge for more mature adults as they seek to remain relevant in their desired sphere of influence. The amount of peer pressure on innovation may be considered limited for mature adults and quite strong for younger individuals. However, the vision of Dubai is not necessarily focused on the young outside the country's native populace but on those who have the means to afford an opulent and lavish lifestyle focused more on peer pressure that rivals any youngster's experience with pressure from their peers.

Estimating the Effect of Dubai's Culture on Innovation

It is obvious that Dubai's native culture has been affected by the 15 million expats represented from some 180-plus countries from around the world. The culmination of such a diverse collection of cultures living and working closely together in such a small geographic and densely packed area supports our position that cultures are influenced by this arrangement. Thus, we posit that how a person perceives life experiences, decision-making, and judgments, regardless of the native culture, is somewhat touched and influenced by Dubai's evolving identity. In Dubai's case, because of the tendency to promote a certain desired value or proficiency (such as technical solutions, green and ecologically responsible initiatives, CSR, etc.), people associated with the culture tend to adopt a mindset that promotes the desired values and behaviors. Those who align with the desired values often tend to adapt more quickly than those who disagree.

Subsequently, a person tends to develop a model of reality that is culturally bound (influenced). They use the model to build the knowledge and experience with which they judge such concepts as innovation. To know how much or little culture impacts innovation is a necessity if Dubai, as a prominent adopter and example of an innovative culture, plans to remain competitive and distinctive throughout the twenty-first century.

Culture and the Environment

When considering culture and environment, we provide the following considerations for Dubai's leadership and organizations working within Dubai's public and private domains for building on their current innovation culture.

1. Continue to make innovation a central theme in the national or organizational culture. This must be a top-down approach whereby leaders are proponents and catalysts for a culture of innovation wherein ideas

are shared openly and business models and strategies reflect and support innovation.

2. Create an open and collaborative cultural environment, free from fear, where creativity and the sharing of ideas are embraced, not diminished or dampened by leadership. Realizing that great ideas are not only generated by innovation pioneers but at all rungs in the organization is essential. Not everyone is an innovator, but everyone does have creative thoughts and ideas that could be combined with others that could lead to an innovation.

3. Recognize that change agents that generate innovation opportunities come from everywhere (both within and external to your organization). Establishing a defined and well-understood process for sharing new ideas for products, services, or processes is essential. Freelancing is encouraged, but there must be a methodology for elevating ideas to the decision makers without their being marginalized or changed to reflect current product offers, services, or processes.

4. Accept that change and risk-taking are realities in any innovation opportunity. If organizations plan to grow, gain competitive advantage, and create value for their shareholders, stakeholders, and the community, a dynamic and responsive change and risk management system that aligns with the selected innovation management system must be in place.

5. Create and maintain balance between innovation and sustainability strategies. In today's rapid-paced global market environment, not every creative idea gets adopted, and if one does, there is a good chance it will require a transition to a sustainment strategy.

6. Encourage an environment of trust, sincerity, diversity, human dignity, and respect for all. An environment of trust and sincerity breaks down many traditional barriers to open and transparent communication. Diversity brings a fertile environment as differing views provide an enriched perspective while creating opportunities for expanding one's thoughts. Human dignity and respect is the bedrock that provides every individual with equal footing, a sense of personal value, and the confidence to openly share what is on his or her mind.

7. Know your customer and industry. Focus on customer and industry needs, not the wants of your organization. Creating "blue ocean" opportunities or "white space" requires that you have a desirable product, service, or process that is either incrementally improved or perhaps a game changer (disruptive) that improves efficiency, value, or

competitive position or opens new market space opportunities (Kim and Mauborgne, 2005).

8. Cultivate an innovation environment and mindset by providing your people with the right tools, time, and training. Along with making innovation a main theme in daily operations, it is of quintessential importance to ensure that your most valuable resource, your people, are engaged in the innovation process, celebrate it, and understand how to package, present, and offer ideas.

9. Challenge your organization with clear and concise expectations. When people are challenged and expectations are known, they have an opportunity to be in synch with others, creating innovation opportunities for real synergy.

10. Minimize conflict through collaboration and openness. Conflict creates adversity, which derails the transfer of tacit knowledge and intellectual capital development (Isaksen and Ekvall, 2010). Communication and collaboration suffer, and the benefits of teaming, creativity, cooperation, and trust are all put on hold.

11. Ensure empowerment and accountability. When people feel empowered to make decisions and are subsequently accountable for their own results, they tend to be more engaged with the organizational entities around them.

In the final section of this chapter, we offer a brief discussion on the use of alliances and why they are important and relevant to Dubai's culture of innovation.

Alliances and Innovation

Both nations and organizations that seek partnering relationships and strategic alliances built on open collaboration and information sharing can open doors to fertile resource creation, competitive advantage, and ultimately, a value-added position in competitive market sectors. As many scholars and innovation management practitioners have cited, there is often more emphasis placed on the outcome of an alliance and little attention paid to the actual structuring of alliances, network density and composition, and the intellectual and structural capital differences between partnering entities (Phelps, 2010). These differences or "structural holes" limit the alliance's ability to access, cultivate, and share knowledge, reducing the opportunity for all players to benefit from the technological and intellectual differences of their partners. Phelps (2010) suggests that adding more members (increasing network density) to the alliance will strengthen the cohort and positively influence exploratory innovation (i.e., the creation of novel technological knowledge relative to existing knowledge stock).

Logically, the pooling of resources (intellectual and structural) in a collaborative effort could be a very productive endeavor with strategic and competitive implications for alliance partners. Intellectual capital is the catalyst for competitive purpose and value, and companies are just not willing to share that freely. In the past, alliances were identified as primary options for smaller companies to improve their competitive advantage. However, in an open innovation environment, countries like Dubai and larger corporations at the international level have been equally successful. For example, top industry leaders such as Apple and Samsung forged a long-term alliance that continues to have trend-leading benefits for both firms. Alliances do have a life cycle (a beginning and an end point) that should be considered when agreements are made. For example, the relationship between Samsung and Apple appeared to be a complimentary and beneficial alliance until Samsung released the Android platform in direct competition with Apple's product line—then they went to court over copyright infringement.

Although some companies do not fare well by acquiring and merging to build competitive advantage (eliminating competitors and diversifying their portfolios), joint ventures and strategic alliances are possible alternatives. However, strategic alliances and joint ventures are alliances that are normally time-sensitive, collaborative approaches that must be built over time to create a scaffolding of earned trust. Building trust often starts with small projects and agreements with the intent to build a collaborative partnership and trust between two entities or companies (and cultures). They are well defined by specific rules of engagement, levels of sharing and responsibility, agreement as to how long the relationship will last, and defined benefits for each participating member. The strategic objective of this type of alliance is often to reduce risk, cost, and loss of competitive advantage while developing innovation opportunities (i.e., products, services, or processes).

Summary

In this chapter, we discussed how Dubai's dynamic approach in pursuing pioneering innovation opportunities has had a resounding ripple effect across the international landscape. There is also little doubt that HRH Sheikh

Mohammed bin Rashid Al Maktoum's commitment is not to opulent land-marks without purpose and value but to building a better economic and CSR-compliant environment for his people and the world in general. His focus is clearly on increased value and competitive advantage for the host population while setting the stage for public and private organizations from the international community to also benefit handsomely from contributing to Dubai's overall vision.

Coupled with the emirate's "all-in" commitment to innovation and its growing track record of innovation prominence across the global landscape, Dubai's hallmark dynamic and vibrant culture has repeatedly been acknowl-edged as the single most important catalyst for innovation and growth across the MENA region. Dubai leveraged its very innovative culture to secure the World Expo 2020 and a firm grip on its prominence as the epicenter for the modern innovation revolution. Finally, we presented key elements instru-mental in building a sustainable culture of innovation—chiefly, the Dubai leadership's tendency to promote a certain desired value or proficiency (such as technical solutions, green and ecologically responsible initiatives, CSR, etc.). Keen and progressive visionary leaders know that people associated with the culture tend to adopt a mindset that promotes the desired values and behaviors. They walk the walk and truly lead by example. In the next chapter, we explore innovation in Dubai's private sector.

Discussion Questions

1. How would you define culture?
2. What are the cultural influences affecting you and your organization? Name five in each category (individual and organization).
3. What are the five unique characteristics of government (political sys-tems) that have an impact on culture?
4. What are alliances and partnerships? Why are they important? As a leader in your agency or organization, what are some of the key consid-erations when entering a partnership or alliance?

Assignments

1. As a leader in your organization, briefly discuss three things you can do to build a culture of innovation in your organization.

2. Although every culture has its own special identity or DNA, there are some variables that can certainly affect the adoption of an innovation opportunity. Please select three to five variables or characteristics that relate to your own organization's culture. Using the discussion in this text and resources in the public domain, briefly provide your definition and understanding of each variable or characteristic and a short example of how it relates to your specific organization.

Chapter 4

Innovation in the Private Sector

Introduction

Driven by the vision of His Royal Highness (HRH) Sheikh Mohammed bin Rashid Al Maktoum, vice president of the United Arab Emirates (UAE) and prime minister and ruler of Dubai, Dubai's seminal goal is to achieve long-lasting prosperity for the emirate. Dubai (the most densely populated city within the UAE) and Abu Dhabi (the capital of the UAE) are the two commercial and cultural centers of activity within the UAE. The UAE has a high-income economy and gross domestic product (GDP) per capita, ranking approximately 19th in the world at the time of this writing. The country also enjoys a sizable annual trade surplus.

Dubai's underlying premise for and strategy toward innovation is rooted in the philosophy of taking something done well and doing it better. We assess this acclimation toward innovation as generally incremental in nature but do not rule out the potential pursuit of disruptive innovation or ideas. The central question many might have is, how does a population of approximately 200,000 Emiratis in a desert community that was once a small fishing village and trading port achieve so much in such a short time span? Some might attribute this to the country's innovation strategy of building clusters of innovation, whereby world business leaders across multiple market sectors are encouraged to share the best ideas in an open and transparent environment, which attracts world-class talent like moths to a flame. Many believe it's the oil revenues that have made this incredible journey possible.

In reality, it takes much more than natural resources to sustain the rapid growth that Dubai has experienced since the turn of the century.

In this chapter, we explore just some of the central innovations championed across key industries central to Dubai's Vision 2020, strategic goals and objectives, and other supporting visions and plans as they relate to those specific industries. Because of the sheer magnitude of advancements made over the past 15 years, attempting to capture the advancements and accomplishments while providing acceptable due diligence and discussion to properly acknowledge the achievements is understandably beyond the scope of this book. Subsequently, we'll focus our discussion on pioneering and innovative achievements and initiatives central to the three strategic pillars of HRH Sheikh Mohammed bin Rashid Al Maktoum's Vision 2020 Plan—sustainable tourism, industrial development, and the financial sector; and the ambitious but noteworthy achievements in sustainable development and green initiatives.

Background

Central to Dubai's current economic growth and sustainment strategy is a three-pronged approach focused on establishing world-class and sustainable tourism, an industrial base, and financial systems to offset the drop in oil and natural-gas revenues (ranked the seventh largest reserves in the world), which are estimated to deplete significantly over the next 10–50 years (depending on which estimate one follows). Commercially, Germany and the United Kingdom are the largest export markets for Dubai.

Dubai is already one of the world's top 10 most visited cities and was also awarded the World Expo 2020, which represents an unprecedented achievement for the region. World Expos are known as the key meeting point for the global community to share innovations and make progress on issues of international importance (e.g., the global economy, sustainable development, and improved quality of life for the world's population). The World Expo is also a catalyst for economic, social, and cultural transformation, generating important legacies for the city and nation hosting this event.

Embracing more than 180 nationalities and cultures, Dubai is already an important international tourism destination (with over 95,000 hotel rooms and 11 million tourists recorded in 2014). It is also home to 63 business councils and a financial center for 18 of the world's top 25 international banks, six of the top 10 law firms, and six of the top 10 insurance companies. Expo 2020 is also expected to provide some 277,000 new job opportunities, having a positive and comprehensive economic impact on small and medium enterprises (SMEs), which constitute approximately 95 percent of all registered companies in the UAE (Woods, 2014).

Ahead of World Expo 2020, the UAE government has embarked on a journey to upgrade its infrastructure, prompting more interest in the country and encouraging business and investment. In sum, many new business development opportunities and projects across all business sectors, to include demands on goods, will drastically increase over the next 5–10 years, and that will certainly energize the overall trade market (Bitar, 2014). World Expo 2020 will also facilitate economic diversification by finding new paths for economic development. According to the latest statistics, in 2015 construction and infrastructure projects announced and underway in the Gulf Cooperation Council (GCC) countries account for $1.9 trillion, while UAE's share accounts for 49 percent of the overall projects. The UAE continues to remain the largest projects market, with around $940 billion worth of projects under execution (Emirates News Agency, 2014).

Leveraging the vision of his father, Sheikh Rashid, Sheikh Mohammed envisioned what could best be described as a "develop for survival" approach to replace the country's oil revenues, which are estimated to drop significantly over the next 10–30 years. Central to Sheikh Mohammed's economic strategic vision is for Dubai to become the international community's leading financial services provider, the world's largest international transportation and redistribution hub, and ultimately the globe's top medical tourism (MT) destination spot.

Current Economic Strategy

Central to Dubai's economic strategy for sustained growth and move toward a consumer-based economy is tourism, the establishment of a robust industrial base, and becoming an internationally accepted financial center. As the footprint of Dubai's development and infrastructure grows measurably by the month, the emirate's influence on and attraction for the international community grows. Foreign investors and those desiring a lavish and almost unrealistic lifestyle gravitate toward the emirate like a moth to a flame. Articulating his vision in the book *My Vision: Challenges in the Race for Excellence*, Sheikh Mohammed bin Rashid Al Maktoum argues that intrepid leadership and trust are essential elements to building the required infrastructure and environment for Dubai to flourish at the level His Highness envisions. Sheikh Mohammed shares a great analogy in this book that epitomizes Dubai's pursuit of excellence and innovation: "Whether you consider yourself a gazelle or lion, you simply have to run faster than others to survive" (Al Maktoum M. bin Rashid, 2006, p. 12). On the heels of Sheikh Mohammed's 2006 book, Dubai faced a four-year economic downturn that spawned much doubt as to whether the emirate would ever experience or sustain the unprecedented growth it saw between 2001 and 2007.

Many articles with mixed opinions and reviews exist in the public domain on Dubai's recent financial crisis (2007–2010), and we encourage readers to pursue due diligence in considering Dubai's exposure to international economic conditions. Some saw this as a bad omen for the future, while others considered it just another challenge on the road to a strong and thriving country with a vision of becoming the world's Rubicon of innovation in the global landscape. History has shown time and time again that sustained growth at a record-setting pace is simply not sustainable in the long run. Culture and a healthy consumer base are essential drivers in the very fabric that establishes the required supply and demand requirements to sustain continuous growth.

At a rudimentary level, an example can be seen in a company that finds itself in a prolonged incremental innovation loop because it lacks a viable innovation opportunity strategy or it has simply run out of ideas on how to grow. Here, the company focuses on incrementally improving its process to save resources or build its cash position in questionable economic times or indecision. When the economy takes a downturn, many international companies jettison their business strategy and vision statements on innovation opportunities, and slip into survival mode or strategy to weather the proverbial storm or economic downturn. We do not say that this is the wrong move for every organization or company, but these are the times when game-changing and transformational innovation opportunities present themselves. In sum, it takes a visionary leader with the commitment to stay the course of his or her convictions to navigate these trying times, much like Dubai's prolific leader, His Highness Sheikh Mohammed.

Sustainable Tourism

This is a very large vertical industry being led by the entertainment, health, wellness, and medical sectors. As the footprint of Dubai's infrastructure grows at a prolific pace each month, its international influence and meteoric rise are attracting significant attention across the global health-care communities. Much like Costa Rica and Thailand, Dubai is developing a very competitive MT presence led by the boutique or concierge business model.

Medical Tourism

Much like Costa Rica and Thailand, Dubai has launched an aggressive effort to improve the quality, affordability, and timeliness of care in both the government and private health-care sectors. Central to the medical industry's transformation and reform are the government's establishment of the Dubai Health Authority (DHA) and the Dubai Health City Authority (DHCA). The DHA and DHCA are chartered to oversee and develop new initiatives and programs such as

1. Unification of health-care policies, improving access to quality and affordable care while reducing the reliance on out-of-country treatment
2. Unification of private and public sectors
3. Development of a premier medical academic institution
4. Substantial investment in modernizing hospitals
5. Establishment of mandatory health insurance
6. Adoption of specialty clinics based on the boutique or concierge business models, which attract a spectrum of complimentary market segments such as pharmaceutical manufacturers and pharmacies, research laboratories, wellness clinics, and so on

Further, Dubai's specialty clinics draw regional clients from the Cooperation Council of Arab States of the Gulf (GCC), seeking cardiac, spinal, dental, and plastic surgery procedures. In sum, the efforts to date have Dubai on the cusp of emerging as one of the international community's top MT destinations. Health within the UAE is an instrumental concern. The life expectancy at birth in the UAE is 78.5 years, and cardiovascular disease is the principal cause of death in the UAE, constituting 28 percent of total deaths; other major causes are accidents and injuries, malignancies, and congenital anomalies (Figure 4.1).

In February 2008, the Ministry of Health unveiled a 5-year health strategy for the public health sector in the northern emirates, which fall under its purview and which, unlike Abu Dhabi and Dubai, do not have separate

Figure 4.1   Dubai Healthcare City (DHCC): Mohammed bin Rashid Academic Medical Center. (Courtesy of Dr. Aaron "Sandy" Amacher.)

health-care authorities. The strategy focuses on unifying health-care policy and improving access to health-care services at a reasonable cost, at the same time reducing dependence on overseas treatment. The ministry plans to add 3 hospitals to the current 14 and 29 primary health-care centers to the current 86. Nine were scheduled to open in 2008 (El Shammaa, 2009) (Figure 4.2).

The introduction of mandatory health insurance in Abu Dhabi for expats and family members was a major driver in reforming the emirate's health-care

Figure 4.2   Dubai Healthcare City (DHCC). (Courtesy of Dr. Aaron "Sandy" Amacher.)

policy. Abu Dhabi nationals were brought under the scheme from 1 June 2008 and Dubai followed for its government employees. Eventually, under federal law, every Emirati and expat in the country will be covered by compulsory health insurance under a unified mandatory scheme. Recently, the country has been benefiting from medical tourists from all over the GCC. The UAE currently attracts medical tourists seeking plastic surgery and advanced procedures, cardiac and spinal surgery, and dental treatment, as UAE health services have higher standards than other Arab countries in the Persian Gulf (Detrie, 2009).

The medical sector in the UAE is based on the English language; its foundation is built on Western medical practice and policy (British and American). An example of Dubai's concerted efforts to change the calculus of health care in the emirate is the development of the Dubai Healthcare City (DHCC). The DHCC or health-care precinct is currently under development with an initial estimated footprint of some 16 city blocks. According to Dr. Azad Moopen, chairman, Aster DM Healthcare,

As Dubai begins to attract medical tourists, I believe there should be more centers of excellence established and Dubai Healthcare City (DHCC) is looking into that.

There will be a huge requirement of professional staff but we are not producing doctors and nurses, as we should. (Saberi, 2014)

In sum, with improved access made possible through centrally locating health-care services and the improved affordability of quality health care within the emirate, both Emiratis and expats working in the country will certainly benefit. Further, the advancements have drawn the attention of many world-class health-care providers who are keen on the prospect of relocating and opening their practices within the DHCC precinct. In order to support ambitious measures like the DHCC, the establishment of a robust infrastructure and industrial base must be considered quintessential elements in the DHCC's evolution and success.

Industrial Development

In the latest estimates from multiple sources tracking international transportation, supply chain, and distribution performance factors, Dubai has quickly established its place as the third largest retransportation port in the world (behind Korea and Singapore). As of March 2014, Airports Council International reported that the rapid growth in Dubai has positioned it as one of the fastest growing airports in the world and ranks it among the 1400-plus airports worldwide as the seventh busiest. While average growth in passenger travel has increased by some 4 percent worldwide, the report goes on to say that passenger traffic increased by over 15 percent (some 70.5 million passengers) in 2013 (compared with 2012) alone, coming a close second behind Malaysia at 19.1 percent. While 30 percent of the world's top-ranked cargo hubs experienced declines in 2013, Dubai's position greatly improved, and it is now the fourth largest cargo hub in the world with the highest annual increase in the cargo movement category at 6.8 percent (Ohayon, 2014). With double-digit growth projected for Dubai's International Airport and the addition of the new Al Maktoum International Airport, Dubai is positioned not only as the major hub connecting the East and the West, but is also set to move up several positions both in the passenger and cargo rankings in 2014 and 2015. According to a *USA Today* article in January 2015, Dubai is now the world's busiest airport for international travelers (Mutzabaugh, 2015) (Figure 4.3).

Under the Smart City policy umbrella, the government of Dubai issued the landmark Dubai Data Law in October 2015. The measure opens the door for potential opportunities for collaboration between the government and the private (or nongovernment) sector through the sharing of data that was previously generated and maintained by government entities. This partnering concept in support of Smart City development is also expected to drive innovation opportunities and entrepreneurship across both segments. The law also defines the type of data available for sharing, the parameters of what can be shared, and how government and private-sector entities can approach the data-sharing relationship.

Figure 4.3   New airport model. (Courtesy of Dr. Aaron "Sandy" Amacher.)

Smart City

As many authors and visionaries continue to profess, the world's migration to urbanization of the "modern" or "Smart City" is moving a lot quicker than many might anticipate. Dubai's rapid growth is perhaps one, if not the most, epic example in the world today. Its meteoric growth in popularity and size clearly places it under the mantle of all things possible in sustainable and responsible urban living, and the city may be primed to become the road-map for all others in the global landscape to emulate and build from. From the city's early days as a small fishing and trade village to the early 1950s, when oil was unexpectedly discovered when drilling for water, the city and the Emirati culture has transformed like no other. Some might contest the relevance of Dubai's opulent and exotic buildings and lifestyle, but one thing is certainly clear; it is primed to become the world's leading example of a net zero city where engineering, technology, and policy achieve world-class energy efficiency and CO^2 reduction goals.

When it comes to the three cornerstones of responsible business practice (social, financial, and environmental responsibility), there will always be differing views on whether Dubai's approach to balancing the competing interests of "people, planet, and profit" is truly a socially responsible model for others to emulate (Figure 4.4).

Internet of Things

Like a celestial sphere that has yet to reach the highest point of achievement, the information technology and telecommunications industries have driven cross-over innovation opportunities of a magnitude comparable with that of Moore's Law. The insatiable appetite for mobile, "on-demand," real-time access to any resource or handheld device in any environment at the stroke of a fingertip, 24/7, 365 days a year has literally permeated all facets of life. At the heart of this fervor is the global information grid (GIG), a menagerie of terrestrial and space-based telecommunications systems that link users to the cloud via Internet protocol (IP) addresses specific to domains within the GIG ecosystem.

With every visionary brushstroke, the blank canvas of Dubai's footprint is filled with the artist's vision. From developing and implementing smart power grids that redistribute power resources across the city's infrastructure to meet changing community requirements, to the growing ecosystem of Internet-connected appliances and intelligent converged networks that link

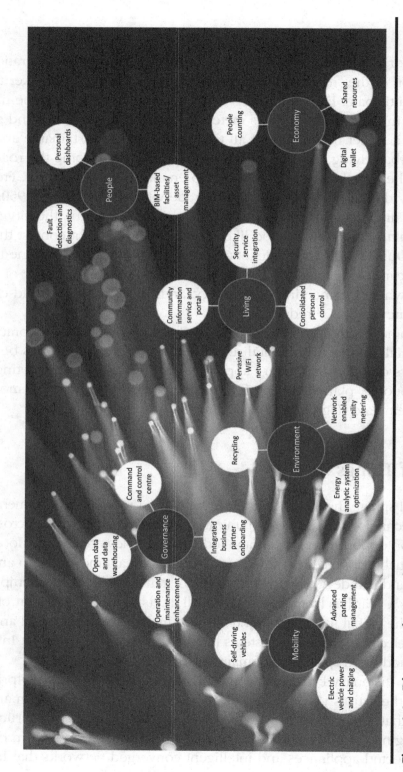

Figure 4.4 Diagram of smart city planning model. (Dubaidesigndistrict (d3). Smart city. Dubaidesigndistrict.com. Retrieved from http://www.dubaidesigndistrict.com/innovation/smart-city-2, 2016.)

roads, airports, railways, and ports, Dubai's realization of a networked city is astounding. Leveraging the computing power of the cloud, Dubai is not only building a robust and reliable IT infrastructure to support an evolving Internet of Things (IoT) presence, it is compiling some of the world's top marks for improvement in the areas of efficiency, safety, security, the reduction of waste, and the optimization of resources and services. Additionally, the development of a fully networked, scalable, and intelligent transportation system is providing the city with the necessary platforms and infrastructure for continued growth and expansion into the foreseeable future. Central to Dubai's commitment to harnessing the power of advancing technologies and the GIG is the necessary policy and guidance to govern the day-to-day operations and future planning of the "City of Innovation."

Policy

Under the Smart City policy umbrella, the government of Dubai issued the landmark Dubai Data Law in October 2015. The measure fosters an environment where there is an increased focus around policy and guidance that incentivizes the transfer of knowledge between the public, academic, and private sectors with the goal of securing benefits for all and job creation. The measure opens the door for potential opportunities for collaboration between the government and the private (or nongovernment) sector through the sharing of data that was previously generated and maintained by government entities. This partnering concept in support of Smart City development is also expected to drive innovation opportunities and entrepreneurship across both segments. The law also defines the type of data available for sharing, the parameters of what can be shared, and how government and private-sector entities can approach the data-sharing relationship.

Renewable and Clean Energy

The world's energy equation is changing, and the demand for electricity will have grown by a hefty 76 percent by 2030 (Bowman, 2012). With fossil-fuel supplies on the verge of extinction for the second time in their cycle of life, the call for clean, renewable, and adaptable energy sources has resonated across the globe with profound announcement. Pundits are calling for nations and states to consider alternatives, with leaders like Germany, Dubai, and the United States adopting aggressive efforts to deploy renewable (wind, water, solar, etc.) and clean (natural gas, clean coal, etc.) resources as their primary sources of energy and electricity. In fact, Dubai's commitment to leading the move to renewable energy was a significant contributor in the UAE hosting the World Future Energy Summit 2016 in Abu-Dhabi.

Of the class of renewable energy candidates, solar power is an integral element of diversifying the city's energy mix as part of Dubai's Integrated Energy Strategy 2030, the Dubai Plan 2021, and the UAE Vision 2021. Coupled with the plans to leverage nuclear and clean coal sources under the current strategy, it's estimated that roughly 30 percent of the emirate's energy and electricity requirements will be met by solar, nuclear, and clean coal technologies, while the estimated remaining 70 percent will be met by natural gas (Al Tayer, 2015) (Figure 4.5).

Solar Energy

Enjoying over 300 days per year of sunshine on average, Dubai has completed the first two phases (200 megawatt capacity) of Mohammed bin Rashid Al Maktoum Solar Park, and the third phase of the park has been launched, which also includes a new Solar Innovation Center, which will be open in 2017. Using photovoltaic (PV) and solar thermal technologies, the projected capacity of follow-on phases in the park are expected to reach 3000 megawatts on completion, bringing the overall footprint of the park to

Figure 4.5   Mohammed bin Rashid Al Maktoum Solar Park. (Bhatia, Mohammed bin Rashid Al Maktoum Solar Park. Constructionweek.com. Retrieved from http://www. constructionweekonline.com/article-34564-uae-dewa-inks-32m-deal-for-dubai-water-networks, 2015.)

over 40 square kilometers, the largest in the region. Although this represents another potential seminal effort in Dubai's Smart City plans, the real impact will come when residential homes and other energy users pursue small-scale solar projects that connect to the city's power grid. This provides opportunities for surplus energy produced at sources throughout the city to be fed back into the power grid to meet other energy requirements and support Dubai's green economy and sustainable development initiatives.

Solar Energy 101

The sun produces an incredible amount of energy, and solar power is now considered a potential panacea for the future energy needs of generations to come. At its basic level, solar cells (wafers, ingots, and modules) are made from doped (negative and positive) silicon. The resulting silicon-based products absorb the sunlight and create electrical charges, which are then routed to a conductor (wire) that results in a direct current (DC) being passed to an external circuit. These silicon "gems" are often formed into 6-inch squares that typically generate 1–2 watts of power each and are connected to others forming "solar panels" or arrays. Examples of devices already in use are solar fields, street and resident lighting, calculators, watches, and so on.

With an average life expectancy of 25 years, each panel and subsystem requires regular cleaning and servicing to ensure that efficacy and performance levels are maintained. For a 40-kilometer footprint solar farm subject to desert sandstorms, cleaning and upkeep will certainly be labor intensive and will require a sustainable source of water on the premises.

Solar Energy Challenges

In recent history, the solar industry has been hampered by purified silicon shortages and international disputes between Chinese, U.S., and German companies involving filings of antidumping and countervailing duty positions with the Department of Commerce and International Trade Commission (Movellan, 2011). For countries like Dubai that are devoted to incorporating solar energy technologies as a cornerstone or hallmark of their sustainable energy development policy and planning process, anticipating life-cycle costs over the long term will certainly require an evolutionary strategy. Currently, the four largest global suppliers of purified silicon supporting the solar industry (and electronics industry) are

- Hemlock Semiconductor Corporation (Hemlock, MI)
- Wacker Chemie AG (Munich, Germany)
- Renewable Energy Corporation (Sandvika, Norway)
- MEMC Electronic Materials (St. Peters, MO)

Although there is much optimism about the growth of solar energy in the region, driven somewhat by the continued reduction in the cost of manufacturing PV panels, the long-time supply and demand battle between the electronics and solar energy industries will not be resolved anytime soon. Competition for and cost of "low density, high demand" resources are often more unpredictable than organizations and government entities anticipate in their modeling efforts. They can also be more sensitive to international trade agreements, tariffs, and geopolitical policy when countries disagree on issues such as human rights, intellectual property, or copyright violations, for example. This can place some solar product and service providers at a potential disadvantage based on their location alone.

Financial Sector

At the center of the third leg of Dubai's vision is the independent and tax-free zone referred to as the Dubai International Financial Center (DIFC). Already in place and extremely popular, the DIFC is an international tax-free zone run under Western financial laws and practices from Britain and North America. Worthy of note is that the UAE's economy, particularly that of Dubai, was badly hit by the financial crisis of 2007–2010. In 2009, the country's economy shrank by 4 percent, and the property sector and construction went into decline. However, tourism, trade, and the retail sector have remained buoyant, and the UAE's overseas investments are expected to support its full economic recovery.

Financial Corporate Social Responsibility (CSR) Initiatives

Responsible CSR and sustainability are usually measured in terms of technical, economical, environmental, and social requirements (Vavra et al.,

Figure 4.6 Dubai International Financial Center (DIFC). (Courtesy of Dr. Aaron "Sandy" Amacher.)

2011). One tool finding traction in the area of financial responsibility is the International Association of Outsourcing Professionals (IAOP) Value Health Check Survey (VHCS) (Figure 4.6).

Designed to improve the health and performance of the outsourcing relationship, this flexible (tailorable) 800-question web-based diagnostic survey tool focuses on five key areas of the business relationship: financial performance, service quality, risk, compliance, and governance. From self-inspection checklists to third-party observations and audits, organizations that regularly and proactively monitor, measure, track, and report their performance in key compliance areas create a better reputation in their industry.

There is a broad range of groups that international financial institutions and businesses have obligations to and agreements with, in addition to government, corporate, civic, and legal obligations. Acquiring a prominent pedigree that distinguishes an industry leader in CSR and sustainability requires a social conscious that goes well beyond the bottom line. One of the prominent hallmarks in that pedigree is the open and transparent evaluation from external sources like the nonprofit group the Aspen Institute, which is focused on global leadership initiatives and the greater meaning of humankind and society (the Aspen Institute, 2013). CSR has two levels of observance: compliance and opportunities. Unfortunately, our business schools have traditionally promoted competition and the idea that engaging in business always results in a 'win–lose' proposition. For many reasons that are not well thought out, CSR and sustainability is looked on as a burden instead of a potential game-changing positive factor that could add huge value and competitive advantage for those who lead by adopting the same.

Leadership

When leadership is united through a common and agreeable vision on innovation, the opportunities for creating and sustaining a vibrant culture of open and transparent communication improve markedly. Complementing the traditional venues of news media releases, websites, and formal communications venues, Sheikh Mohammed and many other high-ranking government officials in Dubai are leveraging smart devices, popular social media platforms, and networks to share their vision with an increasingly connected and mobile international fan base. As of this writing, the UAE's prime minister and vice president has amassed an impressive 3 million followers on Facebook and has built a network of more than 11 million followers across Twitter, Instagram, and LinkedIn (Dickinson, 2016). Further, the ability to share one's thoughts with an international audience of some 11 million people in nanoseconds is trending among other international leaders as shown in the recent study *World Leaders on Facebook* by ASDA's Burson-Marsteller. The value-added proposition of leveraging social media to share one's message with one's followers has second- and third-order benefits. Some of those benefits are the elimination or streamlining of major time-consuming tasks (processes), supporting cast (personnel), travel, and other resources (i.e., material and nonmaterial) associated with a typical public news release or formal speaking engagement.

Summary

In this chapter, we provided our thoughts on Dubai's underlying strategy and philosophy toward innovation—taking something done well and doing it better. We assessed this acclimation toward innovation as generally incremental in nature but do not rule out the potential pursuit of disruptive innovation or ideas. We explored some of the central innovations championed across key industries central to Dubai's Vision 2020, strategic goals and objectives, and other supporting visions and plans as they relate to those specific industries. Because of the sheer magnitude of advancements made over the past 15 years, attempting to capture those advancements and accomplishments while providing acceptable due diligence and discussion to properly acknowledge the achievements is understandably beyond the scope of this book. Subsequently, we focused our discussion on pioneering and innovative achievements and initiatives central to the three strategic pillars of HRH Sheikh Mohammed bin Rashid Al Maktoum's Vision 2020 Plan—sustainable tourism, industrial development, and the financial sector; and the ambitious but noteworthy achievements in sustainable development and green initiatives. Dubai's business strategy and culture is also considered the region's most progressive and perhaps the international community's leading model for an open business environment. Through the savvy adoption of social media networks, Dubai's leadership has achieved "rock star" status and popularity in social media circles, and this phenomenon seems to have taken the international community by storm. In our next chapter, we introduce key initiatives relating to the government sector and HRH Sheikh Mohammed bin Rashid Al Maktoum's key foundational principles and elements that are critical to successfully implementing a true leader's vision in a government structure.

Discussion Questions

1. As discussed in this chapter, what is Dubai's premise or philosophy when it comes to innovation?
2. What are the three key primary sectors for innovation identified in Sheikh Mohammed bin Rashid Al Maktoum's Vision 2020 Plan?
3. Provide a brief discussion on innovative projects or programs of initiatives that Dubai has instituted in the any of the three sectors you've identified above (Question 2). Limit your discussion to no more than three projects, programs, or initiatives (2–4 paragraphs on each) and be prepared to share with other students.

Assignments

1. Pick one of the three sectors (sustainable tourism, industrial development, or financial sector) identified in Sheikh Mohammed bin Rashid Al Maktoum's Vision 2020 Plan. Use any available resources to capture and share at least three of the latest innovations and two potential innovation opportunities for the sector you've selected. Complete a report (3–5 pages) that you can share in a presentation with other students.
2. Considering Sheikh Mohammed bin Rashid Al Maktoum's Vision 2020 Plan, share your personal thoughts and ideas on whether Dubai's strategic vision is a sustainable reality. Pick one of the following positions

and provide the necessary discussion and supporting material in a report (2–3 pages) to share with other students.

a. If you believe it is, explain why you feel this way and the rationale behind your position.

b. If you do not believe it is sustainable, explain your position and the rationale behind it.

Chapter 5

Innovation in Government

Introduction

Developing a vision is by no means a serendipitous event or contrary undertaking. From a general perspective, most visions have a desired future state (i.e., a goal or objective—e.g., to be recognized as the world's "City of Innovation"), a clearly defined purpose (i.e., a satisfied need or requirement—e.g., to build a sustainable economy based on innovative products, services, and processes), and values (i.e., guidelines for how to achieve the vision—e.g., to achieve excellence by taking something someone does well and doing it better). A vision typically begins with an ambiguous thought or idea, and, through an established framework of questioning, discovery, and definition driven by curiosity, it evolves into a more concrete and memorable vision statement that inspires an audience. An example of a vision statement capturing the end state, purpose, and value relevant to the vision of Dubai and innovation could be as simple as, "Become the world's recognized leader in excellence through innovation." In reality, good vision statements are short (i.e., 20 words or less) and announce what it is you are trying to achieve in a clear and concise manner. Again, they should also be easy to remember and inspirational. Finally, if the end state, purpose, and value statement cannot be captured in short form, consider a complimentary vision tag-line approach (five words or less) that people can easily remember (e.g., "City of innovation and excellence").

69

Government Vision

In his book entitled, *My Vision: Challenges in the Race for Excellence*, HRH Sheikh Mohammed bin Rashid Al Maktoum outlines the foundational principles and elements that are critical to successfully implementing a true leader's vision in a government structure. At first blush, the act of sharing a vision is not as straightforward as some might think. Once a vision is shared, achievable objectives and goals must be identified and a successful outcome defined. These goals are then supported by a series of objectives, which are driven by detailed tasks. Once the vision and objectives are understood and accepted, a strategy for achieving those goals and objectives is developed and an engagement plan defining the scope, cost, and schedule for implementing and achieving a successful outcome is completed. From Sheikh Mohammed's perspective, "Vision is not a science, it is not an abstract idea either" (2006, p. 32). In a general sense, it is a coalescence of imagination (creativity), understanding and articulation, process, and action. There are four definitive phases that Sheikh Mohammed shares for leaders to consider in achieving a successful vision outcome (2006):

1. Shape a coherent vision
2. Define achievable objectives
3. Navigate vision development
4. Champion the implementation of the vision outcome

As HRH Sheikh Mohammed bin Rashid Al Maktoum so eloquently summarizes in his philosophy for achieving vision excellence, a leader's role and primary challenge is being able to mobilize and guide the right people and resources at the right time with the common goal of achieving the vision's defined objectives and desired outcome. In the following sections, we share additional fidelity on our assessment of the foundational principles supporting HRH Sheikh Mohammed bin Rashid Al Maktoum's dynamic approach to a successful government vision outcome. In the modern world, innovation is a key component of vision achievement whether in government or in an enterprise.

In his own words, HRH Sheikh Mohammed bin Rashid Al Maktoum stated on the occasion of the inauguration of Innovation Week in Dubai on 22 November 2015, "Innovation is not an option but a necessity. It is not a culture but a work style and governments and companies that do not innovate, risk losing their competitiveness. We have multiplied our

investments in innovation especially in the terms of equipping and training our national cadres, because keeping pace with the rapid changes
taking place in the world requires innovative cadres and environment that
supports innovation" (Gulfnews.com, 22 November 2015). HRH Sheikh
Mohammed bin Rashid Al Maktoum's current vision is supported by his
Dubai Plan 2021, which lays out six strategic goals and 20 supporting
objectives:

- A city of happy, creative, and empowered people
  - Educated, cultured, and healthy individuals
  - People who are productive and innovative in a variety of fields
  - Happy individuals who are proud of their culture
  - People who are the cornerstone for Dubai's development across all
    fields
- An inclusive and cohesive society
  - A vibrant and sustainable multicultural society
  - A tolerant and inclusive society embracing common civic values
  - Cohesive families and communities forming the bedrock of society
- The preferred place to live, work, and visit
  - A city with the best educational, health-care, and housing services
    catering to everybody's needs
  - A vibrant and active city, providing a rich cultural experience and
    globally distinctive entertainment outlets
  - The most secure place
- A smart and sustainable city
  - A smart, integrated, and connected city
  - A city with sustainable resources
  - Environmental elements that are clean, healthy, and sustainable
  - A safe and resilient built environment
- A pivotal hub in the global economy
  - A city that enjoys sustainable economic growth
  - One of the world's leading business centers
  - The most business-friendly city and a preferred investment
    destination
- A pioneering and excellent government
  - Proactive and creative in meeting the needs of individuals and soci-
    ety as a whole
  - Sustainable and innovative in the management of its resources
  - Transparent and reliable

More information on the Dubai Plan 2021 can be found at www.dubai-plan 2021.ae. Vision is also the key component that starts the Strategic Formation Process as outlined in Figure 6.1, "Life-cycle model," found in Chapter 6.

Elements of the Government Vision

In his work, *My Vision: Challenges in the Race to Excellence*, HRH Sheikh Mohammed bin Rashid Al Maktoum shares the integral elements and sage insight he considers when moving a particular vision from a thought to successful project implementation. These key elements are also essential considerations for translating a vision from the tacit to the explicit realm and are paramount for setting the stage for a clear and concise transfer of knowledge as the vision progresses from concept to reality. We have summarized our interpretation (in question format) of the Sheikh's proven approach to initially evaluating a vision:

1. What level of interest does the business community and society have in the vision?
2. What are the perceived benefits (i.e., value addition, competitive advantage, etc.) to all concerned and what are the expected second- and third-order impacts or effects the vision might have on linked or related vision outcomes that are already conceived or that are ongoing? In other words, how do you break the current paradigm to achieve innovative vision achievement?
3. Is the vision a random implementation without a plan or does it have an established, planned, or preliminary phased approach?
4. Is it an achievable vision or one where the outcome is not measurable?
5. Does the timing of the proposed vision fit within the overall strategic vision of the country and society?
6. What is the desired or best approach for implementing the vision?
7. Is the appropriate leadership structure with the right skill sets and buy-in in place to achieve the vision?
8. How will the vision be financed?
9. What is the marketing plan for the expected outcome (i.e., product, service, or process) (Al Maktoum, 2006).

Like those of his father, Sheikh Rashid, who decided to build the largest man-made port in Jebel Ali, Sheikh Mohammed's visions are not without their critics. Regardless, any leader with vision must be prepared to defend his or her vision in the face of any storm, obstacle, or obstruction. Visionaries understand that not every idea they introduce will be met with complete agreement or will be viewed as having features or outcomes that add value by those close to them or the community in general. In the next section, we provide a brief summation of key features that Sheikh Mohammed feels are instrumental in implementing any vision.

Implementing the Government Vision

HRH Sheikh Mohammed bin Rashid Al Maktoum also shares a short list of critical features that he feels are instrumental and emblematic in implementing any leader's vision. In no specific order, our assessment of what features the Sheikh feels are essential for taking a vision to implementation are

1. "The vision must be excellent in form, essence, and implementation" (Al Maktoum, 2006, p. 35).
2. It should be far-sighted and comprehensive.
3. Each element previously provided should include imagination.
4. It must invoke excitement, promise, and anticipation in shareholders, stakeholders, and the community in general.
5. The vision, objectives, and expected outcome must be sound in definition and clearly understood from the leadership team and project team through all levels of the organization or enterprise.
6. It must be challenging so as to test the resolve of both society and the project management leadership team.
7. It should stir action, initiative, and creativity and instill a sense of competition across the business community and society.
8. It should be achievable but challenging (it should push the boundaries of the impossible).
9. It should be perfected before being introduced.
10. It should be mutually beneficial to society in general and not isolated to a particular community or group of people within society.
11. It should be unifying and binding, in that it strengthens trust in the country's leadership and a sense of unity among the members of society (Al Maktoum, 2006).

Implementing an excellent vision requires a clear operational plan with defined phases and achievable objectives, the mobilization of the right resources at the right time, and a well-conceived and well-understood strategy and framework with a specific time frame for completing the vision. In relation to our discussion of how important vision is to innovation opportunities and outcomes, the statement can be made that a sound vision is also a quintessential guiding feature of and contributing element to any type of innovation. Subsequently, the indelible nature and relationship that a vision has with innovation opportunity profiling is certainly what HRH Sheikh Mohammed bin Rashid Al Maktoum does extremely well as indicated by his stellar track record of repeated success in Dubai.

A few of his innovative exceptional achievements over the past 10 years have been such things as an innovation roadmap, the Dubai Smart City, the Mohammed bin Rashid Al Maktoum Solar Park, Dubai Expo 2020, and his Global Initiatives Foundation. However, it should be noted that vision achievement and innovation does not come about by chance. Vision is realized through work, and work without a systematic methodology of implementation just results in chaos and movement but no sustained improvement (see leadership and management axioms on page 92). One systemic methodology that we have found to be successful is our Innovation Opportunity Profile (IOP). In the next section, we introduce the IOP instrument, which we have developed and which continues to evolve as a result of our successes and failures in implementing micro and macro innovations across multiple industries.

Innovation in the Armed Forces

Innovation in government has always posed some unique challenges, however innovation in the armed forces which in most all nations represents the most stoic and conservative elements of the government. Therefore, to find someone who is a true innovator and transformer within the military establishment is rare; however, in the United Arab Emirates (UAE), there have been a few noted exceptions. One of these is Staff Lieutenant General Juma Ahmed Al Bawardi Al Falasi. General Juma is currently serving as adviser to the Deputy Supreme Commander of the Armed Forces, but previous to this assignment, General Juma was the commander of the land forces and commander of the Special Operations Command (SOC).

In both of these assignments, General Juma proved to have a deft understanding of the military requirements of the future, and through his innovative approaches, he transformed both commands to meet modern threats not only inside the UAE but also the country's allied neighbors. One of his innovative approaches was to look outside at other world militaries and combine the best of those militaries into a coherent sustainable approach with a well-thought-out and well-executed transformation plan. General Juma represents a key example of an individual working within the current operational paradigm, but expanding that paradigm by innovative thought and analysis of the future and implementing new ideas from outside the current military establishment, thereby effecting meaningful change in the capacity and capability of the military to execute its national security missions.

Another example of unique initiative and innovation in the UAE military is demonstrated by General Mubarak, Saeed Al Jabri, PhD, when he was director of the Armaments Department of the United Arab Emirates Land Forces. Then Colonel Mubarak recognized the need to restructure the way the land forces had previously looked at acquiring new equipment and the acquisition process used in the execution of supplying and sustaining the forces. He recognized that the current process did not provide adequate lifecycle management of the equipment being considered and the technical evaluations were not as complete as could be to support major acquisitions of equipment. He therefore undertook the task of analyzing what would be the most effective way to provide the inputs necessary to ensure that future acquisitions and equipment buys for the land forces, would be properly vetted to ensure a proper fit with the current operating capabilities and capacities of the land forces; ensuring that viable sustainability of that equipment was also part of the process.

This unique and innovative approach to designing a system that would benchmark the acquisition processes of other militaries, as well as those proven processes that were currently in place, worked well. He was able to create not only an innovative solution, but a solution that would also have or could have a profound effect on how acquisition for all of the UAE Armed Forces could be achieved by concentrating on applying centers of excellence and total lifecycle management analysis and procurement. His proposed acquisition management system was a radical change in the way the UAE Land Forces participated in acquisition management to increase efficiency and effectiveness of the acquisition process. His innovative approach would also result in numerous cost savings during the acquisition and sustainment process of major equipment when utilizing his developed approach. His approach combined a unique system of innovation and benchmarking current successful systems, into a coherent approach that provided the best alternatives for all selected acquisition management solutions.

Building an Effective Initial Innovation Opportunity Profile

Before describing how to implement an innovation driven by a set of objectives supporting a vision, we first need to evaluate the opportunity at hand. Much like the requirements generated in response to a consumer or consumer need, priorities must be set, and the resulting innovation opportunity outcome must be assessed against variables to ascertain if a project is appropriate or viable. The process from vision (need) to outcome (marketable product, service, or process) may require a great deal of creativity and investment of resources. The process from the vision conception phase to a final outcome can be complex and time-consuming. Tracking and monitoring at defined periods (milestones) throughout the phasing becomes necessary to ensure that the objectives of the vision (i.e., value proposition, competitive advantage, etc.), are met and the vision realized.

The IOP instrument (Figures 5.1 and 5.2) serves as both a guide and a tool for undertaking an innovation project (McLaughlin and Kennedy, 2016). Unlike a project charter that monitors the process of implementation, the IOP is an accumulative management tool that coalesces key events, activities, and information across the phases of the innovation opportunity project, such as vision and objective definition, decision-making, benefit (value) evaluation, and so on. The IOP was designed to be coalescing in nature, universal and agile in application, and scalable to the particular innovation project requirements. Figure 5.3, the IOP flowchart, describes the process of organizing the information needed before an innovation project begins.

The following section introduces how the IOP instrument is used and how the information can best prepare an organization for an innovation project. Also evolutionary by intent, the latest version of the IOP instrument can be sourced from our website (www.IPSinnovate.com), and a more in-depth discussion on application is provided in our *Innovation Project Management Handbook* (McLaughlin and Kennedy, 2016), which is available through the CRC Press (https://www.crcpress.com/Innovation-Project-Management-Handbook/McLaughlin-Kennedy/9781498725712).

Innovation Opportunity Profile Flowchart

Completing each process (and subprocess) step in the prescribed order will result in a completed IOP instrument. The remaining information in

Executive summary
Note: Highlights key information from the 11 sections in the profile; provides high-level discussion on recommendations with supporting benefits considerations, exceptions, limitations and assumptions, associated risk matrix or factors; and identifies any associated appendices and attachments (target length - 1 page). Identify related core competency(ies), associated functional needs assessments (FNA), and functional solutions analysis (FSA), applicable certifications, standards, and waiver requirements, budgetary documents, test plans, etc.

Section I. Operational profile key points of contact

Name	Title and position	Department	Contact number/email
1.			
2.			
3.			
4.			
5.			

Section II. Operational system requirements statement

1. Key performance parameters	First tier	Second tier	Third tier
2. Key performance indicators	First tier	Second tier	Third tier
3. Key performance measurements	First tier	Second tier	Third tier
4. Critical success factors	First tier	Second tier	Third tier

Section III. Customer/user profile types user profile (person, group or business unit operating or using the system or capability)

Customer type	Intended use (statement of key user requirements)
1. User 1	
2. User 2	
3. User 3	
4. User 4	

Section IV. System-mode profile (manner or way system or capability can operate)

System or capability mode	Mode of operation
1.	
2.	

Figure 5.1   Innovation opportunity profile—Side 1.

this chapter is introductory in scope and should show the reader how this flexible and unifying tool can be a favorable compliment to an innovation project team's charter, which we introduce and cover in more depth in the *Innovation Project Management Handbook* (McLaughlin and Kennedy, 2016).

Section V. Functional profile (Evaluation specific essential functions in system or capability modes identified in section IV)	
System or capability mode	Essential function (requirement)
1.	
2.	

Section VI. Certification, standards, and waiver requirements (internal/external offices, groups or agencies, and/or standards guiding implementation and adoption)				
Entity title	Internal or external	Certification and testing requirements	Standard and designator	Waiver requirements

Section VII. Operational profile (elements, architecture, and test plans — likely be in attachments and appendices)		
Elements, architecture and/or test plan title	Applicable functional system and/or capability	Attachment of appendix number

Section VIII. Data management and resource sharing plans (describe how information is managed, and how results are shared and disseminated)		
Responsible agency	Plan title	Justification statement

Section IX. Project budget and financial information (justification)			
Responsible agency	Account/budget code	Amount	Justification statement

Section X. Coordination and approval			
Name	Title	Approved/disapproved	Date
Comments:			
Name	Title	Approved/disapproved	Date
Comments:			

Section XI. Appendices and attachments
Attach core competencies source documents, functional needs assessments, functional solutions analysis, budgetary documents, architectural and system drawings, certification and guiding standards, waiver processes, test plans, data management plan, resource sharing plan, etc.

Figure 5.2 Innovation opportunity profile—Side 2.

Establish the Organization's Innovation Management System

Within an organization, it is essential that the organization develops and evolves a repeatable and sustainable innovation management system (processes,

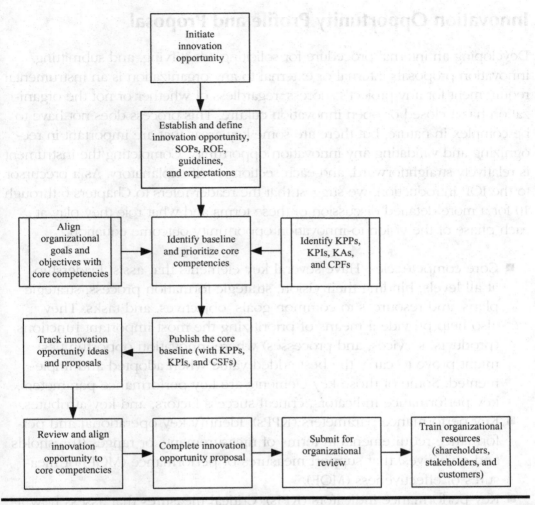

Figure 5.3   Innovation opportunity profile flowchart. SOPs, standard operation procedures; ROE, return on equity.

procedures, guidelines, and expectations). This approach should be wired into the organization's DNA and culture through recurring training and awareness sessions and leadership buy-in and support, and it should subsequently be formalized and recognized as an organization best practice. In sum, everyone in the organization should be familiar with how to submit an idea or an innovation opportunity. After identifying an innovation opportunity, the organization's established management system should facilitate the training, initiation, tracking, determination, implementation, and follow-on phases involved in sustaining the potential opportunity. We must reiterate that training and awareness should also focus on shareholders, stakeholders, and customers where feedback serves as an important tool in other steps throughout the innovation process.

Innovation Opportunity Profile and Proposal

Developing an internal procedure for soliciting, identifying, and submitting innovation proposals internal or external to any organization is an instrumental requirement for any project's success, regardless of whether or not the organization has a closed or open innovation culture. This process does not have to be complex in nature, but there are some key areas that are important in recognizing and validating any innovation opportunity. Completing the instrument is relatively straightforward, and each section is self-explanatory. As a precursor to the IOP introduction, we suggest that the reader refers to Chapters 6 through 10 for a more detailed discussion of these terms and what role they play at each phase of the vision-to-innovation opportunity outcome equation.

■ Core competencies: Have several key elements that assist leadership at all levels, binding their vision, strategic formation process, strategic plans, and resources to common goals, objectives, and tasks. They also help provide a means of prioritizing the most important functions (products, services, and processes) where innovation opportunities might prove to carry the best added value when adopted and implemented. Some of those key elements are key performance parameters, key performance indicators, critical success factors, and key attributes.

■ Key performance parameters (KPPs): Identify key operational and performance requirements in terms of measurements or ranges (thresholds and objectives) that support measures of performance (MOP) or measures of effectiveness (MOE).

■ Key performance indicators (KPIs): Critical measures that assess how a product, service, or process performs. These are of primary concern in Step 3 (operational assessment), and they should assist the innovation team in determining how something is happening, what is happening, and why it is happening.

■ Critical success factors (CSFs): Unique to each organization, these are critical factors that define procedures, processes, or activities that a business depends on for survival and are typically directly linked to the organization's core competencies. They are also instrumental to achieving the organization's goals, objectives, business strategy, and plan.

■ Key attributes (KAs): These are measurable and testable criteria that a product, service, or process must have and are best captured or displayed as key steps in a process map. They are also instrumental in supporting KPPs, KPIs, and CSFs.

Executive Summary (For Innovation Opportunity)

By necessity, the executive summary builds as the ensuing sections are populated and information becomes available. In essence, it should be the final piece of the profile before submission for review and approval. The executive summary provides a mechanism to define the project and its potential outcomes. The executive summary frames the subject in terms of the expected outcome. The dynamic nature of the environment reinforces the immediate need for information and decision-making superiority. The remainder of the executive summary would capture the key takeaways of the aforementioned considerations and supporting documentation in a short concise manner.

Section I: Operational Profile Key Points of Contact

In Section I, "Innovation Champion (Initiator) and Contact Information," the individual who is proposing the innovation opportunity (need/idea) or a sponsor (supervisor, someone knowledgeable about the process, etc.) will provide his or her specifics. The assignment of tracking numbers is the responsibility of the organization's innovation management point of contact (this may vary by organization). This section captures the operational profile tracking number, title, team lead (key team members by department and role; to include contract and third-party support [by company]), project start date, estimated completion date, sponsor information, audit agency, and date of recurring audit.

Section II: Operational Systems Requirements Statement

In this section, you are looking to capture the operational system requirements statement (to include KPPs, KPMs, KPIs, and CSFs) for your innovation improvement opportunity. First, second- and third-tier (priority requirement) KPPs, KPIs, KPMs, and CSFs are those required and desirable elements and factors that improve the existing performance elements and factors meeting expectations. The next step is to complete "Innovation Opportunity Proposal," which should provide as much detail as available on the proposed improvement or gap, the goals and objectives, the assumptions, the limitations, and the known constraints. Identify information as objective (i.e., factual, source from reference, etc.) or subjective (i.e., perceived, estimated, no specific reference available, etc.).

Section III: Customer/User Profile Types User Profile

In Section III, "Key Shareholders, Stakeholders, and Customers," list all those instrumental to this specific proposal. Management can add members to the continuation section (Section V) or as an attachment. Key players are typically executives (C-suite), department heads, process owners, clients, suppliers, and so on. In Section III, the customer profile (customer types), your goal is to capture all individuals, groups, or business units operating or using the system or capability. You will identify the intended use by each user identified. In our example, potential individual users could be the chief executive officer, chief financial officer, department head of business unit, or C-suite official within the group or organization.

Section IV: System-Mode Profile

In Section IV, the IOP is validated; the assigned or owning champion or sponsor of the proposal reviews the previous sections and all supporting materials and makes a determination on whether to pursue the proposal (i.e., move toward establishing an innovation team lead and members). The sponsor/owner then may request additional supporting materials or further review by another source (i.e., key stakeholders, shareholders, or customers), or may simply decide not to pursue the proposal and to close it out. In identifying an effective user profile for the set of user types identified in Section III, "Customer Profile," the goal is to identify who will use the product, process, or service and the probabilities of them using the product, process, or service.

Section V: Functional Profile

According to Musa (1993), the system-mode profile defines the way the product, process, or service can operate. Depending on your selected project and concentration (product, process, or service), your modes of operation may vary significantly.

Section VI: Certification, Standards, and Waiver Requirements

In the functional profile section, the innovation opportunity lead and team will evaluate each system mode identified in Section V, "System Mode Profile," with a focus on functionality testing, efficacy, and purpose. A number of tools are discussed, beginning in the next chapter, that will help define and build the IOP.

Section VII: Operational Profile

In building the certification and waiver authority profile, the goal is to identify who will certify your functional profile findings and to what established standards and expectations. Further, it is also used to identify any potential waiver authorities for your current product, process, or service performance standards when expectations are not met (Federal Communication Committee [FCC], the Federal Aviation Authority [FAA], any recognized airworthiness certification agency, etc.).

Section VIII: Data Management and Resource Sharing Plans

In the operational profile section, simply identify any elements, architecture and engineering drawings, guiding requirements documents, and test plans associated with the innovation opportunity. Those elements, drawings, test plans, and supporting documents should be included as attachments or appendices to the IOP form.

Section IX: Project Budget and Financial Information

As most innovation opportunities are measured in value added against cost or resources committed to achieve the innovation, the need for budget and financial estimates are significantly important. The level of detail captured (i.e., one-time cost or recurring on a monthly, quarterly, semiannual, or annual basis), the estimated cost of maintenance and sustainment (annual), percentage increase on current system or performance cost, and the difference pursuing the proposed improvement). Remember, budgetary estimate profiles can be an ongoing affair, as they often require significant coordination with shareholders, stakeholders, and customers to ensure accuracy.

Section X: Coordination and Approval Authority

Achieving a smooth coordination and approval process through the right authorities can also be a lengthy process. As your IOP is routed through the organization (to include sections requiring shareholder, stakeholder, and customer buy-in or approval), requests for additional information might certainly arise at any level in the routing process.

Section XI: Appendices and Attachments

The final section on the IOP form is self-explanatory. This will be your essential reference list for all supporting documentation and correspondence that supports your case for approval. This section should also identify any dissenting or alternative positions and comments received during the routing process. Further, alternative views should also be captured in the executive summary, so when you reach this stage, we suggest you revisit your executive summary and ensure that these comments are included and that the owning individual or business unit is identified in each statement. Conversely, you should also consider adding a list or comment capturing the key individual(s) and business units that are in full agreement with the profile as presented.

Innovation Project Team Charter

Finally, the Innovation Team Project Charter (ITPC) is a common project management tool that can help identify, synchronize, monitor, and report innovation team implementation efforts across the enterprise (i.e., shareholders, stakeholders, and customers; and objectives, responsibilities, and outcomes) (McLaughlin and Kennedy, 2016). Like the IOP instrument, the ITPC is tailorable and flexible by design; sections can be added, modified, or deleted to meet the innovation opportunity and project team's requirements. Please keep in mind that this instrument, like the IOP, best serves the innovation project team when its members are geographically separated and the tool is automated and hosted on a web- or cloud-based platform. This allows one central access and a collection point for updates, changes, and reporting. The ITPC should be utilized in conjunction with the IOP instrument. Both are living documents that evolve over your project's life cycle.

An example of an ITPC is provided for consideration in Figure 5.4. Each section has a brief discussion on what the specific section is intended to capture. Each section is presented briefly below.

- Section I: "General Information"
  - Project title: short title for the innovation opportunity project.
  - Project description: short description of the innovation opportunity you wish to pursue.

Innovation team project charter (tracking #: _____)

I. General information

Project title	Short title of the incremental innovation project				
Project description	Short description of the incremental innovation you wish to achieve.				
Prepared by	Team leader name				
Date	DD/MM/YY	Version	1	Expected completion date	DD/MM/YY

II. Project objective

Detailed description of the innovation project objective.

III. Assumptions and limitations

Identify known assumptions and limitations. Update as required.

IV. Project scope

Identify the focus, objectives, and timeline in as much detail as possible. Include the boundaries of the innovation project.

V. Project milestones

Identify inch stones and milestones that are critical in achieving your objective(s).

VI. Impact statement

Potential impact	Affected domains (departments, activities, etc.), processes, machine centers, etc.
Identify potential initial perceived benefits and add others as the project proceeds through each of the steps.	Identify areas that will be affected by your innovation project. For example, all departments, activities, and machine centers.

VII. Roles and responsibilities

Sponsor (decision maker) **Name and position**	Provides overall direction on the project. Responsibilities include approving the project charter and plan; securing resources for the project; confirm the project's goals and objectives; keep abreast of major project activities; make decisions on escalated issues; and assist in the resolution of roadblocks.
Innovation team lead (project manager)	Leads in the planning and development of the project; manages the project to scope. Responsibilities include: develop the project plan; identify project deliverables; identify risks and develop risk management plan; direct the project resources (team members); scope control and change management; oversee quality assurance of the project management process; maintain all documentation including the project plan; report and forecast project status; resolve conflicts within the project or between cross-functional teams; ensure that the project's product meets the business objectives; and communicate project status to stakeholders.
Team members(s) — Others have requested to be added but approval from their respective department head is required.	Works toward the deliverables of the project. Responsibilities include: understand the work to be completed; complete research, date gathering, analysis, and documentation as outlined in the project plan; inform the project manager of issues, scope changes, and risk and quality concerns; proactively communicate status; and managed expectations.
Subject matter expert(s)	Provide expertise on a specific subject. Responsibilities include: maintain up-to-date experience and knowledge on the subject matter; and provide advice on what is critical to the performance of a project task and what is nice-to-know.

VIII. Resources, project risks, and success measurements. These areas will be captured in the next version of this plan.

Figure 5.4   Innovation team project charter (ITPC).

- Prepared by: team leader or responsible administrator for tracking the instrument drafting, updating, and making changes to the instrument.
- Date: version and expected project closure date (DD/MM/YY).

▪ Section II: "Project Objective(s)." Give a detailed description of the innovation project vision, goals, and objectives.

▪ Section III: "Assumptions and Limitations." Identify known assumptions and limitations germane to the innovation project outcome. Update as new assumptions and limitations are discovered.

▪ Section IV: "Project Scope." Identify and define the focus, objectives, and time requirements or time line in as much detail as possible. Scope and requirements (defined objectives) should not change, as "requirements creep" can cause real issues (increased cost and delays in schedule). Also include the boundaries of the project. In general terms, define what is achievable and what is beyond the scope of the project. This should leverage information also available in your IOP instrument.

▪ Section V: "Project Milestones." Identify within project planning and tracking tools inch and milestones critical to the innovation team achieving a positive innovation opportunity outcome.

▪ Section VI: "Impact Statement." This statement should capture the potential areas impacted by the innovation opportunity outcome and affected domains (i.e., departments, shareholders, stakeholders, service providers, etc.) within the enterprise. Also include external stakeholders and shareholders involved with accomplishing a successful innovation outcome. In the area entitled "Potential Impact," make an initial assessment of the anticipated innovation outcome benefits and continue to update the benefits as the project moves through each step of the journey. In the "Affected Domains" section, list the internal and external shareholders, stakeholders, and community your innovation opportunity outcome is likely to affect.

▪ Section VII: "Roles and Responsibilities."

- Sponsor (decision maker) name and position. This individual is the person who typically provides the vision and helps define the objectives and goals of the project. He or she provides overall direction on the innovation project outcome and subsequently makes the final determination if the outcome was a success. Responsibilities include approving the project charter and plan, securing resources for the project, confirming the project's goals and objectives, keeping abreast of major project activities, making decisions on escalated issues, and assisting in the resolution of major and critical roadblocks.

- Innovation project team leader (project manager). Leads in the planning and development of the project; manages the project to scope. Responsibilities include developing the project plan, identifying the project deliverables and resources (team members), identifying risks and managing the risk management plan, controlling the scope and change management, overseeing all aspects of quality assurance and compliance with the project management process, overseeing and maintaining all documents generated in support of the innovation opportunity project (i.e., status reporting and forecasting), managing problem resolution and disconnects between cross-functional teams throughout the project's life cycle, ensuring that the project's eventual outcome achieves the defined business objectives of the vision, and developing the preliminary innovation outcome for the sponsor to report to the shareholders and stakeholders and the community.
- Innovation project team (IPT) members. Capture the names, departments, and contact information for all team members. IPT members are instrumental and primary to the innovation outcome success. Responsibilities include (but are not limited to) assisting in the development of the project plan; understanding the work to be accomplished (i.e., objectives and goals); executing the project plan; providing the necessary research, data gathering, reporting, and documentation as outlined in the project plan; reporting to the innovation team project manager on potential issues, scope changes, risk, and quality concerns; proactively communicating status and managing expectations within their realm of assigned responsibilities; and completing all assigned tasks associated with the innovation opportunity.
- Subject matter experts (SMEs). Every project will require support from SMEs who provide exceptional knowledge in a specific subject area. They can be internal or external to the innovation project's organization. Adding SMEs to meet every requirement of the project is simply not feasible, however. Adding SMEs to the IPT is a project manager's decision, and the value-added propositions they provide should be supported by the IPT members. Responsibilities may include (but are not limited to) providing their expert insight and guidance on a relevant subject area, maintaining up-to-date knowledge on that area in relation to the expected innovation opportunity

outcome, and providing timely support and input in their subject matter expertise that is critical to the IPT members as required.

■ Section VIII: "Resources, Project Risks, and Success Measurements." This section should identify the key resources that are required to achieve the proposed innovation outcome, a more in-depth discussion on the potential risks, and the success measurements defined in the IOP instrument. An updated ITPC instrument can also be found on the www.IPSinnovate.com website.

Summary

In this chapter, we have demonstrated the importance of having a vision as well as a methodology to implement that vision, one that supports innovative initiatives, associated goals, objectives, and tasks. Additionally, we briefly introduced two tools that can be employed across the spectrum of innovation opportunities—the ITPC and the IOP instrument. We described how the IOP instrument is used and how the information can best prepare an organization for an innovation project. To reiterate, simpler projects may not need to complete all sections, so the reader must use his or her best judgment so as not to introduce unnecessary complications that can slow the innovation opportunity decision. When the process becomes complex and convoluted, tracking and monitoring its progress may be an important function that should not be overlooked. The IOP is both a guide and a tool for undertaking an innovation project. Further, unlike the ITPC, which monitors the process of implementation, the IOP is a management tool for assessment, decision-making, and benefit evaluation. Finally, consider using the IOP tool as you begin to investigate the merits of the potential innovation. More complex projects may require an extended version, available from the https://www.IPSinnovate.com website. Further, as with other forms and tools offered in this workbook, this tool can be automated online (Internet or intranet) or placed in convenient locations (in hard copy) throughout the facility.

Discussion Questions

1. Name five key elements cited by HRH Sheikh Mohammed bin Rashid Al Maktoum for building an excellent vision. What are your personal

thoughts on the importance the elements have in developing an excellent vision?

2. What is an innovation management system and why is it important for organizations interested in sustainable innovation success?
3. Following the IOP flowchart (Figure 5.3), select an innovation opportunity project within your organization and pencil down some initial thoughts as to how the project relates to each step.
4. Name two innovation opportunity tools from this chapter's discussion. Explain their use and discuss the three key elements in each tool. How are the elements you chose important to the innovation opportunity performance acceleration process?

Assignments

1. In a five-page report, discuss HRH Sheikh Mohammed bin Rashid Al Maktoum's key elements and features for building an excellent vision. What are your personal thoughts on the importance of each element and feature in developing an excellent vision?
2. Identify a process, product, or service that has the potential to become an innovation opportunity project. Using the information you gathered during the exercises, complete the IOP executive summary section and submit your final product to another class member for review and feedback. Discuss the feedback in a short discussion and update your executive summary accordingly.
3. Using the ITPC provided in this chapter, identify any innovation opportunity project in your organization. Complete Sections III through VI to the best of your ability and knowledge. In your own words, provide a brief assessment of the value an instrument like the ITPC could bring to the project and potential problems with implementing such an instrument in that project.

Chapter 6

Innovation and Leadership

Introduction

The relationship between innovation and leadership can best be described as covalent and complimentary. One without the other simply diminishes its quality and outcome. In this chapter, we introduce and elaborate on the commonalities and relationships that bind the two terms. We start our discussion with an introduction to general leadership axioms and logics in business and management, and we examine how a leader's vision, commitment, and approach to innovation are essential in setting the tone for an organization's innovation culture. The chapter wraps up our leadership and innovation discussion with leadership and best practices, dynamic capabilities, and effectively managing risk in an innovative culture.

Axioms of Leadership and Management

In our observations, studies, and analysis, we have repeatedly observed that leadership involvement is the quintessential ingredient in successful innovation cultures in business, government, or any endeavor. In the United Arab Emirates (UAE), and particularly in Dubai, that direct involvement of leadership has been demonstrated over and over again to be the critical catalyst in stimulating major initiatives and the never-ending pursuit of innovation excellence. We have also recognized the sagacious focus that Dubai's leadership places on innovation as a prevalent hallmark in the pursuit of excellence. Central to Dubai's leadership approach is its unwavering commitment to innovation and its adherence to the "axioms of leadership and management."

These axioms have been encouraged and fully incorporated across the enterprise, from day-to-day operations to the very systems and processes that have Dubai clearly positioned as the world's leading innovation culture. Central to Dubai's meteoric rise and success is the adoption and implementation of the axioms of leadership and management. Sheikh Mohammed has set the tone and created an environment where leadership across every domain and market sector inherently creates visions that traverse the entire enterprise, from top to bottom. It is a mindset and not open to compromise. We offer the following leadership and management axioms for the reader's consideration. They are general in nature and by no means all-inclusive.

1. *Vision is realized through WORK.* Work must begin with a meaningful vision. That vision must provide a clear and unifying focus supporting the desired result, one that every team member within the organization can understand, internalize, and support. Visions must be achievable—with either internal and/or external resources. There must also be an implementation methodology and structure and the commitment to make it possible. Without these basic requirements, it becomes an empty promise for employees.

2. *All work is a PROCESS.* Just as a vision can provide a unifying focus to work, the application of a focused, systematic, data-driven, and fact-based methodology is required to improve competitive advantage, reduce waste and variation, and provide value. As Lean focuses on reducing waste and Six Sigma on reducing variation within a process, the marriage of the two provides a nice blend in improving value for both the customer and the organization. For example, pipeline and portfolio management are most efficiently managed when the work process data is reliable and proactive. Without focused policies and procedures driven by methodologies like N²OVATE™ and LEAN Six Sigma; real project and program control; people unified in the vision of meeting defined internal requirements and satisfying customers; and continuous process improvement, productivity and performance degenerate into a functional activity with questionable value to the shareholders, stakeholders, and the customer.

3. *Processes that provide customer satisfaction are CRITICAL and cross-functional.* The internal supplier/client relationship (chain) spans the organization both horizontally and vertically. Both internal and external relationships have shareholders, stakeholders, and customers. Thus, it is not uncommon to find that outputs of some processes in a relationship

become inputs for other processes and relationships that contribute to customer satisfaction. In some cases, satisfying internal clients ultimately contributes to satisfying the external customer as well. Further, failure to acknowledge that satisfying internal and external clients in any process could lead to diminished customer service and the potential for delays in responding to customer complaints and attempts to correct problems. Past case studies have proved that problem-solving is more costly than problem prevention.

4. *Critical processes result in external CUSTOMER SATISFACTION.* Understanding a customer's needs (requirements) and tracing them back through the enterprise is a common approach in identifying processes essential to customer satisfaction. This requires identifying every process step, procedure, and measure of performance (MoP) critical and subordinate to satisfying the customer's basic needs. Without an understanding of critical and subordinate processes and how they work, customer satisfaction is a hit-or-miss affair. For example, an organization's marketing department and senior leadership often use past performance on meeting or exceeding customer requirements as selling points to new and potential clients. Although this axiom is not at the top of the axiom list, it is truly the ultimate measure for any company or organization.

5. *Customer satisfaction depends on the RELIABILITY of critical processes.* Regardless of internal measurements, an organization's reliability will ultimately be evaluated by the customer. In a basic sense, reliability is the culmination of the organization's ability (processes) to perform and provide the promised service dependably and accurately. This means doing what is promised *and* delivering what the customer expects for each and every transaction. From key performance indicators (KPIs) and measurements (KPMs) to critical success factors (critical to quality [CTQ]), there are many factors often captured on balanced scorecards reported at varying levels within an organization that contribute to the overall reliability picture. Each organization must decide which KPIs, KPMs, CTQs, and variables they wish to include in their reliability profile. Additionally, these factors should align with their core competencies, vision, and business plan. In sum, reliability should be measured and thresholds set. If performance falls below established benchmarks, immediate action should be taken to identify the cause.

6. *Reliability is an inverse function of VARIABILITY.* Making good on promises to customers and clients should be every organization's chief

goal and sustainability objective. An organization that can predict and ultimately identify, address, and react in a timely and effective manner to address variability are few and far between. An organization that has a data-driven and fact-based methodology and understanding of their internal and external processes is often in a small class on the top shelf of their market sector. They are also in a better position to predict (with confidence) what adjustments they will need to make as their market sector shifts as new products, services, or processes are introduced; or improvements or changes are made to existing products, services, or processes within the sector. As a precursor, an organization must be confident that their processes are capable of delivering the desired results. An accepted ISO 9000 and Lean Six Sigma quality is to deliver the required quality at least 99.9997% of the time. This confidence is possible only through controlling the causes of variation in the process of management, administration, service, or manufacturing. Regardless of the market sector, controlling and reducing variation at the process level is the nexus of preventing errors.

7. *Reducing variability as the means of improving customer satisfaction decreases costs, increases profits, and makes the VISION possible.* It is through a customer-focused vision that leaders and management express the commitment necessary to enable the workforce to begin the task of continuous improvement. Continuous improvement is the process of reducing variation and eliminating non-value-added activity. Avoidable non-value-added activities comprise a significant portion of an organization's typical operations budget. More importantly, since they are often mistaken for necessary work, they rob the workforce of the opportunity to efficiently spend their energy satisfying customers.

Variability is often categorized in the cause–effect pairing. It can take two forms in this instance at the process level: common causes and special causes. Please note that variability can also be categorized as a problem–solution or input–output set. Common causes are those that are inherently part of the process and affect everybody in the process (i.e., quality of suppliers, adequacy of work instructions, training, goals, etc.); special causes are those that are not always present, are obscure, and are not necessarily common to everyone in the process, and they occur because of a unique set of circumstances. They can be special to an individual or set of individuals (i.e., suppliers are changed, a worker is out sick, one person misreads the work instruction, new training was not given to all, etc.). As leaders, managers, and employees work together to eliminate special causes and reduce common causes, variability reduces, and the service, product, or process becomes more uniform (i.e., more reliable) and conforms more to internal requirements and to the demands of the customer. This conformance to internal requirements and basic customer demands can reduce rework, improve work quality, and reduce non-value-added steps that distract the workforce and drive costs up.

In summary, we recommend that every organization consider the seven axioms we have provided here, coupled with the N²OVATE™ methodology, to achieve innovation success. Some of the immediate key benefits follow:

- Competitive advantage—by delivering improved quality of goods and services and reduced cost for obtaining desired results, higher margins and increased levels of customer satisfaction are possible.
- Once processes are defined, measured, and controlled, they become more reliable and establish a rational basis for planning, programming, and pipeline and portfolio management.
- Costs are better managed when they are predictable.
- Productivity is at a maximum and costs are at a minimum under this system (i.e., no new technology, no sunk costs).
- Workers and managers understand their jobs and where they fit in the overall vision. They can also act with knowledge and an eye on *improving* what they add to the resulting goals, objectives, and outcomes.
- Enterprise can be proactive and focus their combined energies on *innovation strategies*, not problem-solving.

As we show in later chapters, the N²OVATE™ innovation methodology fits nicely with Dubai's leadership vision and commitment to taking what is done very well and doing it better. N²OVATE™ provides the not only the establishment of a desired goal or objective; it also provides the necessary tools and philosophy to accomplish the same. The methodology is also industry agnostic and tailorable to any organization's existing structure and management system. It requires teamwork and most of all, leadership buy-in and support. We are talking about quality innovation leadership and management that encompasses the entire workforce (internal and external). As we have maintained through this initial discussion, leadership and management in business are coherently linked principles in innovation, but they are markedly different. In the next section on logics in business management and leadership, we hope to share our insights into these differences and how they relate to innovation.

Logics in Business Leadership and Management

Innovation leadership is only as good and effective as the organization's innovation culture and existing structure. If the organizational culture is not open and transparent or prepared to act in a concerted manner (as catalyst and stimulus) in adopting innovation, the enterprise will most likely have trouble promoting, adopting, and capitalizing on their innovation pioneer's innovative thinking and ideas. In order to be effective, leaders must be adept at understanding and articulating the organization's logic of leadership and management in regard to innovation at all levels throughout the organization. They must also advocate and support clear channels of open and transparent communication and support a well-structured leadership and management cycle (Figures 6.1 and 6.2), which provides a paradigm within the organization to promote innovation, continuous improvement, and sound business management.

In order for an organization to maximize its human talent and resources and its pursuit of innovation, it must be able to identify, mitigate, and/or eliminate as many as possible of the distractions of the day-to-day business processes that add no value to, stifle, or interfere with innovative thinking. In order to do this, an organization must commit to an enterprise-wide culture or philosophy and the supporting processes. The organization's culture should also be flexible and readily adaptable to fluid and fast-moving changes in the market sector and be capable of shifting its emphasis from problem-solving and competing with outdated or legacy business processes to a work environment that is proactive, predictable, and capable of producing predictable work systems and processes. The result is that the organization will be able to free up human resources for cross-functional application and process improvement.

The logic of leadership and management, as shown in Figure 6.3, is representative of how innovative organizations and enterprises can share an organizational innovation methodology. Graphical representations allow all members of the enterprise to understand their individual roles and responsibilities as well as their contributions to the enterprise as a whole.

This starts with everyone in an organization or enterprise understanding the pyramid that represents the logic of leadership and management. As we walk through the logic pyramid, we have shared with the reader how each

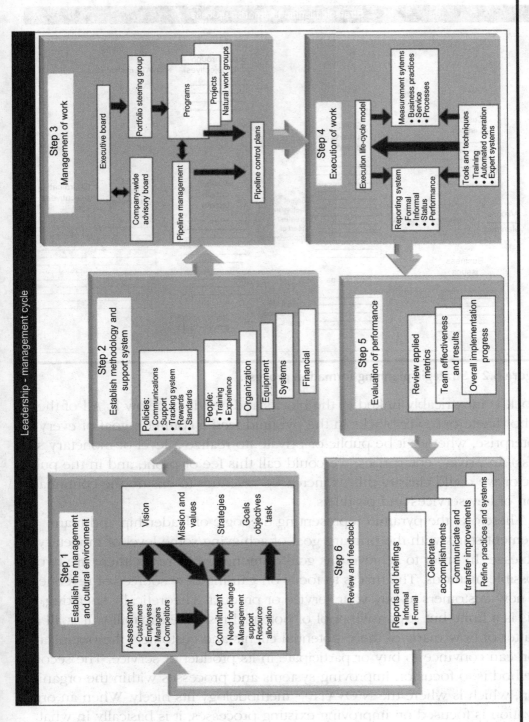

Figure 6.1 Life-cycle model.

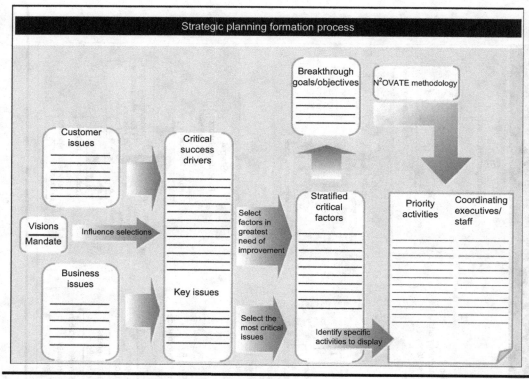

Figure 6.2   Strategic planning formation process.

block is inextricably linked to the blocks and activities below it. All of the subordinate or lower blocks in the pyramid feed a common goal of every enterprise, whether it be public or private (to realize a level of monetary success). In private enterprises, we could call this fee or profit, and in the public sector we could classify this as increased revenues to ensure the continuation of key services and products.

Therefore, the pyramid representing the logic of leadership and management starts with the primary goal of achieving some level of monetary increase. In order to achieve this goal of monetary increase, there are two possible methods. The first is to focus on gaining new sources of revenue or new customers to buy your service or product. Theoretically speaking, this is a finite but expansive pool of potential resource capability. It is all a matter of how many of these potential clients and customers the organization can convince to buy or participate in its product or service. The second method is to focus on improving systems and processes within the organization, which is where the N^2OVATE^{TM} methodology fits nicely. When an organization is focused on improving existing processes, it is basically in what we refer to as the incremental innovation loop with a goal of reducing waste

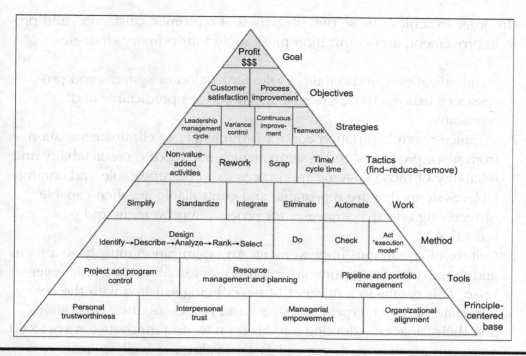

Figure 6.3 Logic of leadership and management.

and improving the profit margin through efficient operations. Although there are variations on how an organization approaches process improvement, one relative approach that the reader might be familiar with is Deming's "define, measure, analyze, improve, and control" (DMAIC) model. The N²OVATE™ methodology expands on Deming's model by providing detailed process maps that help organizations make fact-based and data-driven decisions on innovation propositions.

We acknowledge that when an organization is in an incremental innovation loop, the returns are usually limited in comparison to those changes driven by new products, services, or processes. In sum, incremental innovation is often associated with preserving or building profit margins and sustaining cash flows. There is a certain amount of value realized on its resources in the amount of savings a given process or system improvement can provide as a return to the enterprise. In order for an organization to maximize competitive value, it must not only have strategies in place that concentrate on customer satisfaction and gaining new customers, but also a fact-based and data-driven systematic approach focused on increasing revenue by way of increased efficiencies and productivity.

In order to achieve these two objectives of customer satisfaction and process improvement, an organization must apply four primary strategies:

1. Standardization (predictability): Standardization of systems and processes or making those systems and processes predictable and repeatable.
2. Variance control: Variation control is the ability to eliminate variation from work processes and systems, which adds to the predictability and reliability of those systems and processes to be repeatable and controllable. Systems that are repeatable and controllable are then capable of receiving effective strategies for process improvement and cost reduction.
3. Culture of continuous improvement: An organization must have a focus and inner drive for continuous improvement in all areas of the enterprise. This results in a mindset of never being satisfied with the current state of the enterprise's systems and processes, their capabilities, and their capacity. Adopting a focus on new and innovative ways to do work can increase customer satisfaction values, as well as create new ways to improve current systems and processes to produce better and more efficient outcomes. These usually will result in monetary savings as well as decreased variability within the systems and processes and increased reliability for both enterprise internal customers as well as the external buying customer.
4. Teamwork: Today's enterprises are extremely complex and diverse with no single system or process being the purview of single entities or individuals; therefore, in order for the strategies to work, one of the paramount strategies is teamwork. Teamwork not only provides the crucible for breakthrough ideas in pursuits relating to both customer satisfaction and systems and process improvement but also allows for the penetration of current paradigms within the organization, allowing new ideas from outside sources to gain a foothold and stimulate innovative and creative solutions.

As with all strategies, in order for them to be effective, there must be some focused tactics to ensure that the strategies remain in focus with the organization's core competencies and daily endeavors. They must also relate to personal metrics that can be applied by every individual and their performance, and their specific contributions to the enterprise or organizational goals and objectives as they relate to KPIs, key performance parameters

(KPPs), and CTQs. These tactics are universal and also consist of activities that are focused on finding, reducing, and removing non-value-added activities. With the exception of some regulatory requirements such as paying taxes, maintaining the books for outside audits, and so on, all systems and processes should be constantly and continuously reviewed for the value they add to organizational goals and objectives. The metric for considering whether they add value or not goes back to the primary objectives, which, stated as a question, could be, do those steps within the enterprise add to customer satisfaction or do they result in increased systems and process improvement? If the answer to either of these questions is no, the next question to ask is, of what value are they to the enterprise in their execution?

Second is to look for where systems and processes produce rework or a duplication of effort. This can be complex in that in many organizations, duplication or rework is a manifestation of nonintegrated systems and processes or, in very large organizations, of limited communications between different divisions, sections, or functions. Instead of reengineering and integrating systems to eliminate rework, it is easier to create duplication, which increases variation in the overall efficiencies of the organization and enterprise. Increased variation inevitably leads to less reliability, increased costs, and the diversion of human resources from the key focuses of customer satisfaction and process improvement.

Third is to determine where the enterprise produces scrap. And while we mainly think of scrap as being a byproduct of production in manufacturing-type settings, many large businesses lose sight of the scrap that is produced in many of their administrative processes; such things as multiple printings, for example, of questionable reports and briefings, along with scrap that may be produced by ill-conceived technical solutions and unnecessary upgrades, resulting in high monetary loss of current invested capital.

Fourth is to identify excess time and cycle time that is prevalent within systems and processes. Each of the first three adds to the fourth, which is the increase in time it takes to perform a system and process. As the old adage says, time is money, and wherever you can reduce the amount of time it takes to effectively implement a system or process or reduce the time or cycle time to carry out a daily work–focused activity will almost always result in monetary savings and decreased exposure to the addition of non-value-added activities, rework, or scrap. Cycle time is the focus of those repetitive processes and the length of time it takes to return to the beginning of that process for each cycle. Again, reducing cycle time by reducing steps within that cycle usually results in higher reliability as a result of reduced variability.

As these tactics provide the focus for the enterprise human capital to concentrate their daily efforts in order to succeed, they must have a standardized system of work that helps them realize the application of these tactics. The work is a systematic approach to finding a solution for every enterprise problem, system, or improvement, and it consists of five major steps. The five recommended steps to follow (in order) in creating a systematic approach to the final solutions are

1. Simplify: The very first activity in looking at systems or process improvement or problem-solving is to look at how you can simplify the current process activity. It has been said that it's easy to take a simple problem and make it complex; however, it is much more difficult to take a complex problem and make it simple.
2. Standardization: By standardizing the way we do things throughout the organization for like-type activities, we reduce variation and increase reliability across the organization, which usually results in cost reductions.
3. Integrate: As we simplify and standardize, the natural fallout is that we find that there are many activities that can be integrated one with another, either totally or partially. This integration results in reduced overall steps for systems and processes, and when you reduce the steps in a system or process, you reduce exposure to the introduction of errors or the possibility of increased variation within that system or process.
4. Eliminate: As you simplify, standardize, and integrate, you also identify steps that are no longer required or may be outmoded or out of date and can be candidates for elimination. This further reduces the exposure to the introduction of variation, systems errors, or rework within the focused systems and processes.
5. Automation: Finally, when you've looked at the system, process, or problem through the steps of simplifying, standardizing, integrating, and eliminating, you can then finally automate that system with a greater assurance that the system will be in control or statistical control. With a system that is in control and is automated, we further reduce the possibility of the insertion of errors or variation within that processor system. Additionally, automation provides for a repetitive process to be performed with higher reliability and greater accuracy and speed.

With a systematic way to perform work using the five steps outlined above, we need to apply a certain methodology within those steps to ensure that each of the steps maintains the accuracy of the outcomes we desire. One of the most effective methods in all systems, process, and reengineering work is Deming's "plan, do, check, act" (PDCA) model. In 1993, Deming modified the Shewhart cycle to "plan, do, study, act" (PDSA) (Deming, 1993). This method proved to provide an effective problem-solving methodology that affords a systematic approach to problem-solving, allowing solutions to be tested and verified before full implementation, thereby reducing the scrap and rework of effective systems and process improvement efforts. Under the PDCA methodology, the "plan" step consists of identifying the issues, fully describing them, providing an analysis using a number of tools and techniques, rank ordering those possible solutions, and selecting a possible or best identified solution. The "do" step is a test step, which allows us to test the solution under a controlled scenario. In the "check" phase, we can validate that the solution in fact provides the desired outcomes. The final phase, which is "act," we are able with confidence to implement a fully developed tested solution. This phase requires the institutionalization of the process improvement or the innovation. This can best be achieved by the application of the execution life-cycle model or method, as shown in Figure 6.4. This methodology provides four main steps and four supporting steps to achieve systematic and sustainable implementation.

The four main steps consist of design, deploy, operate, and sustain. Following the steps ensures the implementation of a solution ingrained into

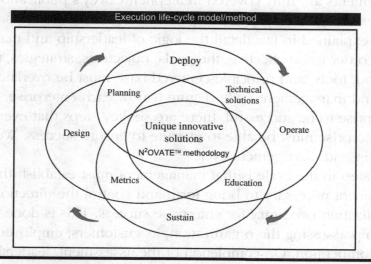

Figure 6.4   Leadership and management cycle.

the enterprise. In addition, the four supporting steps—planning, technical solutions, education, and metrics—will ensure a robust implementation and execution with a coordinated effort between all the enterprise assets to ensure a successful execution.

The PDCA methodology allows for the implementation of many tools to help with the process improvement, systems reengineering, or problem-solving scenarios. These tools fall into three major categories, the first being project and program control, the second resource management and planning tools, and the third pipeline and portfolio management tools. There are so many of these tools and resources that can be used, and as they are adequately covered in many other publications, we will not spend time outlining their different uses and approaches here.

As with all approaches, the logic of leadership and management relies on a principle-centered base that is the bedrock of good organizations and interpersonal relationships within enterprises. Stephen Covey's principle-centered leadership philosophy is an example of a good base from which an organization should build. His stated philosophy is based on four key principles, which are paramount for any good organization:

1. Personal trustworthiness
2. Interpersonal trust
3. Managerial empowerment
4. Organizational alignment

These elements are fully covered in Stephen Covey's publication *Principle-Centered Leadership* (Covey, 1991).

We have explained in fair detail the logic of leadership and management; however, in order to be effective, the goals, objectives, strategies, tactics, work, method, tools, and principle-centered base must be overlaid on the leadership and management cycle (Figure 6.4) of each enterprise. In order for an enterprise to be successful, there are six key steps that every organization or enterprise must be able to execute to ensure success. We call this the leadership and management cycle.

The first step in the cycle is that management must establish the culture and environment necessary to bring forth and control the direction of the resource utilization necessary for enterprise success. This is done first by the key leadership assessing the organization, its customers, employees, managers, and competition. On completion of the assessment, leadership can then create the vision necessary for an enterprise to pull together toward one visualized end state. The vision is then supported by a stated mission and values, selected strategies to which goals, objectives, and tasks can be applied. This provides the overall framework and direction for the human resources within the enterprise to understand their participation in meeting the overall enterprise end state.

One way to document and achieve success for the items in the first step of the leadership and management cycle is to apply a strategic planning process. While there are many strategic planning processes available, we have found use of the strategic planning formations process, as shown in Figures 6.1 and 6.2, to be highly successful in applying not only the standard strategic planning methodologies but also in the integration of innovative thinking within the process itself. This results in key breakthrough objectives and goals, which not only best serve the requirements of the enterprise, but leads to paradigm breaking innovations for future implementation. Once this is accomplished we move on to step two.

Step two involves establishing the methodologies and the support system necessary to implement all of the actions in step one; this includes such things as creating the policies, which include communications, support, tracking systems, rewards, and standards; focusing on people, their training, and their experience; creating the proper organization to implement the strategies; providing the proper equipment so that the workforce has the necessary tools, along with the systems and the financial support necessary, to reach the end state. Once a support structure is in place, we move to step three, which is the actual management of work.

Step three involves creating the necessary internal structure, from the executive board down to programs and project teams, to pipeline management and pipeline control plans, which allows work to be planned for and controlled. Once the management of work is in place, we move to step four, which is the execution of the plan, or the actual work implementing the action plans; and setting the stage for creating the measurement systems and the business practices, services, and processes necessary to control work. This also includes the tools, techniques, training, and automated operations in expert systems necessary to facilitate all of the systems and processes needed to produce the products and services for customer satisfaction and continuous process improvement.

In the final step (step five), a proper reporting system for the both formal and informal processes provides information on the status and performance of how the work is being performed. Once the reporting system is in place, we can move to step five proper, which is the evaluation of performance.

This basically applies to three main areas: first, the review of applied metrics—those metrics that are incorporated to know what we were doing, how are we doing it, and where we can make improvements; second, team effectiveness and result—how well we are using our human capital and resources and their contributions to the overall in-state; and third, overall implementation progress—how well we are improving the systems and processes that we have, how well the systems and processes in place are functioning, and whether they meet the stated goals and objectives without excesses in repetitive systems, redundancy, scrap, rework time, cycle time, and non-value-added activities.

Once effective evaluation of performance is carried out, then we move to the final step, step six, which is review and feedback; these are the reports and briefings, both formal and informal, that allow the management back in step one to continuously review how well they are moving toward the stated end state of the enterprise. This step also allows celebrating accomplishments and communicating and transferring improvements in refining practices and systems; this review and feedback is essential because it links the whole process back to step one, which allows for the continuous updating of vision, mission values, strategies, goals, objectives, and tasks, thereby providing a continuous loop of improvement in the overall leadership and management cycle as well as in the work being performed within the cycle.

Once an enterprise has in place both the logic of leadership and management and the leadership and management cycle, it has created the controls and environment necessary to free up their human capital, and particularly their leadership, to focus on a culture of innovation. So, what is a leader's role in building a culture of innovation? The next section discusses how leaders can best help their organizations build the right innovation culture to achieve their business goals and objectives.

A Leader's Role in Building a Culture of Innovation

In dynamic organizations with an established history of continuous innovation success, we often find that their leadership team is central to the success story. Beyond their roles in recruiting, retaining, and developing team capabilities that directly contribute to the organization's dynamic capabilities and core competencies; they are the single most influential element in establishing the organization's identity and attitude toward innovation. As the measure of creative liberty and innovation success within these organizations is often attributed to the organization's leadership (Prather, 2010), leadership also sets the tone for organizational climate and culture by modeling the level of acceptance, support, and behavior they expect the organization's team members to emulate.

When the leaders are engaged in the innovation equation, they tend to bring an alignment between vision and action that directly impacts the potential value and success of innovation opportunities. Instrumental to the leader's role in the organizational climate and propensity toward innovation is to keep a close eye on the pulse of the organization's innovation climate and culture. Through active, deliberate, and determined engagement at all levels throughout the organization, these leaders become the fulcrum point for successfully aligning the intrinsic capabilities of their innovative employees (pioneers) and subsequently aligning those capabilities with the organization's core competencies, business strategy, and vision.

Create other leaders and that creates sustainability.

Mr. Paras Shahdadpuri, Chairman Nikia Group

The biggest role for him (a leader) is to actually implement plus identify the strength of those ideas that are coming from your people. And then power those ideas, and then actually lead them into implementation.

Mr. Nanab Shaji Ul Mulk, Chairman, Mulk Group

Cultivating an Innovation Culture

Companies must innovate to grow, stay close to their customer, stay current in their field or market sector (industry), and remain on the lookout for incremental and disruptive innovation opportunities. Being of entrepreneurial spirit helps leaders, subordinates, and peers ask the right questions, those that can trigger innovation opportunity generation. The advantage that entrepreneur-minded organizations have in today's international business landscape is that they tend to survive based on their ability to innovate, sustain, and capitalize on cross-industry technology developments. That said, cultivating a positive culture for innovation starts with leadership. Regardless whether it is at the individual, first-level supervisor, department, or CEO level of the organization, someone leads the initiative or introduces the seed of thought either by choice or by chance. In reality, respected leaders build the mountain and rise with the mountain. In response to the question "What can leaders do to create cultures of change and innovation?" we offer the following recommendations for the reader's consideration.

1. Lead by example: Demonstrate the behavior and conduct you expect from the innovation experience and culture. The leadership sets the tone, and subordinate leaders will most generally follow. People know when your actions do not align with the verbal messages, e-mail traffic, and corporate letterhead that demonstrates your expectations, code of conduct, business strategy, and rewards system. People know when you're sincere and when they're respected, appreciated, and trusted. Do not be marginalized by a vertical hierarchy of managers and supervisors who are not in line with your direction. Be visible, action oriented, and on point by knowing your people to the greatest extent possible. Success is best achieved when expectations are delivered in person, not via e-mail, announcement board, or second-party interpretation. Be an accountable, responsible, objective, and respected mentor and coach—grow the leadership that will eventually replace you. "Walk the talk and talk about success."

2. Focus on your customer, organization, and industry (sector) needs: Consider crossover applications and opportunities with other industry segments. Select and appoint a chief innovation officer and provide them with the resources to champion the organization's innovation process once you reach a decision to take an idea beyond the creative thought phase (McLaughlin and Caraballo, 2013).

3. Support, foster, and enrich an organizational culture wherein innovation is considered a core competency and strategic objective: Provide people throughout the organization with regular training, tools, and time to corroborate and collaborate, open and freely without fear of attribution. Encourage, support, and plan recurring collaborative opportunities (both internal and external) for people to share tacit and explicit information to generate new knowledge and intellectual capital. These events should also be spontaneous, planned, and measured (what to share and when to share). Train and equip your people for success, and celebrate those successes as an organization.

4. Challenge the current state of play and accept the reality that there will be failures and setbacks: The blame game is not productive and diminishes opportunities for people to share what they learned from the event and their ideas on how to change the outcome the next time around—these are wonderful opportunities for continued process

improvement. Leaders should regularly question the decisions, pat answers, and assumptions that result from challenging organizational strategy, vision, and process.

5. See the bigger picture: You may be the one in charge and responsible for the organization and its future, but that does not always make you the resident expert on all subject matter. This requires you to immerse yourself in all facets of the industry, your organization, and your primary resource—your people. Be humble and honest about your capabilities and be open to the input of others when it comes to sharing road maps—"What do you mean here?"—and strategy. Dreaming is alright ... sometimes you meet someone that provides that one crucial ingredient or thought that makes the connection or leap to the next level a reality.

Leaders and Establishing Best Practices

At the foundation of any discussion on successful innovation best practices is a strong link between strategy, technology, a focus on creativity, and the intentional creation of buy-in and engagement. Supporting the critical touch points that link critical elements like strategy, innovation, and technology is a company's preponderance toward establishing informal and formal domains. In these domains, enthusiastic and disciplined networked experts can illuminate short-, mid-, and long-term opportunities that contribute to the development of each individual participant, group, or culture and ultimately the competitive position and value, business model, and strategy.

Further, by leveraging the intellectual capital of informal domains of expertise, companies can cultivate and harvest creative ideas and convert them to actionable knowledge and innovation. Finally, domains incorporate the diverse concerns and priorities of three vital components: the strategic options and decisions of the corporate executives, the opportunities offered by new technology and research and development, and the evolving external environment in which a company operates, determined by a company's specific scenario.

Codes of conduct and rules of engagement are essential to any domain's survival. Considered the next great opportunity for boosting a company's innovation activities, Schröder and Hölzle's (2010) generic framework and concept of community–company interaction quality (CCIQ) explores the social factors (communication, mutuality, recognition of effort, cohesion, and the impact on innovation) that influence a company's collaboration efforts with virtual communities (VC). Based on a framework capturing activities (governance and company capabilities), sentiment (norms motivation and incentives), interaction (frequency and intensity), and the technology channel, the CCIQ process attempts to answer many questions about the VC relationship (intellectual property rights, licensing, compensation, ethical behavior of companies and the individuals involved, etc.). Successful innovators establish, train, equip, and execute with timing, precision, and magnitude of effort—the CCIQ process is a necessity.

Culture of Open Innovation

Companies that create a culture of open innovation supporting the organizational climate and strategy are usually in a better position to act on creative ideas and turn them into game-changing innovations. Further, these companies know what defines who they are and commit to identify inhibitors and roadblocks (barriers: silos, internal structure, finances, and others) that are obvious but overlooked in day-to-day activities. Building a company-wide innovation capability takes support from all levels of leadership and management. Birkinshaw (2011) provides six conditions directly supporting sustained innovation:

1. A shared understanding of who the company is and where it's headed
2. An organization structure and process to support the innovation environment
3. The necessary tools, training, concepts, and techniques to enable innovation
4. The ability to celebrate differing views from diverse sources and to accept failure
5. The establishment of informal and formal collaborative venues and environments that promote interaction and the sharing of thought
6. The ability to take excursions (slack time) from the daily beat of the drum

Healthy and successful innovation cultures also have key innovators or pioneers that have a deep subject matter expertise in one area and a lot of breadth in others; they work hard at stimulating observation, are powerful observers, and are always asking why things are done a certain way and not another. They also tend to be great networkers, always experimenting with their products and business models. Finally, cultivating a strong innovation culture takes a robust commitment to investing valuable resources, developing an environment where everyone has their role in promoting a successful innovation event.

Dynamic Capabilities

In reality, environmental turbulence is only one of many dynamics driving both private- and public-sector entities to make a concerted effort to identify, understand, and pursue dynamic capabilities to adapt to these uncertain times and the fluid nature of the international landscape. So what is a dynamic capability, and why is it important to leadership within any industry or market sector?

Dynamic Capabilities Defined

In a broader context, dynamic capabilities are routines (procedures, processes, or routines) performed at varying levels within an organization. At the organizational level, they are high-level routines (or a collection of routines or processes) that, together with implementing input flows (inputs and outputs from other processes or routines), provide the organization's leadership and management (decision makers) with an objective view or a set of decision options (actionable information) for producing significant outputs to meet a particular objective or goal. The key is objective, fact-based actionable information that is free from personal feelings and motives. Further, emphasis should be placed on the idea of *routine*—behavior that is learned, highly patterned, repetitious, or quasi-repetitious, founded in part in tacit knowledge—and the specificity of objectives (Zollo and Winter, 2002). When these routines are process mapped and shared across the agency, a common understanding and a set of parameters can be established with an idea of open and transparent communication.

Dynamic Capabilities in Rapidly Changing Environments

Dynamic capabilities are those skills needed to build internal and external competencies within an integrated workplace conducive to a changing environment. In other words, these are skills that determine an agency or an organization's ability to "integrate, build, and reconfigure internal and external competencies to address rapidly changing environments" (Teece et al., 1997). The idea and recipe for pursuing dynamic capabilities is industry and sector agnostic. For federal agencies, developing dynamic capabilities might start with experience accumulation, knowledge articulation, and knowledge codification in a deep dive of their operational routines. Within any given government agency, there are traditional functions, one of which is continuing education and training. For example, learning competencies associated with these efforts are often outlined and guided by regulations or directives to facilitate a deliberate and effective learning process. Dynamic capabilities supporting the learning process complement and support the organization's culture, core competencies, and strategy. The resulting tacit-to-explicit, explicit-to-tacit knowledge exchange can generate new ideas codified for explicit use. This provides an incredible opportunity to harvest tacit knowledge within the agency, which is often difficult to access when employees are reluctant to share their ideas and thoughts for fear of ridicule or the appearance of looking less knowledgeable in front of their peers, or because they simply aren't sure if their ideas are that important to the agency. These are sometimes termed *latent* or *hidden* dynamic capabilities, and learning environments show tremendous promise for building trust ladders between leadership and employees.

Competencies aren't essentially physical matters; they manifest themselves in ways such as human capital (leadership), structural capital, processes, and strategies that build the very fabric that makes a company what it is and what it can grow to be—without them, an agency's destiny can turn toward incoherence and a lack of focus. Growing leaders to function in a demanding, dynamic, and fast-paced environment is paramount.

Dynamic Capabilities and the Leader

Integrating, building, and reconfiguring internal and external competencies address rapidly changing and high-velocity environments. These environments influence any organization becoming a management and leadership challenge. In fact, the most important dynamic capabilities for any organization are its leadership, strategy, and culture. There are three avenues that agency leaders can employ in preparing and adapting their culture and capital structure to be more responsive to high-velocity and volatile environments:

- Sound and experienced leadership (concern for the human capital, engaged to take advantage of opportunities when they arise, result oriented, etc.)

- Ability to recognize and to effectively manage change
- Becoming the catalyst for engagement with dynamic capabilities

Leadership coherence is paramount—coherence focused on proven and dynamic capabilities and competencies, providing leaders across the organization with an opportunity to focus on congruent organizational strategies that build on and fuel growth, innovation, flexibility, and resilience. In reality, when an organization deviates from the things they do best (core competencies), the risk and rewards, they venture into the unchartered waters and risk running aground. Dynamic capabilities that support an organization's core competencies are built brick by brick and form the foundation of the strategic framework (architecture). The benefits of having a working knowledge of your dynamic capability roadmaps are significant and directly correlate with how effective and efficient the organization operates both internally and externally with shareholders, stakeholders, and their customer base. The resulting roadmaps serve as references or guides for personnel when faced with turbulent and volatile environments. Mapping of dynamic capabilities can also build leadership competency, support organization succession plans, and contribute to future strategic planning, programming, and capital investment. In theory, executive leadership groups and dynamic managerial capabilities perform an instrumental role in preparing and adapting an organization to capture and identify innovation opportunities. As agencies move through preparing and adapting their organizational climate, opportunities develop or surface through the collective sensing and seizing of those opportunities and the reconfiguring of resources to exploit them.

Much like private industries have had success with open and transparent communications up, down, and laterally within a company, government and nonprofit entities have the distinct opportunity to adopt, mimic, or modify these practices to meet their specific needs. Tantamount to adopting this approach is to create a culture and environment wherein creativity is celebrated, employees feel valued for their contributions, and rewards exist for those that bring value to the organization. Unfortunately, most organizations simply have trouble recognizing their employees for innovative ideas chiefly due to organizational culture (norms), leadership oversight, policy, and so on.

So you have a very clear process in place where you can actually keep the life of creativity of the people.

Mr. Nanab Saji Ul Mulk, Chairman Mulk Group

Finally, in comparing the public and private sectors, dynamic capabilities and leadership in both domains are viewed as essential core competencies and prolific hallmarks of great organizations. These organizations also have a flexible and determined approach in building human capital that is responsive and agile to innovation and change-driven environments.

Risk Management

The greatest risk is the risk of riskless living.

Stephen Covey

Risk and uncertainty are common elements in virtually every decision we make, both personally and professionally. Every organization is subject to internal and external factors that can add varying levels of uncertainty and impact the outcome or achievement of the intended objective. In setting the stage for this discussion, a common and universally accepted definition of risk is appropriate. Drawing from the intent of the International Standard for Organization (ISO) 31000-series directives on risk management (2009), risk can be summarized and defined as the impact of internal and external influences, known or unknown, inherent to achieving organizational objectives. The ISO 31000-series proposed definition is a significant evolution from other renowned standards (such as the British, Australian/New Zealand, Institute of Risk Management, Guide to the Project Management Body of Knowledge, etc.), as it accounts for opportunity (reward) and not just consequence (or threat). We feel this positive dimension and change in philosophy (the "yin" to the "yang") offers balance and offsets the traditional negative connotations many leaders and managers have historically associated with risk.

Relative to our position regarding a leader's or manager's role in creating innovation cultures and managing strategic change within an organization, we feel that a more precise definition of risk management in relation to a leader or manager's activities is germane to our discussion. From this perspective, risk management involves analyzing, identifying, assessing, attenuating, and socializing the cadre of internal and external factors relative to the ethical decision-making process and the desired or intended outcomes (as determined by the desires of stakeholders, shareholders, and the community). This definition also includes the presentation of and accounting for potential for both negative and positive impacts and outcomes associated with any decision. Further, we acknowledge that every leader and manager must face his or her ego-based (self-interested) and benevolent (good for others) decisions, and all decisions bring some form of risk. At the strategic level, risk-taking is an essential reality and integral factor associated with strategic planning, business model development, and organizational innovation culture evolution. Subsequently, beyond acknowledging the ever-present dimension and impact that risk adds to achieving organizational objectives, we feel that analyzing risk is the primary activity in executing any decision-making process.

Analyzing Risk in the Operational Environment

Primarily, acknowledging the presence and potential impact of risk is an essential precursor to any decision. Seasoned leaders are well acquainted with the realities and potential impact of risk. They often view and assess risk based on their sphere of influence or span of control, and they develop their own internal risk profile relative to a specific set of conditions and experiences. Based on a decision maker's experience, tolerance for risk, and ability to assess, process, react, and manage changing variables in the decision process, each leader or manager develops (or learns) to gather certain data points through inquiry or reason, analyzing the (or reassigning) priorities as the situation unfolds. Assessing risk in the decision-making process is not a one-time activity. Successful leaders develop a routine of inquiry (i.e., questioning) relative to risk. Depending on the situation and circumstances, they typically develop a series of general questions that help to frame their current understanding of the risk profile or baseline of the current state of play in any decision-making process. We offer the following questions as potential starting points for new and experienced leaders to consider:

■ What are the known and potential unknown origin(s) or causes of the risk?
■ What are the potential drivers of the risk?
■ How may risk appear or manifest itself?
■ When might risk appear?
■ Where may risk appear?
■ What are the potential impacts of risk on the outcome?

This is not a complete list of inquiry by any means, but it does provide a starting point for those leaders who do not actively employ risk profiling in their decision-making process. In addition, there are other internal and external tools that a leader or manager could enlist to help identify and assess potential risk (impact and consequences). Depending on the time available for assessing the risk profile, we offer the following suggested tools or sources for the reader's consideration:

- Consulting subject-matter experts
- Utilizing surveys, focus groups, and third-party audits
- Performing quality, safety, compliance, security, functional, and operations inspections
- Conducting business-case and/or formal analysis

Further, we mentioned previously the notion of a leader or manager's propensity for risk. It is not only important for leaders and mangers to evaluate their own propensity for risk but also to gage their position against their organization's strategic climate and cultural position of risk. In most cases, this assessment of alignment between personal and organizational risk profiles is an essential activity and is one that is avoided in many organizations. Potential sources for identifying your organization's strategic and actual position on risk-taking can be found in

- Published vision statements, strategic documents, and business models
- Risk-prediction models endorsed by your organization
- Regulations and policy
- Senior mentors and past practice

Risk and the International Community

With cross-border integration and globalization a growing reality, cultural acceptance for ethical risk management still has a variety of different meanings and interpretations. One approach to assessing risk across innovation cultures is to employ the "Uncertainty Avoidance Index (UAI), which essentially measures a culture's tolerance to uncertainty and ambiguity" (Ellingson, 2009, p. 50). Using numerical ratings, the risk is assessed on three key variables: the probability of the event/risk occurring, the impact (financial and nonfinancial), and whether or not control mechanisms exist to mitigate or control the risk. Cultures with high UAI (numerical) ratings tend to be more controlling (with more rules and attempts to control the outcome), while those with lower scores tend to have fewer rules and less control of the outcome.

Additionally, not every risk-predicting model or risk checklist will provide a clear-cut path for making a risk-free decision. Further, assessing the impacts of that decision becomes more ambiguous as you move from your domain to the enterprise level and beyond. Finally, our own subjectivity and propensity toward accountability and ethics will always influence our assessment process—the higher moral ground is essential, and objectivity is also quintessential in accurately assessing risk. In what is virtually synonymous with implementation, the decision maker will manage risk by creating an actionable phase to guide the risk and reward process or mitigate the potential impact that risk might bring to all players involved—the organization, stakeholder, shareholder, and/or community.

Risk in the Operational Environment

Regardless of how we perceive risk, as leaders and managers, we all react to various circumstances based on our experience—our sensitivity toward risk also varies across the spectrum of our daily activities. In dealing with risk every day, how leaders, managers, and cultures react to the decision-making process can vary dramatically. At the individual manager level, facing any decision involving a high level of risk is an emotional event marked by fear, uncertainty, and intense reflection. Our fears and uncertainty come from what we value most—sincerity, authenticity, ethics, integrity, humanity, human dignity and respect, and so on; managers learn over time (through trial and error) to weigh the magnitude of their decision in light of their propensity for risk (risk aversion), the chances for success or failure, and the potential impact (regarding the result).

Managing risk in the operational environment, the leader and manager are responsible for time-sensitive actionable processes that often manifest themselves at the tactical and operational level. Actionable processes, such as identifying, assessing, analyzing, synthesizing, evaluating, learning, educating, and providing feedback up, down, and laterally within the organization, are essential. In evaluating risk and return, managers must also identify windows of opportunity (i.e., increased value for the shareholder or improved competitive position in the market place) and plan, organize, coordinate, and act in an ethical manner to optimize return while managing (minimizing) the impact of associated risk.

Conversely, managers must also be actively engaged and prepared to act quickly if mitigation and damage control are required when a decision is

damaging or undesirable or has unplanned effects on shareholders, stakeholders, or consumers. Largely, some leaders manage risk with a focus
on their intellectual capital (people), a personal sense of accomplishment
(pride), and perhaps the reward (prize). For others, it may be a cultural matter of implementing higher levels of control in order to eliminate risk or the
unexpected. Lorenz's chaos theory (the butterfly effect) is of some relevance
to this discussion (Lorenz, 1963). For all managers, any decision will have
second- and third-order effects. These effects might be characterized as a
"ripple" effect, which may have a long-standing impact on related entities
that may never be revealed in our lifetime. In our opinion, the true essence
of managing risk is to consider how our decisions affect the collective
whole, not just our immediate audience at that moment.

Executing and managing risk are essentially transparent and relative
terms when considered for application in the operational environment. With
that said, execution requires empowerment, understanding, trust, collaboration, and the internal strength and intestinal fortitude to make an ethics-
based decision at the most opportune time. Further, execution requires a
firm command of your environment, the key players, and the variables;
and the best possible assessment of the state of play to ensure the mini-
mization of risk. In order for a leader or manager to address the realities
of risk within their sphere of influence or span of control, they need to
seek understanding and acknowledgment of that risk by identifying where
risk originates and how, when, and why it may appear. This starts with an
objective self-assessment of the leader or manager's internal compass setting and their own propensity toward risk and risk aversion, and a clear
understanding of responsibility.

Recognizing what level of decision a leader or manager can make on
their own in their current position is also instrumental in effectively executing the risk management strategy. Having credible, reliable, and accurate information on an apparently "low-risk, high-return" proposition might
require an immediate decision, but if it is out of your realm of responsibility, it may not provide the expected results or outcome, as key variables
and factors may be outside your control. If information is not qualified
in such a way, we face potential "assumptions and limitations" versus
viable information on which to act. Risk management is a dynamic, evolving, and active process requiring the manager's uninterrupted attention.
Information, variables, and environmental conditions can change rapidly
and keeping your finger on the pulse of the contributing elements is a
daily event.

Most notably, the source, packaging, relativity, and age of the information are important factors to which a manager needs access when executing risk-management strategies. Each manager develops their own persuasions and processes for implementing risk management across the spectrum of low- to high-level risk. For example, when faced with a time-sensitive or high-risk decision, the general approach could be to

1. Sharpen the focus, broaden perspective; elevate intensity and sensitivity
2. Seek clarity and the best possible understanding of the situation at hand (who, what, where, when, how, and why)
3. Assess, analyze, and evaluate the objectives, sources, agendas, vested interests, key players, impact, outcomes, and timing
4. Make a decision and follow the results as they play out

What is important to mention here is that any level of decision can spawn one or a series of follow-up or follow-on decisions that cascade and occur through the organization. Decision makers should make every effort to anticipate the impact of their decisions on other entities within the organization as well as those outside in supporting roles. Having their proverbial finger on the pulse of the organization is not enough. They should fight for feedback beyond the boundaries of their domain and across the enterprise. They should also be prepared to provide support for internal and external entities and be prepared to react to new situations that alter the level or makeup of risk.

Important Considerations in Risk Management

The following list of examples is only representative of three different levels where risk is a factor and by no means is it all-inclusive. From a cultural perspective, the risk of globalization and cross-border integration are overarching themes that amplify the growing concerns of Americans who feel that outsourcing, off shoring, and crowdsourcing are counterproductive to "keeping Americans employed." From an organization and business point of view, key factors the leader and manager should focus on are

1. The viability of a company's objectives and strategies, and how they might fare in a culturally diverse environment or how they might compare if cross-border integration became a key factor in their particular market sector

2. The impact or outcome of the decision to assume risk and the chances for success
3. The distinct interdependence of risk and opportunity— that risk creates opportunity and opportunity creates risk—is a seminal consideration for leaders and managers

We emphasize that ethical risk-taking is an essential hallmark in respected strategic decision-making processes. In fact, an organization's navigational heading and attitude toward risk-taking is often a reflection of their ethical climate and cultural stance on control and change. Risk-taking should also be viewed through multiple lenses (i.e., tactical, operational, and strategic). When decisive action is taken, risks can manifest themselves in ways that simulations, estimations, and assumptions simply did not account for based on uncontrolled or unknown factors or variables. Leaders and managers need to accept the reality that one person will rarely make an informed decision of significant magnitude in today's professional environment without the help of their supporting cast.

In summary, the manager should seek to learn by gaining the best possible understanding of contributing factors and the current state of play before making any decision that may impact those around them, the organization, and the community. Yes, there are situations that will arise requiring the manager to go with their gut feeling or to make a quick decision. When that becomes the norm for a manager and the manager appears cavalier about the decisions they make, there's an increasing risk that they're not considering key factors or the magnitude of the decision, and a mentor should be sought out at the earliest opportunity.

For those effective and respected leaders and managers, assuming coaching and mentoring roles for their subordinates (direct reports) can provide excellent opportunities for them to learn and gain experience and confidence through the delegation of low- to medium-risk decision-making processes. This is also conducive in building a knowledge-generating organization. Put another way, if managers have the opportunity to empower their subordinates to make decisions within their spectrum of responsibility, all reasonable efforts should be made to push those decisions down to the lowest level so that the human capital within the organization can gain experience and learn. This is essential for organizational health, growth, and idea generation. Further, it's a rich and rewarding experience for all—a total game changer.

For some managers, risk is the proverbial elephant in the room that's ignored when they're faced with a time-sensitive, indiscernible, or complex decision that takes them to the limits of their knowledge or ethical boundaries. Risk and uncertainty is innate to every decision we make, and acknowledging, understanding, and managing risk is a dynamic and changing process that impacts stakeholders, shareholders, and the domains and ecosystems that are commonly referred to as "communities."

Summary

By necessity, every enterprise, whether public or private, must move forward and seek new ways to adapt their organizational culture and dynamic capabilities (processes) to a resource-disparate environment where the demand for changing needs is constant. Organizations that do this well have a much better chance of emerging from this time of opportunity with an agile, responsive, and tempered culture built to withstand virtually any environmental uncertainty. This recent trend has focused not only on the impact that dynamic capabilities have on the organization in changing environments but also the implications that dynamic capabilities may have on an organization's strategy development and leadership.

In sum, leaders and managers should make every effort to concentrate on building learning environments within their organizations—dynamic capabilities that compliment or function like core competencies—while focusing on leadership, financial capital, staff relationships, reputation, technological know-how, and strategic thinking, all of which contribute to the overarching and long-term strategy of building a flexible, enduring, learning, and innovative organizational culture. Further, the authors have provided a comprehensive literature review of key scholarly works providing a general definition of what dynamic capabilities are, potential ways to develop those capabilities (to include competencies), and how those capabilities may influence the leadership growth approach.

Discussion Questions

1. What are the seven axioms of leadership and management? Please explain each as they have been presented in this chapter.
2. In order to achieve the two objectives of customer satisfaction identified in this chapter, four primary strategies were discussed. What are they and how do they relate to your organization?

3. What are dynamic capabilities? Please explain in your own words.
4. How do dynamic capabilities relate to core competencies?
5. In your own words, what is a leadership's role in developing a culture of innovation within your organization?
6. What is risk management and why is it important to your organization's innovation climate and culture?

Assignments

1. Revisiting our discussion of the axioms of leadership and management, elaborate on how each axiom relates to your organization and your position within your organization. Are you satisfied with the efforts made across the enterprise or do you have recommendations for possible improvements? Please explain.
2. Referring to Figure 6.1, showing the logic of leadership and management, pick two levels within the pyramid and discuss how they are related. For example, compare the "tactics" and "strategies." How are the elements of tactics (non-value-added activities, rework, scrap, and time/cycle time) related to strategies (standardization, variance control, continuous improvement, and teamwork)? Please explain each.
3. Identify and define in your own words three dynamic capabilities within your organization. How are they related to your organization's core competencies and what is your personal assessment on your organization's ability to meet your defined dynamic capabilities?
4. Does your organization have a risk management plan? If so, what is your contribution to this plan and how would you recommend improving the overall strategy and your particular contributions to the strategy?

Chapter 7

Organizational Diagnostics: Through the Looking Glass

Introduction

For most businesses or organizations, innovations occur as a chance event (or are event-driven). Typically, a critical need or requirement drives the organization to produce a product, service, or technology. Generally, the company or organization assembles or forms a team or set of teams to address an identified need or requirement. The organization then plans and directs activities focused on expending capital resources that are often limited to achieve a benefit that far exceeds the overall investment cost. When innovation becomes a key objective for the organization, it can be difficult to plan for the chance events or opportunities that often present the best cases for innovation. Further, the difficulty is often in repeating the innovation success multiple times in a reactive environment. For sustained innovation success, we feel a proactive and determined strategy is required for any business or organization postured to take advantage of potential innovation opportunities and discovery. Further, the terms *organization*, *business*, and *company* are used interchangeably and are intended to have the same meaning.

By our definition, a strategy is simply a plan to accomplish one or more objectives (goals) to meet a need or perhaps a set of requirements. To ensure sustained innovation success, businesses and organizations need a long-term plan that is consistent, sustainable, and repeatable over time and resistant to frequent modifications and changes. The objectives must be measurable and the plan logical in order to succeed. The organization must commit to a long-term strategy combined with the resolute desire to ensure that the innovation effort succeeds.

The next logical step after assessment and diagnostics is the development of an innovation management (IM) system and strategy. In simpler terms, innovation must be a corporate (executive) strategy, accepted and promoted by management, who operationalize it on a daily basis. Innovation is generally conducted on a project basis with two important but different aspects characterizing innovation. The first is in identifying the innovation project (Chapter 9); and the second is in implementing (managing) the innovation project (Appendix I). The administrative component occurs at the level of leadership (executive/director) and above within the organization; and the operational component functions as a project management (PM) strategy dedicated to achieving sustained innovation success. The operational component or PM strategy also includes the education and application of methodologies, tools, and techniques we present in this book, which support an agile and sustainable approach to success in innovation for any organization.

For a long-term commitment to innovation to be successful, each organization or business needs to understand its own strengths and weaknesses. Accomplishing this requires an introspective examination of the organization's preparedness for innovation. This assessment permits not only an understanding of where the organization is at present but what it will take to become more innovation proactive. "Jumping in" to innovation without first understanding certain elements of the organization can prove disastrous. Innovation is more than a process; it is a strategic function dedicated to sustained long-term performance and improvement.

The first step in developing a successful innovation effort is to understand the organization and propensity toward innovation. A typical and normal reaction is that we all understand the company or organization—but this understanding is based on our own set of experiences and knowledge. Further, every other supplier, employee, and user (customer) have their own perceptions, which govern their understanding of the organization. We maintain that an overall objective assessment of the organization is required—one that seeks the perceptions of others across the enterprise in order to establish an unbiased baseline. The process initially begins at a high level, and then subsequent evaluations will drill down with a focus on the organization's culture and work environment.

Assessment

An assessment is an evaluation of existing conditions. The objective of assessments is to provide a baseline from which to improve the organization. An assessment differs from an audit or critique in that no standards are yet established. Assessments are more of a general evaluation rather than an audit, which is highly specific. An assessment is also cyclical by its very nature and is typically generated for information purposes. For example, an innovation assessment provides information that identifies critical elements, such as

- What employees value
- How employees best understand innovation
- Whether the environment will support an innovative culture
- How innovation benefits the organization, customer (user), and employees

Figure 7.1 displays a typical process associated with the assessment cycle. There are levels of innovation assessment, beginning with a general evaluation of innovation "fit" within the organization. At this juncture, we highly recommend that organizations conduct an "organization fit for innovation"

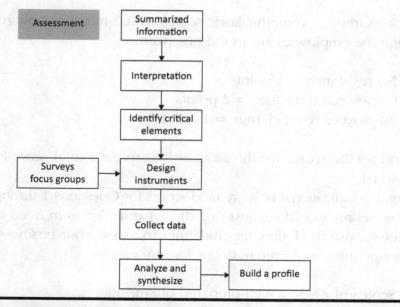

Figure 7.1   Assessment cycle (diagnostic evaluations for innovation opportunity).

assessment to determine overall acceptance and support for innovation (see Appendix II).

Scoring and Interpretation

The intent of these questions is to determine if the organization has an effective IM system in place or needs to develop an IM strategy. In our experience, few businesses or organizations have actually developed innovation as a strategy. Most businesses and organizations know that they need innovation but are unsure how to effectively implement the concept at the strategic, operational, and tactical levels.

Scoring

Score this instrument in the following manner:

- First response = 3 points
- Second response = 2 points
- Third response = 1 point

For example, overenthusiastic scores would measure how resistant to change the employees are in the organization.

- No resistance = 3 points
- Occasional resistance = 2 points
- Employees resist change = 1 point

Add up the scores for the 12 questions to get a total score for each individual.

Total organizational fit score (add scores for Questions 1 through 12): _____

Low scores would suggest that the organization is in need of innovation. Therefore, use the following guidelines to assess your business or organization's openness and preparedness for innovation:

- Scores of 31–36 = Well-prepared organizations.
- Scores of 25–30 = Opportunities for innovation, improvement needed.

- Scores of 18–24 = Innovation is not a strong value; innovation needed as a working strategy.
- Scores less than 18 = Innovation is unimportant or the business or organization needs a redirected focus. Lower scores indicate the potential for improvement and further delineation of program needs.

Actions

Realistically, scores should fall in the 18–25 range. Higher scores indicate that a business or organization is producing innovations on a regular basis and does not require further evaluation. Lower scores signify the need for innovation and the need for change. A proactive approach is to examine the scores and decide whether

1. The organization is not ready for innovation.
2. The organization is ready for innovation.

For those not ready, the choice to proceed or retreat is evident. Proceeding forward requires an evaluation of those lower scores, and we offer the following questions for those businesses and organizations that desire change to consider

1. Are these short-term or long-term concerns?
2. Are these structural (policies and procedures) or subordinate (leadership, climate, history, etc.) concerns?
3. What are the resource requirements?
4. Is the organization ready to change?

Answering these questions will help provide a realistic evaluation of what it will take to initiate a culture change that supports innovation. Assuming the culture can change as the innovations become more commonplace, we emphasize that recognizing and acknowledging the need are crucial for developing an effective strategy and a successful management process.

If innovations were common to the organization (business), then a more comprehensive evaluation would provide more detailed information. The assessment is also more specific when the organization wants to evaluate its ongoing innovation effort. A comprehensive innovation assessment tool is discussed in the next section.

Comprehensive Innovation Assessment

For those ready for innovation, we suggest proceeding with the next round of assessments and evaluations. The goals and objectives of these assessments and evaluations are a deeper understanding of the business or organization's strengths and weaknesses and its propensity for evolving its current culture and structure to become one that is more innovation-centric. Becoming an innovative business or organization is a journey. Central to that journey is a concerted effort to maintain open and responsive channels of communication up, down, and laterally within and outside the organization. The promise of success is never a guarantee, but the aperture of opportunity expands greatly when accomplishing assessments with objectivity and full disclosure, and in an open and honest manner. In summary, assessment instruments provide more focused information for decision makers to assess and consider. Part of the process of implementing an IM strategy is the alignment and transformation of the organization to a proactive status.

This simple assessment is only the initial evaluation of the business or organization's posture regarding innovation. We must reiterate that in no way does this assessment by itself provide the basis for a definitive action plan or strategic decision. The next step is to evaluate how executives, directors, managers, and employees judge their company or organization's innovation success.

Innovation Readiness

If the organization is open to innovation and can readily formulate a broader definition of innovation success, then further assessment can continue. The next assessment we offer is the innovation readiness (IR) assessment, which evaluates the seven critical components of a successful IM program (explained in further detail in Chapter 8). These components establish the essential steps required in evaluating and implementing innovation projects. This assessment is one that Innovation Processes and Solution (IPS), LLC and NorthStar Meta-Group Intl., will evaluate for our clients. The score will highlight areas of positive achievement and needed improvement. These assessment tools are instrumental in developing the business or organizational profile.

Scoring

The IR scoring portion of this instrument represents a method of assessing the organization's strengths and weaknesses. Each statement is a characteristic of innovation (seven major components. When a respondent evaluates a characteristic favorably, identify it as a "strength." Conversely, when a respondent evaluates a characteristic negatively, identify it as a "weakness." The IR position is the sum of positive scores minus (–) the sum of the negative scores. To score the IM portion, convert all statement scores into one of three IR score categories:

- 1: When the respondent scores a 4 or 5 (a positive response).
- 0: When the respondent scores a 3 (a neutral response).
- –1: When the respondent scores a 1 or 2 (a negative response).

Consider Table 7.1, "Example of Innovation Readiness (IR) Instrument Scoring," as an example.

Interpretation

There are seven total IR scores, one for each component. The sum total is the IM score. It is prudent to recognize that for those businesses or organizations in an advanced stage or culture of innovative performance, achieving a score of 70 would be difficult; and for those on the opposite end of the innovative performance scale, it would be difficult to score –70. Typical scores will range between 20 and 50. A common mistake is averaging the scores. Do not average scores as the overall average could be very close to zero and negate the purpose of the assessment. Sum the scores for each N²OVATE™ category. Examine the range or distribution of scores. The higher the score, the better prepared the organization is for innovation at the operational level. Lower scores indicate targeted areas that require improvement or modification before implementing an innovation strategy. Large deviations between scores indicate a lack of consensus in regard to preparedness (Figure 7.2). Total scores for the 50 respondents demonstrate this lack of consensus. Rather than

Table 7.1   Example of Innovation Readiness (IR) Instrument Scoring

	Needs and New Ideas Component	Strongly Disagree 5	Disagree 4	Neither Disagree nor Agree 3	Agree 2	Strongly Agree 1	IR Score
1	Managers are open to new concepts.			X			0
2	Employees are naturally creative.				X		1
3	What the user needs is important.				X		1
4	Unhappy users require immediate attention.					X	1
5	Employees can easily bring new ideas to their supervisor.			X			a
6	Needs must add value.			X			0
7	Users generally need what is often not available.				X		I
8	The organization rewards new ideas.				X		I
9	The agency/ organization/ division/ department is open to new ideas.		X				-I
10	The organization has strong ties to its internal and external users.			X			0
						IR Scores	4

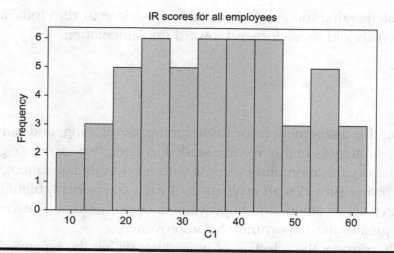

Figure 7.2   Total innovation readiness (IR) scores for 50 respondents.

this being considered as a negative indicator, we recommend that additional steps be taken to determine the reasons for the disagreements.

The IR instrument can also assess a present process or IM system. Use the scores more as indicators than solid, empirical numbers.

To determine which N²OVATE™ category is most (least) capable, average the scores across the number of respondents (the sample), and construct a "radar chart" (Figure 7.3) across the seven categories (seven steps). Remember that averages will be close to zero. A positive response indicates compliance with the process step (more to follow in Chapter 9). A negative response suggests that additional effort is required to improve that step

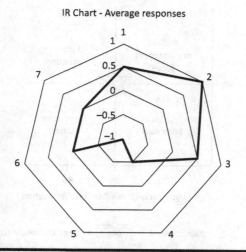

Figure 7.3   Radar chart of respondent averages.

before implementing the entire process. Scores close to zero indicate that organization should move forward toward implementation.

Actions

Conducting this assessment prior to designing, developing, and pursuing any innovation strategy is highly recommended. A composite score (Figure 7.4) provides the organization and business with an overall assessment. Each of the seven scores provides an evaluation of each component, highlighting both positive achievement and improvement opportunities. The lower the score, the greater the opportunity for improvement.

Carefully consider the selection of individuals within the organization or company to complete this assessment. These individuals must be at a supervisory level, with a minimum of 2 years of experience with the company or organization. The authors also recommend that the organization provide training with this assessment before it is distributed and the resulting data analyzed. We must emphasize that the use of this assessment is extremely beneficial as a precursor to implementing an innovation strategy. The assessment provides valuable insight and information on the perceptions of those individuals responsible for implementing, maintaining, and evolving the intent of your organization or company innovation plan. Further, consider the value in the scores rather than the absolutes. By design, the IR instrument is also a versatile assessment tool that is useful for auditing and continuous improvement.

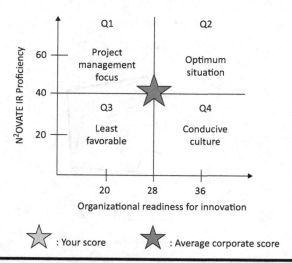

Figure 7.4 Composite innovation readiness (IR) score.

Why Do Diagnostics?

Consider the situation when you have an illness that requires the attention of a physician. You make an appointment to meet with the doctor to discuss your symptoms and find a remedy. When you enter the office, the doctor or nurse begins by collecting your vital signs, interviewing you as the patient, and recording information for the physician. We call this situational analysis. When the physician enters the examination room, they do a visual of your condition (an environmental scan), ask questions (begin a causal inquiry), examine your chart (examining passive data), and carry out further examination (collecting active data). Using their knowledge and experience and the prevailing information (seasonal factors, common symptoms, etc.), the physician makes a diagnosis. If conditions warrant (conflicting information), they may do a "what-if" analysis—using a process of elimination to reach a diagnosis.

We use a similar process to understand why innovation can bring benefit to an organization and use this information to suggest a "best" strategy. Unlike those who only sell a "cure" (a method), we at IPS, LLC, determine the best method (strategy) based on the organization's present situation (needs). This may mean creating a one-of-a-kind (proprietary) strategy for each organization.

To complete the evaluation accurately, use an evaluator with experience working with or at multiple locations. The best evaluator is an intuitive person, one who would rather understand the existing organization than judge it for compliance. The evaluator has to demonstrate a professional attitude and demeanor and respect for the organization. Begin the process by completing a situational analysis. Follow the process (Figure 7.4) until there is enough information to choose an appropriate innovation strategy.

Diagnostic Elements

Situational Analysis

Performing a situation analysis consists of examining the elemental units that describe the situation of interest. Identify and describe the following:

- Location (where the situation takes place)
- The "event" (the underlying purpose or reason for the event)
- Outcome (presumed and actual)

- Context (in which the situation exists)
- Assumptions (made and presumed)

When examining an organization for its present and future innovation capabilities, consider not only the encounter (event) but also the preconceived notions (bias) the evaluator has before assessing the situation. This includes any assumptions made before the evaluation begins. Evaluate with this context in mind (the pressure on the client to demonstrate positive results), where the evaluation takes place (location), and the expected/actual outcome. Often, evaluators orchestrate their reviews based on what they expect and want to occur. This "bias" will cloud the judgment of the evaluator. Complete a situational analysis without preconceived notions. The experience and discipline of the evaluator are critical.

Consider as an example the situational analysis performed by a police officer when evaluating a minor traffic accident. Often, there are two or more conflicting accounts of the accident. The officer must evaluate the situation without bias to make a report. The officer must take into consideration the location, existing circumstances, driving conditions, time of day, and so on. The situation analysis determines the prevailing conditions in which the accident occurred. The experience and expertise of the evaluator keeps them unbiased as to the situation. Next, evaluate the environment in which the organization operates.

Environment Scan

An environmental scan involves examining the organization from a cognitive and sensory perspective (Aslakson et al., 2014). The evaluator examines the surroundings to develop a profile of the environment in which the innovation does or could occur.

The environmental scan consists of

- Visual assessment (place, presence, posture, people—body language/facial expressions)
- Verbal assessment (tone, clarity, communication effectiveness—talking vs. listening)
- Cognitive assessment (knowledge, experience, preparation)
- Setting assessment (atmosphere, mood)
- Emotional assessment ("feel," comfort factor, emotional state)

A visual assessment is critical to establish a baseline. Place is the physical location (i.e., office, restaurant, pub); presence is the authority, rank, or title of the people attending; posture involves physical items (i.e., seating arrangements, furniture) and people (i.e., body language, facial expressions, eye contact).

Next, evaluate the verbal cues received through the encounter. The content should be clear, direct, and easy to understand. Tone measures rhythm, style, and intent (friendly vs. conformational). Finally, evaluate the effectiveness of communication (value, delivery, content).

Every environmental scan assumes that we have some knowledge and experience of the event. Knowledgeable and experienced evaluators are prone to asking more questions. Those with less knowledge (experience) will listen and learn. A good rule of thumb is to include both approaches in an interview.

The setting is the characteristic that evaluates the atmosphere in which the event will occur, involving items such as setting (which could be positive, neutral, or negative) and overall "mood." If one of the members of the encounter is uncomfortable, this will affect the result and could sabotage the meeting. If this is detected, try to diffuse it with appropriate humor or a welcoming demeanor (which invites a person into the encounter), or identify and eliminate the reason for this discomfort.

Finally, the emotional component is the evaluator's own state of mind in entering the event. Concerns such as preparedness, anxiety, behavior (extrovert vs. introvert), trust, intuitiveness, and confidence are critical. Since no one is perfect, prepare a strategy to deal with emotional issues, those of both the evaluator and the other person(s) involved in the encounter. Next, consider the type of information (data) collected.

Active Data (Information) Sources

Both situational analysis and environmental scanning result in a large amount of data (information). Active data is real-time information, collected by the evaluator in real time. Active data consists of counts and categorizations. An example of active data is the information collected from an environmental scan. It can include observations, experiences, perceptions (emotions, opinions, beliefs), and measurements. The goal is to find a pattern and link the data to a particular attribute. The information is more descriptive than strictly numerical (quantitative) information. For example, temperature can be both quantitative (73 degrees) and qualitative (pleasant or mild). This type of data reduces inconsistency but is open to the effects of bias. This information source provides an excellent analysis of short-term events.

Active data contains valuable information. Websites such as Facebook permit and encourage expressions and observations and offer a forum for experiences. This is generally unstructured data, but data scientists are actively tracking this data for economic and competitive information. For innovation evaluations, capture and record information directly related to the situational elements and environmental scans.

Passive Data (Information) Sources

Passive data is time-dependent information not collected in real time by the evaluator, and analysis of the data can occur in various formats. Assessment-type data is passive in that the respondent (data source) is not directly in contact with the evaluator. Passive data reduces bias, since the evaluator cannot directly influence the source. This information source provides longer-term information. Data sources can consist of individual respondents, databases, organizational records, government statistics, and so on. Passive data can be descriptive, measured, and categorized. It is the most frequently used; however, we use active data (short term) for most decisions.

Passive data's usefulness decreases with time. It can provide nearly use-less information if the intention and purpose is misaligned. If measured incorrectly, it can cause problems or catastrophes. Relying on passive data only is dangerous, and it can distort the true reality.

Assessment instruments (surveys) collect passive data. This information helps to determine the larger picture, provides a history of the occurrence, and describes what individuals think and act on as a group.

Summarize the Information

Summarizing the observational and situational analysis data is key to under-standing the organization in real time. When summarizing the data, consider the following:

- Patterns and trends (in behavior and actions)
- Verbal emphasis (what employees talk about)

- Convergent and divergent views (what individuals agree on or disagree with)
- Attainable versus unattainable goals/objectives
- What is important (unimportant) to employees/management
- Similarities and differences (personality types, work ethic, loyalties, etc.).

Summarize the information into a usable format. Continue to update while continuing to work with the customer (user). One suggestion is to build a profile.

Building a Profile

Build a profile of the organization. Use the information collected from the situational analysis and environmental scans. An organizational profile is a short but concise description of

- The organization's health (growth, stability, customer/user satisfaction, cost containment, resource usage, mission/vision alignment, etc.)
- The amount and success of value adding (what value is added and by whom)
- Leadership and decision-making success/failure
- Employee/management relations/communications (including aspects of trust, commitment, honesty, engagement, etc.)
- Influence of customers (users) and resource providers (i.e., stakeholders)
- Innovation efforts (value/benefits) (what worked, what failed)
- Organizational properties (efficiencies, effectiveness, products/services, etc.)

This is an example of what a profile contains. Each organization has its own unique set of needs and its own description. The more complete the description, the better and more efficient the choice of strategy for sustained success. The profile is a living document and should be updated when major events occur. Knowing the organization is a key to success. It helps prevent missteps (false starts), aligns personnel, demonstrates the competency of the organization, and promotes better communications. We must iterate that the security and confidentiality of the data is a primary concern.

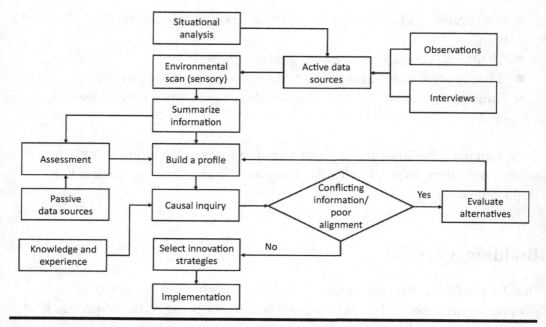

Figure 7.5 Diagnostic evaluation for innovation opportunity.

Causal Inquiry

The evaluator is well prepared to conduct a preliminary causal inquiry after completing the first four steps (Figure 7.5). The developed profile provides invaluable information regarding the organization.

A causal inquiry is a logical process of identifying reasons (causes) to explain the results of a specified event (in this case, the results of the organizational profile). Causal inquiry is part "connecting the dots" and part data interpretation. The evaluator combines his or her own knowledge and experiences to determine if the organizational profile matches reality or is somehow different. Often, reality (situational analysis and environmental scans) conflicts with the data obtained during the assessment phase. This results in further "what-if" analyses and the examination of alternatives.

When the data matches (or aligns), the next step is to review the available strategies, that is, to identify a strategy or modify an existing strategy. The project is ready for the N²OVATE™ process (discussed in Chapter 8).

Before implementing an innovation strategy, the organization needs to diagnose its present situation. Like Alice in Wonderland, the organization must peer through the looking glass. Often the need for innovation arises from an existing program or possible innovation opportunity. Conducting the review occurs after the assessment phase is completed but before the best innovation strategy for implementation is identified. Figure 7.1, "Diagnostic Evaluations for Innovation Opportunity" details the steps involved. The technique begins when an organization (company or business) expresses interest in working with IPS, LLC. Prior to performing any work, we first carry out an analysis of the present environment, including an assessment interpretation. Analytics is the information collected; diagnostics is the interpretation and follow-through.

Strategies for Innovation

Organizational Scale

For the business sector, strategies for innovation can occur anywhere along the leadership structure or chain of command. Businesses or organizations usually implement the innovation strategy, but the directive for innovation often comes from a higher authority. Strategies usually begin at the "C-suite" level, which is responsible for approving such initiatives. Certain entities within the governance system have some level of discretionary spending allocated at the beginning of the year, which they directly control. Here is where the policy now changes from requiring organizational or business leadership and the chain of command to implement and succeed. Policy directives require information and interpretation at the subordinate levels in the organization. This continues until the operational level is reached (e.g., at the division or department level).

The interpretation requires a thorough understanding of the mission, values, and purpose statement for developing a viable strategy. Smaller organizations may or may not have considered innovation as a strategic objective. In either case, what is often unknown is the type of strategy deployed. Knowing the type of innovation strategy deployed provides information on how to update or correct that strategy, which permits and encourages the concept.

Existing Strategies

Many organizations subscribe to innovation and its benefits but struggle to achieve a sustained track record of positive results, which require a specific and focused strategy. Often, innovation is part of a greater organizational or business strategy to promote value, efficiencies, and lower costs. Yet, effective innovation efforts require a separate, unique strategy and vision. Some of the more common existing innovation strategies are *blue ocean*, *disruptive*, *early adopter*, and *fast-second*, which focus on achieving effectiveness as an overall strategy for innovation.

When companies create blue oceans, they break from their traditional strategy to infrequently pursue differentiation and low cost simultaneously (Buisson and Silberzahn, 2010). This limits the overall success that innovation can deliver. According to Buisson and Silberzahn (2010), blue ocean and fast-second strategies simply do not fully explain successful innovation, and they maintain that innovative success is secured through four kinds of breakthroughs—design, technology, business model, and process breakthroughs. Breakthroughs occur infrequently and often by chance. Additionally, Kim and Mauborgne (2005) assert that "by driving down costs while simultaneously driving up value for buyers, a company can achieve a leap in value for both itself and its customers" (p. 83); and that building new market segments requires a consistent pattern of strategic thinking, one that never uses the existing competition as a benchmark. These "leapfrog" innovation strategies may only come once or twice in the life of the organization. Missing are the benefits of change and incremental improvement. An example of the "leapfrog" innovation strategy is the iPod, which changed the face of the recorded music business. In fact, raising the social "cool factor" of your product line is definitely desirable; maintaining and sustaining that product line as more companies enter the market segment tends to narrow your profit margins as increasing supplies and lower demand drive down market share. Apple's iPod entry redefined the market standard and made other competitors retool or become irrelevant. As Apple looked for new opportunities to expand their spectrum of influence, the cellular handset industry emerged as a new frontier waiting for a unifying champion—enter the iPhone.

Developed by Christensen (1997), the disruptive innovation theory challenges the traditional framework of sustainment strategies by altering the product or delivery methodology and displacing the existing process. Raynor (2011) adds that Christensen's theory can be employed to either enhance innovative concepts that currently exist or create balanced portfolios of innovation initiatives. The seminal principle in Christensen's theory is that companies innovate faster than the customer base demands. A good example of this is Apple's innovative "i" products. Disruptive innovation can also have a negative side, as it can cause disruptive effects within the organization. It is most useful on an organizational scale when product redefinition is required. Organizations that need to redefine themselves can find this strategy useful.

Perhaps a better example comes from the aircraft industry's leading provider, Boeing Aerospace Corporation. Sticking to a proven record of accomplishment of forging solid foundations before moving forward, Boeing has learned to listen to its customers while creating new and balanced portfolios that meet customer needs (Masters, 2007). With global business ethics gravitating more toward social responsibility, global partnering, and "greener" solutions, Boeing's new business model and integration of new aerospace structure technology (composite wings and fuselage), big sky interior, and the global supply chain approach was fresh and destined for success. This large-scale global collaboration between Alena, Boeing, Fuji, Kawasaki, Mitsubishi, Spirit, and Vought at seven production sites around the world displays a diverse set of highly integrated partnerships that did not exist in the commercial aircraft industry. These new approaches broke new ground, and Boeing's new collaborative business model may become the roadmap for international collaboration and innovation effectiveness in more than just the aviation and aircraft-manufacturing industries. Therefore, some innovation strategies follow a "homegrown" approach.

In order to examine internal innovation strategies, the next section examines different methods of categorizing innovation types. These simple descriptors will assist in evaluating the strategy's effectiveness, intent, and future sustainability.

Innovation Strategy Types

Classifying or categorizing types of strategic innovation is critical to success and future growth. Clausen et al. (2012) identified five unique strategies that businesses/organizations often employ:

1. Ad hoc—random innovations (strategies created on a project basis)
2. Supplier based—driven by newer technology, new products
3. Market driven—consumer (client or competitor) or user driven
4. R&D intensive—a traditional approach whereby innovation emanates from one source
5. Science based—reliance on patents, science, and research
6. No strategy (author added)—no discernible strategy or plan

Clausen et al. (2012) maintain that results support the idea that the differences in innovation strategies across firms are an important determinant of the probability that those firms will repeat and sustain success. More concretely, they found that firms pursuing the strategies "market driven," "research and design (R&D) intensive," and "science based" were more likely to be persistent innovators. Persistence is as critical as a defined strategy.

To determine, in a simplistic manner, the strategy deployed requires some form of self-assessment. Use the following set of survey statements with a 5-point or 7-point Likert scale. The agreement/disagreement scale provides a method of establishing the prevailing strategy that an organization could deploy. Assign a value of "1" to "strongly disagree" and a value of "5" to "strongly agree" (using a 5-point scale; a 7-point scale would have more gradations, adding the phrases "somewhat disagree" and "somewhat agree"). Distribute to the director level and above (a minimum of 20–30 participants). Calculate an average response for each group and then transfer the averages to a "radar chart" as shown in Figure 7.6.

Strategy 1: Ad Hoc Strategy

1. Innovations are often unplanned.
2. Innovations are event based rather than strategic.
3. Innovation is a common workplace word.
4. It seems that innovations appear only when needed.
5. Innovation is discussed on a regular basis within the organization.

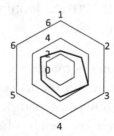

Analysis of present innovation strategy

Figure 7.6   Radar chart: predominance of strategy type.

Strategy 2: Supplier-Based Strategy

1. New technology drives the agency or organization to innovate.
2. When a supplier changes a part or product, our organization must innovate.
3. Our suppliers have a great deal of influence on what and how we innovate.
4. Working with suppliers is a way to determine our innovation needs.
5. We rely heavily on our suppliers to innovate.

Strategy 3: Directive-Driven Strategy

1. Directives determine what and when we will innovate.
2. The innovation strategy is focused on new directives.
3. When the organization meets directives, innovation efforts can be successful.
4. We value user needs to guide our innovation strategy.
5. Directives guide our strategic efforts.

Strategy 4: R&D Emphasis Strategy

1. R&D creates most innovative/products/services//technology.
2. R&D's primary function is innovation.
3. Administration and R&D set the strategic vision for innovation.
4. Innovation proceeds only with the approval of R&D.
5. The engineering department creates and manages innovation.

Strategy 5: Science-Based Strategy

1. The agency/organization relies on patents to advance innovation.
2. A focus on science and discovery is the result of the organization's innovation policy.
3. The agency/organization is focused on research for its innovative products or services.
4. The agency/organization regularly advances the field of science and technology with its innovation.
5. A strong research focus continues to be the strategic vision for the organization.

Strategy 6: No Strategy

1. There is no specific or declared strategy associated with or to innovation.
2. There is a strategy, but it lacks any relevant enforcement.
3. The strategy is weak and possibly not applicable.
4. No plans exist to implement an innovation strategy.
5. Innovation is a strategic goal but remains to be implemented.

For those organizations with a strategy, evaluate one of the first five strategy types. Analyze the averages of the 20 respondents to determine the predominance of innovation strategy type. Example of 20 respondents (director level and above) averages:

7.2: typical scores for one dimension
The average points to the third strategy (directive driven).

Many businesses or organizations have no strategic emphasis on innovation. A "no strategy" approach is evident in those businesses/organizations that give only lip service to innovative activities. Corporate-level executives can ask for an emphasis on innovation, but if the culture and environment do not work in its favor, the attempt to implement it will fail. If the organization has failed to deliver successful innovations, then a "no strategy" type may be the best descriptor.

When analyzing the data, examine the range of strategy types selected. Variation is the choice of strategy type. If respondents choose more than one strategy type, this indicates a lack of clarity, poor follow-up, or communication difficulties. Multiple choices for a predominant innovation strategy suggest that no clear strategy exists. Use the results to drive a discussion on modifying or creating a viable strategy. Those organizations that "pass" with good agreement should be considered ready for a more detailed and specific strategy.

For those who experience difficulties, consider an additional step. Examine the mission, vision, and purpose statements of the existing strategy.

Mission, Vision, and Purpose Statements

To understand and implement the strategic component, the business or organization must first examine its mission, purpose, and value statement.

These statements provide a view of what is important to the entity, the environment that innovation must thrive in, and commitments made on activities such as innovation. These statements provide the reason for the existence and the goals and aspirations of the organization. The choice of words is critical, since these uniquely describe the organization and its intent. Not only is the choice of words important; also, the arrangement and emphasis of the language as key elements contribute to the overarching mission of the organization.

Innovation may often be an outcome of the mission, vision, or purpose statement. If so, then the words that describe how the organization will achieve such a goal are critical. Therefore, examining these statements provides an insight into how the organization attempts to achieve these goals. For most businesses, the mission, vision, and purpose statements begin at the C-suite level. Businesses and organizations that develop strategies must adapt to all directives. Innovation is a common directive for many businesses. These businesses often create similar descriptive statements—innovation as a key strategy.

A simple method of assessing the innovation strategy of any organization is to examine the language of these statements. Each business must search for keywords (Table 7.2) linked to innovation success. Some common language is shown in this table.

Innovation cannot thrive in an organization committed to unrelated goals or objectives. Therefore, innovation may begin by correcting or updating the organization's purpose for existing. Expecting innovation success from a business dedicated to some other goal or objectives is ludicrous. Yet, language exists to recognize innovation without any effective support mechanisms. Examine, first, these strategic descriptors of purpose and objectives. Review them to determine if these documents are pro, neutral to, or have a negative slant on innovation. If a conflict exists with innovation descriptors, chances are that innovation will not succeed, as there is no declared

Table 7.2 Keywords Supporting an Innovation Strategy

Success Measures	Environment	Commitment
Reduced costs	Cooperative	Matching resources
Efficiencies/effectiveness	Creative	Long term
Added value	Recognition and rewards	Dedicated personnel
High performance	Trust	Leadership

directive to meet this objective. If the mission, purpose, or vision statements do not contain this language, then the strategic elements may not exist to support innovation. If innovation is present, then these descriptors may send a mixed signal.

Financial results are not enough of a driver for innovation. The environment that supports creativity, cooperation, and coordination must be present if all are to participate. Otherwise, innovation may be limited in scope and benefit. Finally, management must lead the effort by committing resources and personnel for success. Changing the mindset to one more open to innovation may be difficult to accomplish, may be time-consuming, and may upset many within the organization. Those organizations without a corporate vision that promotes innovation will need to start at this very step.

Most large businesses or organizations have developed a unique culture. This culture may come from its past history, its mission, or its directives. For example, the Central Intelligence Agency (CIA) has a unique culture developed to support its ever-changing mission. As technology is such an integral part of the CIA's mode of operation, innovation is a natural part of its mission and existence. Another natural is 3M, which continually produces and releases new products and new technology. It is almost an acronym for innovation. What about a government entity such as the Internal Revenue Service (IRS)? The IRS's focus is on the collection of taxes and fees. Does this lend itself to innovation or will its mission and purpose require an adjustment or a culture change to operationalize innovation?

If descriptions of the culture do not include words such as cooperative, collaborative, or challenging, then innovation is secondary or at best attuned to innovation (a very weak alignment with innovation). That culture, which has developed over time, is the direct result of a specific strategy deployed. If innovation is not an instrumental thread in that culture, then it will be difficult to deploy. Begin by changing the culture with a strategy that supports innovation success for the long term. Remember that success breeds success. Use a proven methodology to demonstrate success at the project level (i.e., the N²OVATE™ process—described in Chapters 8 and 9). Use these successes (with both outcomes and personnel) to develop the fundamentals of the organization's new strategy.

Smaller businesses may or may not have considered innovation as a strategic objective. For these organizations, the focus will be on innovation projects that result in incremental improvements as well as large-scale projects. For innovation to successfully "pay back," the organization needs a comprehensive methodology and strong management leadership and support.

Many businesses or organizations have no strategic emphasis on innovation. A "no strategy" approach includes those businesses and organizations that give only lip service to innovative activities. Setting a goal (such as innovation) and then providing no plan to achieve the goal produces little value. C-level executives can ask for an emphasis on innovation, but if the culture and environment do not work in its favor, the attempt to implement it will fail. Without a system-wide strategy, innovation exists as a random and uncontrolled occurrence. Planning for these events is more chance than choice.

Compatibility with Organizational Outcomes and Functions

Compatibility is an issue when aligning an innovation strategy with organizational structures. Reasons for this disconnect include the complexity of the innovation attempted and the type of organizational structure selected. Innovation complexity ranges from incremental improvements up to radical changes such as in disruptive innovations, discoveries, or significant patents. The more complex the innovation, the more heavily invested the organization will need to be in that innovation. Both the amount of resources and the threat of risk increase with each subsequent innovation stage. Contrasting the innovation complexity with organizational functions, systems, and management creates nine unique innovation strategies. Figure 7.7 profiles these innovation strategies.

Businesses and organizations are searching for strategies that will produce sustained success. Leaders and organizational decision makers must understand that the intent and form of innovation is different depending on its application in an organization. The innovation strategy needed to improve the decision-making process is very different from improving the performance of a product or service provided to users. Trying a "one size fits all" approach will be both frustrating and unproductive.

From the authors' perspective, different outcomes and applications require different innovation strategies. Given that customers (users) want innovative outcomes, this was the first strategy we developed. The strategies presented in this book address process, product (technology), and service applications. The innovation strategy should complement the overall organizational structure. To examine for discrepancies and identify opportunities, first determine which organizational structure (tactical, functional, or strategic)

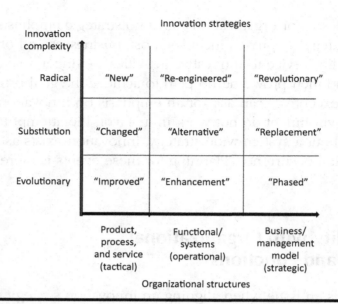

Figure 7.7   Innovation strategic grid.

needs the value-added results of innovation. Next, select the desired level of complexity—there are three distinct types:

Type 1: Evolutionary—ongoing improvement for improved performance
Type 2: Substitution—a replacement of an existing system or practice
Type 3: Radical—new, unique, resets the existing paradigm

For example, consider a medical office practice:

Type 1: New policies and procedures instituted to eliminate wait times
Type 2: A new doctor replaces a retiring physician
Type 3: Medical office now includes traditional and nontraditional practices

The business or organization must decide on the most appropriate choice. On the horizontal axis are three organizational structures. The structure refers to where the innovation strategy is applied. There are three categories of structure:

1. Product, process, and service: This has an external (user) focus (tactical).
2. Systems: Internal operations, practices, policies, and procedures (an internal focus) (functional/operational).
3. Strategic: Leadership and decision making.

It is common to want innovation to occur across all three structures. Realize, though, that the strategies could be different.

The internal grid is made up of keywords that suggest the appropriate strategies to employ. The organization could determine that the incremental approach works best for all three functions. Yet, for the business management model, the approach is different. Different functions may require modified strategies. For example, an innovation strategy for HR is not compatible with one for the accounts/finance department, although there are many common elements. Organizations may want three separate strategies for its external focus product, process, or service functions yet want only one strategy for its internal systems and business model. The N²OVATE™ model (with modifications) will work successfully for all nine strategies.

Creating individual strategies for each element in the grid is beyond the scope of this book. This text will discuss the strategies for innovating products, processes, and services across all three dimensions of innovations (Chapter 9). Look for publications to develop these additional strategies for successful sustained innovation.

Constructing an Innovation Strategy

Rather than constructing a new set of values, a new mission, or new purpose statements, begin first with an assessment of internal and external capabilities. Perform a "SWOT" analysis (S—strengths, W—weaknesses, O—opportunities, and T—threats). Table 7.3 describes some characteristics to consider when determining the elements that constitute a SWOT analysis. This list is not exclusive, but it does consider the issues when attempting a SWOT analysis (Bevanda and Turk, 2011).

Strengths, Weaknesses, Opportunities, and Threats Analysis

A SWOT analysis is useful for developing the elements of an innovation strategy. Consider a concept such as innovation. How can an organization design an innovation strategy to maximize its strengths (opportunities) and minimize its weaknesses (threats)? A SWOT analysis is an excellent tool for assessing these four characteristics. The SWOT characteristics are useful for developing a mission and value statement. This is how an innovation strategy begins. The next steps in constructing a strategy that consists

Table 7.3   List of Characteristics Considered When Performing a SWOT Analysis

Characteristics	Positive/Negative
Financial	Profits, net income, ROI, return on assets (ROA), return on equity (ROE), costs, taxes, fees, etc.
Strategic	Marketplace standing; number of competitors; competitive advantage; product, service or technology competency; history; product line; product life cycle
Resources	Availability, cost, supply chain, integration, outsourcing, staff competency, storage, global capacity
Knowledge	History, accountability, learning culture, technical competency, inherent versus learned, creativity
Operational issues	Staffing, capability, delivery, maintenance, training, global response, turnaround time, business processes
Long term versus short term	5-year planning horizon, immediate needs, enterprise solutions
Standards, quality, reliability	Measures, best practices, quality practices, warranty, guarantees, etc.
Customer/user relationships	Satisfaction issues, consumer behaviors, complaints, effective responses

of developing a process, identifying outcomes, constructing control metrics, assigning responsibilities, and validation.

Gather a team of executives, directors, and managers. For each category (e.g., strengths), brainstorm a list of characteristics (Table 7.3) of the organization that are a defined strength. Brainstorming is a process rather than a chaotic generation of ideas. Brainstorming consists of topic selection, individual idea generation, writing (list of ideas or concepts), listing the ideas, and evaluation. The result of the exercise is a list of items related to the topic. Further evaluation can consist of ranking the ideas/concepts.

Begin with strengths; consider the questions in Figure 7.8 and do the same for the remaining four categories. Be prepared for discussion and negotiation. The primary intent is innovation. For every strength, there is a potential weakness (Evans and Wright, 2009). Address threats (both internal and external). The four quadrants will help in developing a sound strategic innovation policy.

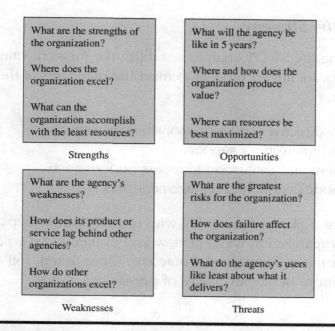

What are the strengths of the organization? Where does the organization excel? What can the organization accomplish with the least resources? Strengths	What will the agency be like in 5 years? Where and how does the organization produce value? Where can resources be best maximized? Opportunities
What are the agency's weaknesses? How does its product or service lag behind other agencies? How do other organizations excel? Weaknesses	What are the greatest risks for the organization? How does failure affect the organization? What do the agency's users like least about what it delivers? Threats

Figure 7.8 Questions to answers when completing a SWOT analysis.

Ghazinoory et al. (2011) report that using a SWOT analysis to help develop an innovation strategy is unique. Yet, it follows that a well-managed business or organization will be more successful. The innovation strategy should build on strengths and opportunities while considering the risks, threats, and weaknesses. Be aware that a weakness may already be visible to your customer or user.

The organization can construct a well-developed mission, value, and purpose statement; create metrics to measure innovation progress; and manage the process to produce acceptable results. Additional critical elements of a successful strategy are

1. Communication of message and intent
2. Empowerment of teams to execute projects
3. Leadership to guide execution and follow-through
4. A strategy securely embedded in department and division policy

What remains is a strategy for lasting and results-producing innovation.

Assembling the Strategy

After completing the SWOT analysis, establish the mission, value, and purpose statements. Identify a process to meet the outcomes of these descriptors, to include

1. Leadership directives (roles, responsibilities, actions).
2. Degree and intensity of support.
3. Measurement and evaluation to assess performance.
4. Review, modification, and replacement policies.

Implement at a planned pace. Try with one division or department before implementing organization wide. Review and evaluate—be willing to change and modify for the most successful outcome. Once tested, roll out to the entire organization. Be keenly aware of persistence issues.

Persistence

This is a critical element of any innovation strategy. Even the best ideas fail at times to achieve a desired performance level or to meet specific needs. Humans learn more through failure than success. Given this advice, an organization's innovation strategy (and efforts) must prevail in the face of occasional failures. Persistence is more than just innovating repeatedly; it is also a mindset. Pharmaceutical organizations that innovate by discovering or inventing a new drug may fail repeatedly before achieving success. Persistence is a corporate or organizational trait that allows the organization to resist failure but learn from its mistakes. Include measures that track persistence, consistency, and lessons learned.

Implementing an Innovation Strategy

Finally, the remaining item is to implement an innovation strategy. As with any strategy, "one size does not fit all," meaning that a single strategy is not applicable throughout the organization. So often, organizations determine that a strategy conceived (designed) at the executive level will apply to the entire organization. These strategies have a short shelf life, given their inability to adapt to various corporate, operational, and user requirements and situations. Recognizing the need for an adaptive strategy is the first step in developing sustained innovation success.

Strategies need refinement, requiring periodic adaptation. Figure 7.7 highlights nine unique areas that require an innovation strategy. Of course, much of the process is transferrable, but each area requires a unique combination of tools, resources, management commitment, and support. Consider these five competencies as the organization develops its adaptive innovation strategy:

1. Involvement (leadership, managerial, employee)
2. Proven success rate (number of projects, success/failure rate, risk)
3. Employee and user awareness (communication effectiveness, feedback, idea generation)
4. Commitment (determination of overall support)
5. Resources (ability to execute without hardship)

Developing these strategies is not complex but requires some combination of all five competencies. Avoiding one or more is an invitation to failure.

Developing a basic strategy requires the use of the tools described in this chapter. After aligning the values, mission, and purpose statements, develop a SWOT analysis to determine the elements of the strategy. Create a process flow diagram, identify critical junctures, and determine conflict points. Next, check the strategy against the five competencies for compliance or potential vulnerabilities. Have a team review the strategy before implementation. Create evaluation "points" to ensure accomplishment. Conduct a review session after the first 3–6 months. Modify what is not performing well. Follow up with yearly reviews.

Strategies will build and evolve over time. A final key element of a strategy is the evaluation of outcomes (results). Innovation is not magic and will not always generate spectacular results or a cure for every problem. It will follow a set method, and the results should satisfy an unfulfilled need in some form. In essence, innovations should meet certain (and identifiable) factors that define whether the innovation is productive.

Success Factors

For innovation to succeed, it must meet a set of success factors that define its value to both the organization and the user. These success factors define whether the innovation project (or strategy) accomplishes its objectives. Success factors come from the organization, its leadership, and the customer

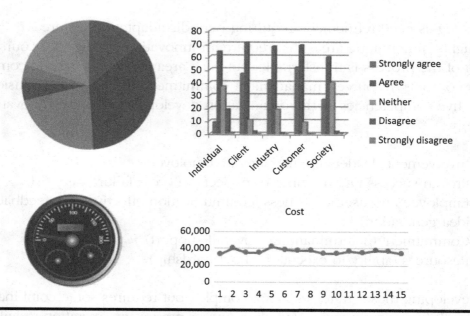

Figure 7.9 Typical dashboard (scorecards).

(user) and measure accomplishment. Determining these success measures or factors enables the organization to measure progress, highlight problems, or identify opportunities. The user and the organization meet its objectives and goals by generating these metrics. Each project or each department will have a different (but related) strategy. These success factors become "dashboards" or "scorecards" for the entire innovation effort (Figure 7.9). By monitoring these dashboards, management can easily identify problems and/or opportunities.

Success factors define a measure (metric) tied directly to an objective or goal. These "dashboards" work both for an individual project and to monitor the overall innovation strategy. The focus is first on outcomes and then on the process necessary to achieve these outcomes on a recurring basis (sustained success).

From a strategic perspective, the success factors will evaluate the "health" of the innovation effort. Typical strategic success factors will measure items such as

1. Number of successful projects implemented (completed)
2. Return on investment (ROI)—more benefit from the innovative approaches
3. Value generation
4. Customer (user) acceptance
5. Quality or satisfaction

Project success factors typically measure the following:

1. Outcomes
2. Efficiencies (time related)
3. Effectiveness (ability to meet objectives and goals)
4. Risk avoidance
5. Costs/savings

Success factor innovation is a method of linking value to performance (performance measures success), as shown in Figure 7.10. Create a success factor based on the need and benefit desired. Be sure it links to a performance measure (performance and innovation are dependent on one another). Align these measures (internal and external) so that each measure supports the intended outcome. Test and evaluate to determine effectiveness and applicability. Refine, if necessary, and implement when complete.

As discussed previously, metrics are critical for sustaining a strategy. Success factors measure performance, progress, and effectiveness. These measurements act like a set of competencies or factors that define success. As part of a coordinated strategy, meeting these factors will determine project outcome success. If an innovation project (effort) meets these factors,

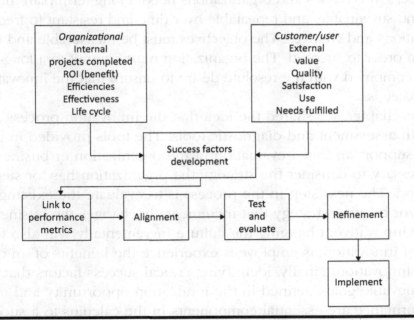

Figure 7.10   Success factors.

it has achieved its objective, met the appropriate needs, and provides benefit as defined by the organization and its leadership and customers (users). Identifying success factors for smaller projects is just as critical. If these are to be accepted and then implemented, values and performance must meet consistent standards. Success factors define the completion criteria and act to sustain that success. Be sure to establish these success factors prior to project or strategy implementation. In addition, use only established or approved success factors so that the benefit and the control ability is more readily identifiable.

So often, managers and leaders look solely to the outcome without deciding (agreeing) on success criteria. Ultimately, the customer or user is the judge. Yet, projects must meet internal criteria for acceptance. The success factor-based approach is one that ensures that the objectives are clearly stated, easily aligned, and simple to check on progress and accomplishment.

Summary

A strategy is simply a plan to accomplish one or more objectives (goals) to meet a need or perhaps a set of requirements. To ensure sustained innovation success, businesses and organizations need a long-term plan that is consistent, sustainable, and repeatable over time and resistant to frequent modifications and changes. The objectives must be measurable and the plan logical in order to succeed. The organization must commit to a long-term strategy combined with the resolute desire to ensure that the innovation effort succeeds.

In this chapter, we shared the idea that the innovation process begins with both assessment and diagnostic tools. The tools provided in this discussion support an initial evaluation of the organization or business. Next, it is necessary to consider the strategy the organization has for sustaining innovation. The next step in the process is to evaluate the existing strategy and/or create a strategy that incrementally changes the business to be more innovative. Changing the culture incrementally will also foster a spirit of innovation as employees experience the benefits of an organizational innovation. Finally, identifying critical success factors that align with achievable goals defined in the innovation opportunity and measuring performance are essential components in the calculus to a successful outcome.

Discussion Questions

1. Typically, a critical need or requirement drives an organization to produce a product, service, or technology to meet an internal or external capability gap or offering. Generally, the company or organization assembles or forms a team or a set of teams to address an identified need or requirement. The organization then plans and directs activities focused on expending capital resources that are often limited to achieve a benefit that far exceeds the overall investment cost. When innovation becomes a key objective for the organization, it can be difficult to plan for the chance events or opportunities that often present the best cases for innovation. Considering your own organization and a recent innovation opportunity you either have knowledge of or were a part of, provide a brief synopsis of
   a. The innovation opportunity
   b. How the innovation team was assembled
   c. The current state or result of the project from concept to implementation.
2. Developing a basic innovation strategy requires the use of the tools described in this chapter. After aligning the values, mission, and purpose statements of your organization,
   a. Develop a SWOT analysis to determine elements of the strategy identified in this chapter.
   b. Create a process flow diagram and identify critical junctures and conflict points.

Assignments

1. Pick two tools presented in this chapter. Define their use, apply the tools to an innovation opportunity project, and provide a one-page discussion on the value that the information your selected tools provides to your leadership (decision makers) in achieving a positive innovation project outcome.
2. Compatibility is an acknowledged issue when aligning an innovation strategy with organizational structures. Reasons for this disconnect include the complexity of the innovation attempted and the type of organizational structure selected. Innovation complexity can range from incremental improvements to radical changes, such as in disruptive

innovations, discoveries, or significant patents. The more complex the innovation, the more heavily invested the organization will need to be in that innovation. In your personal opinion, evaluate the innovation opportunity using the discussions provided in this text along with resources in the public domain to present your assessment of the project and outcome in a three to five-page paper.

3. A SWOT analysis is useful for developing the elements of an innovation strategy. Consider a concept such as innovation. How can an organization design an innovation strategy to maximize its strengths (opportunities) and minimize it weaknesses (threats)? Share your thoughts in a two to three-page paper supporting your position with the information provided in this text and information available in the public domain.

Chapter 8

Selecting an Innovation Project: Projects That Add Lasting Value

Introduction

Once the corporate innovation strategy is underway (or in development), a more practical, project-focused (tactical) strategy can begin to be fully implemented. In this chapter, we focus our discussion on the development and application of the project innovation process. Projects yield tangible and intangible benefits. The focus is on the external applications of innovation primarily, as this is the touch point where the customer or user determines the value in the innovation. The information and generic process presented in this chapter is intended to result in some level of tangible or intangible improvement for the organization or customer. Our practice is to develop a highly customized set of agile and responsive strategies tailored to each business or organization, whether the innovation opportunity is new, improved, or changed. To demonstrate the process, we focus our discussion on improving an existing process.

Due to the unique nature of innovation, we encourage the reader to revisit the set of project methodologies that we presented in Chapter 7. In the initial stages, prior to selecting a specific project type, the organization's management must first identify desired project outcomes suitable for a particular innovative approach. Identifying external (customer driven) and internal (business-driven) outcomes for a specific project is best accomplished through assessment and diagnostics.

Since pursuing innovation opportunities is typically associated with a project-based approach, this chapter highlights our N²OVATE™ methodology from that mindset. The N²OVATE™ methodology is an exceptional approach to effectively validating the organization's best innovation project candidates for potential implementation. Often overlooked in the initial stages of innovation, project validation is another key tactical strategy that we feel is critical for individual and ongoing innovation project success. The N²OVATE™ methodology acronym stands for

Step 1: N—needs and new ideas
Step 2: N–normalize and nominate
Step 3: O—objectives and operationalize
Step 4: V—verify and validate
Step 5: A—adapt and align
Step 6: T—tabulate and track performance
Step 7: E—evaluate and execute

This next-generation methodology is built on the ENOVALE™ framework developed in the book *Chance or Choice: Unlocking Sustained Innovation Success* (McLaughlin and Caraballo, 2013a). A derivative of ENOVALE™, the N²OVATE™ methodology was developed to fit all market-sector profiles.

In order to present this methodology, the authors use a hypothetical case study using all the required seven steps. The case study will follow a project from idea generation to acceptance or rejection. The case study uses the tools and techniques as in a real project. Remember, this initial phase develops and validates an innovation project that can produce true value. Actual project implementation is the focus of the next chapter (Chapter 9).

The case study, as always, requires at least one need and one outcome that has quantifiable value. An assumption is that the need is critical and remains unsatisfied. In this chapter, we provide a synopsis of the case study elements. Read the full case study, located in Appendix I, to get the full perspective of the proposed innovation project.

Case Study Synopsis

Nakra defines medical tourism (MT) as "patients seeking a more affordable health-care outside their own countries" (2011, p. 23). The industry is a $79 billion business (Chou et al., 2012) with 20 million medical

tourists per year. Rather than just a business, it has become a phenomenon, and it is growing at over 20 percent year over year. Marketplace
forces, such as globalization and the reorganization of public and private
health systems, are driving this phenomenon, which occurs outside of
the view and control of the organized health-care system. One reason
for the increase in MT is the high cost of medical services (contrast the
$50,000 cost of knee replacement surgery in the United States with a cost
of $10,000 in Costa Rica [Koster, 2009]). Another driver of MT is the lack
of service quality and the overall services expectation (sharing a sterile
hospital room with a stranger). For example, some individuals seek privacy, while others seek better services. One benefit that MT providers
have offered are luxurious facilities, improved levels of service quality,
and a better overall experience than traditional providers of health care
have offered in the past.

To be successful in any country, leaders of the facilities (and government
proponents) must have a "grasp of operating costs and how they used this
data to fine tune pricing of their services, taking into account their integrated health delivery system, value proposition, preliminary target market
identification, and the building blocks for their health tourism products"
(Todd, 2015, p. 1).

Given this information, the United Arab Emirates (UAE), namely the emirate of Dubai, has decided to invest heavily in MT, especially serving the
high-end customer/patient. The competition for these patients in this unique
market segment is fierce. Given this fierce competition, the prospective
innovation project focuses on medical procedures that require either therapy
and/or rehabilitation. The quantifiable and measurable primary outcome is
patient satisfaction (five-star treatment); cost is secondary. Using this example, we use the N²OVATE™ model to determine project efficacy (viability).

Step 1: Need Analysis and New Ideas

Figure 8.1 details the stepwise process for determining whether the need has
value.

MT is one of Dubai's recognized industries for future growth in Dubai's
Tourism Vision 2020 and the UAE's collective Vision 2021 plans. For Step 1,
examine the need(s) in terms of available data. The exact need is for a
first-class inpatient rehabilitation and exclusive five-star care services facility
(DeMiccio, 2015). The value proposition associated with the need is

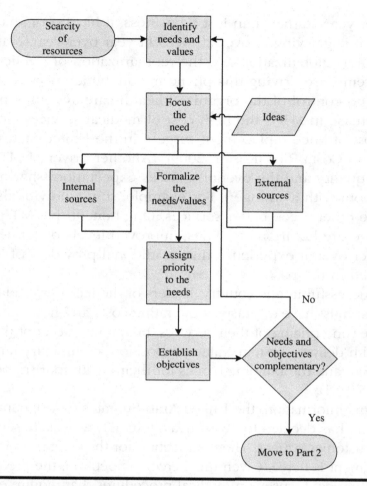

Figure 8.1   Step 1 (Part 1): Needs and new ideas.

1. Immediate
2. No competitor capable of offering this service
3. Dubai is a high-end market
4. First-class services available
5. Highly skilled medical personnel
6. Is family-centric (offers entertainment to family members accompanying the patient)

Objectives constitute

1. First-class services (five-star—lodging, meals, travel, entertainment, concierge service)

2. Capacity to handle various rehabilitative procedures (personnel, equipment, layout)
3. Ability to accommodate family members
4. All-inclusive "resort-type" setting
5. Cost must have demonstrated value

The objectives must complement the needs identified in the Step 1 criteria. As such, the selection process moves to part two of the first step.

Part 2 requires the decision as to which type of innovation would seem to fit best. Recognize that an incorrect decision carries little penalty as it is early in the process. In relation to our case study, this proposed innovation seems to fit in the "New" category. To be more specific, the new application category (uses existing resources, has never been tried at this location) provides the service provider with the opportunity to identify numerous innovations and meet a presently unsatisfied need, and excites the consumer (patient) to make a purchase decision. Therefore, for Part 2, follow the "New" need analysis verification.

The need exists for this five-star surgical procedure rehabilitation service (one of the objectives). Figure 8.2 identifies the innovation type that must meet three criteria (viability, capability, and sustainability). Viability refers to the usability of the item, capability refers to whether it meets objectives consistently, and sustainability refers to the life cycle of the item. For this MT/rehabilitative services case study example, the three criteria of needs are

Viability: Sets performance standards, has lasting appeal, and is difficult to replicate.
Capability: System must be inclusive and cost-effective and yet exceeds the patient's expectations
Sustainability: Services must meet strict guidelines of quality, service, and adding more value than previous experiences

If the initial decision makers identify a number of needs, then it may be best to complete a needs analysis. Complete a needs analysis using the needs analysis tool (Figure 8.3) for the key objective(s). Rate each need criterion element (item) as it meets the objective(s). If the criteria are acceptable and meet the overall objective(s), the project can proceed.

Once the need is established and verified, the next step (see Figure 8.4) can proceed. Before forming the team, assess individuals on their innovation perceptions of the work environment. Figure 8.3 verifies

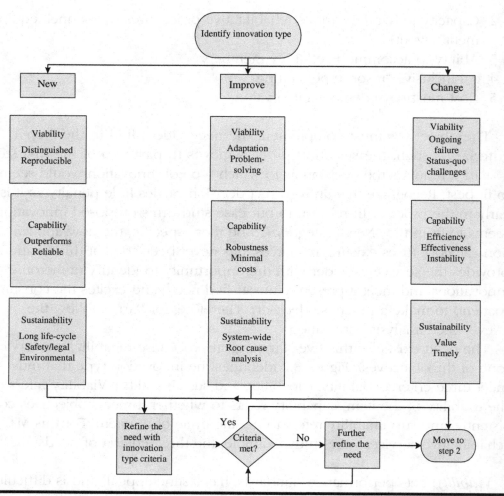

Figure 8.2   Step 1 (Part 2): Needs analysis.

Viability	Rating	Sustainability	Rating	Capability	Rating
Distinctiveness	3	Excellent reputation	5	Inclusive	5
Five-star service	5	Adds significant value	4	Cost-effective	3
Difficult to replicate	5	Strict standards - Service	4	Exceeds patient expectations	4
Lasting appeal	5	Full experience	4	Profitable	5
Strict performance standards	4	Strict quality standards	5	Impeccable Service	5

Figure 8.3   Needs analysis tool.

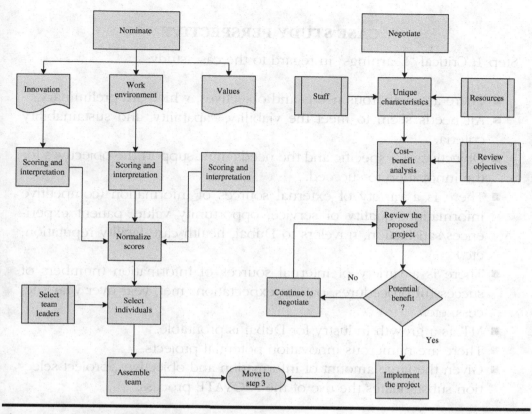

Figure 8.4   Nominate and negotiate.

the need and highlights the complexity in meeting the objectives. The needs analysis tool is optional but especially useful when there are many competing needs and objectives.

One item that is often overlooked at this stage is the opportunity for more innovation from the need/value pairs. It is the potential to identify possible innovation opportunities from lesser need/values pairs. Often, complementary needs will align and provide an additional innovation opportunity. For the example presented, experimenting with various service offerings may lead to more profit. Never underestimate an unfulfilled need!

Finally, ideas, which enter into the process, are a way of identifying needs (wants, desires) or requirements. Ideas work better when paired with value, but the idea must evolve into a need. Once the need is identified, the next step is to move to the "nominate and negotiate" step.

CASE STUDY PERSPECTIVE

Step 1: Critical "Learnings" in regard to the case study:

■ There are numerous needs and objectives, which are preliminary.
■ All needs seem to meet the viability, capability, and sustainability criteria.
■ Objectives are specific and the needs must support the objectives for the innovation to succeed.
■ There is a variety of external sources of information (competitive information, quality of service, opportunity value, patient experiences/satisfaction, travelers to Dubai, health-care facility reputation, etc.).
■ There is a variety of internal sources of information (numbers of successful procedures, patient expectations met, year over year success, etc.).
■ MT as a growth industry for Dubai is profitable.
■ There are numerous innovation potential projects.
■ Given the large amount of information and objectives, project selection substantiates the use of the N²OVATE process.

DISCUSSION QUESTIONS

1. How would you rate and rank the information available to aid in decision making?

Step 2: Nominate and Negotiate

Step 2 is an integration of team formation and negotiation. Figure 8.4 describes one possible path for nominating team members based on survey information that measures three attitudes: perceptions of innovation, work environment, and value of innovation. Although not completely comprehensive, these short surveys take less than 5 minutes to complete. This generates information that is useful for choosing team members. More often than not, these teams may be short lived and complete project selection in 3–10 hours. We recommend the use of a team to secure varied ideas and a different perspective. Choosing implementation teams (those who will manage the project) requires similar evaluation.

Surveys are contained in Appendix II. Each survey listed in this book is in picture format, and active Excel worksheets are available on request or to download from the www.IPSinnovate.com website. Appendix II also contains instructions, calculations, and interpretations with each tool. All three surveys use a five-point Likert scale. The respondent chooses a value from one to five that best matches (expresses) their perceptions or beliefs regarding each statement, placing the numerical value in the "My Choice" column. The surveys each measure three factors or dimensions. A dimension (factor) is a concept (an element) that influences (differentiates) the topic. For instance, "new" (an element or type of innovation) is a differentiator of innovation perception/belief.

Overall Survey Evaluations

The dimension with the largest average is the preferred perception or belief. However, a large range (greater than 1.5) would indicate inconsistency (large shifts) in the response, reducing the ability of the average to predict a consistent belief (perception).

Whichever of the three components of each survey scores the highest average is the preferred method. In other words, you are looking for a range value that is less than 1.5. Ranges greater than 1.5 indicate mixed feelings or opinions. Responses from this small survey are not meant to be fully conclusive but will provide an understanding of what the respondent perceives (understands) about their work environment, what they value and how they best understand innovation. Like individuals (i.e., those that share similar sentiments regarding innovation) will work best on a team. Selecting the team is something management should do before launching the project. This then completes Step 9 (Part 1).

The time has come to assemble the innovation team, name the team leader(s), and evaluate the resources. Once team members identify with a particular innovation type (or combination of types), they are selected to best achieve the project objective. Individuals (team members) who score the highest on the "improve" dimension would be the first-choice candidates. By choosing candidates with similar perceptions, the team leader reduces dissonance within the group, focusing energies on improvement and the project objective(s). Adding other team members to augment the team (i.e., for various reasons such as experience, knowledge, technical capability, etc.) may be an option to complete the team. For those not aligned with the "improvement" philosophy, we recommend you use these members as resources rather than full-time team members.

For this example, choose a team size of between five and seven individuals with an emphasis on knowledge and experience with purchasing and inventory systems. Remember that a diverse workgroup is critical, so add personnel that can "think outside the box" while remaining focused on the objective.

Negotiation

Negotiation is normally an integral part of this process. Figure 8.4 details the negotiation phase. During the initial conversations surrounding the proposed project, the team evaluates various project objectives/outcomes (costs, profit potential, return on investment [ROI], capital requirements, existing competencies, etc.). The team considers both known and unknown information to determine the ultimate fit with the organization. Disputes and individual differences among passionate team members are expected and will require negotiation. Negotiation may require an arbitrator to resolve conflicts. Negotiate outcomes versus internal capabilities. Be sure to represent the customer's voice clearly. Keep discussions at a high level at this stage. The remaining N²OVATE™ process will evaluate the efficacy of the potential innovation project. Be sure that team members agree to the outcomes/objectives and the unique characteristics of the proposed project. If they do not reach consensus, negotiate until the team achieves a majority consensus.

This provides alignment to the outcome/objective and for a unifying message. Agreement on what the innovation will accomplish and what benefit (value) it will provide is critical. Remain open to the possibility of change as more information becomes available. Consider negotiation whenever disagreement occurs. Never let a situation get out of hand, and negotiate the outcomes to a majority consensus.

With the team selected and objectives/outcomes revealed, it is now time to refine the outcomes with process, product, and customer needs (requirements).

CASE STUDY PERSPECTIVE

Step 2: Critical "Learnings" in regard to the case study:

- Use a team to assist executives in making a decision.
- Use the assessments (surveys) to help determine the perceptions of team members to help form a well-aligned group.

- The N²OVATE™ process for project selection generally takes 3–10 hours.
- Negotiation is a critical innovation skill during the early stages of project selection.
- Negotiate to align not disagree.
- The early stages of project selection are exploratory; be creative, challenge standards and norms.
- For the MT case, it is a question of narrowing down the number of objectives and concentrating on between three and five needs.

DISCUSSION QUESTIONS

1. How can Dubai offer a five-star service for those that require rehabilitation time—how is it like a multiple-week cruise or extended-stay holiday?
2. If needs do not align with objectives or outcomes, are these needs worth pursuing?

Step 3: Objectify and Operationalize

With needs evaluated, the next step is to evaluate objectives. Figure 8.5 provides a flowchart of the process of evaluating objectives (objectify). The purpose of evaluating objectives is so that these become the outcomes of the innovation effort. The end user judges the outcomes that represent the benefit and value both given and received by the innovation project. Too many objectives, and the outcomes becomes difficult to measure and evaluate; too few objectives may indicate the inability to sustain the success. Refining the objectives requires a standard, and the specific, measurable, achievable, relevant, and time-based (SMART) criteria is both simple and useful. The SMART criteria also assist in developing a clear definition of and path toward the project's objective(s). For the MT case study, there are five defined objectives, each of which could require an operational definition.

An operational definition defines the word, statement, or phrase while identifying parameters and measures. All of these descriptions (of the objective) may require an operational definition. For example, the descriptor

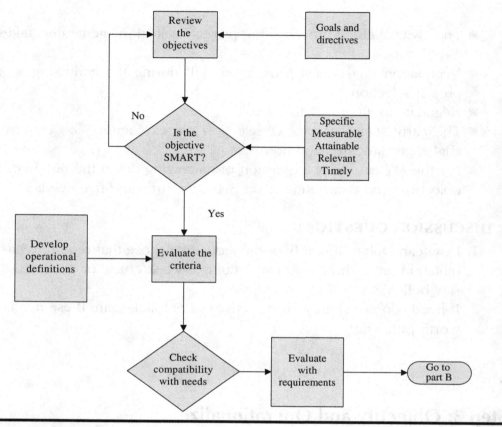

Figure 8.5 Objectify.

"five-star service" requires an operational definition. "Five-star service" attributes include

- Highest service quality possible (medical facility/hotel standards)
- Patient focus (patient comfort, full access to medical staff, patient concierge, etc.)
- Minimum response time to patient
- Dedicated employees (operating in a collaborative culture, proactive communications)
- Management customer (patient) focused

Often, this is one of the first tasks of the team, which should be captured in the Innovation Opportunity Profile (IOP) and the Innovation Team Project Charter (ITPC) introduced in Chapter 5. For "five-star service," the objective is articulated in SMART terms, which are easily understood by internal and external shareholders, stakeholders, and customers. If any one of the SMART criteria are compromised (e.g., poor or inaccurate measures), the ripple effect could be catastrophic and significantly impact the final project outcome or success. Therefore, it is necessary to examine and evaluate the objectives using the SMART criteria, which supports the need for synergy and alignment while ensuring that the lines of communication (i.e., up, down, laterally) both within and outside the organization remain open and transparent. Figure 8.6 is a matrix of objectives and SMART criteria.

After weighting the SMART criteria (using the importance scale below the matrix), evaluate each objective in terms of its defined priority level and importance. The priority of objectives should also be documented in Sections II and III of the IOP and summarized in the executive summary. All associated tools like the resulting SMART criteria should also be added to the IOP instrument as an attachment or an appendix. If the objectives

SMART criteria evaluation weighting	5	5	5	5	5
Instructions: score each objective as to its SMART format. Use a simple five-point Likert scale to rate importance.	Specific	Measureable	Attainable	Relevant	Timely
First-class services	5	5	5	5	5
Capacity for handling various rehabilitative procedures	5	5	5	5	5
Ability to accommodate family members	4	4	4	4	5
All inclusive "resort-type" setting	5	5	5	4	5
Cost must have demonstrated value	4	5	4	4	5
Score	135	140	135	130	150

Importance scale
1 - Very unimportant
2 - Unimportant
3 - Neither unimportant nor important
4 - Important
5 - Very important

Figure 8.6   SMART criteria evaluation tool.

are overlapping, consider an operational definition to eliminate similarities. The overall score is located in the bottom row of the matrix (Figure 8.6). The higher the cumulative score, the more critical the criteria become. Locate a blank chart in Appendix II. For our MT case study criteria, this analysis verifies the overall importance of all the objectives. The resulting SMART objectives should only be used as a foundation for innovation outcomes. The number is less critical; the viability is the important factor.

Scoring

Identify a weight for each objective criteria. Consider the weight and its overall importance to the specific criteria. The weights (for the SMART criteria) can change based on the importance criteria. Objectives with low weights (three or below) may be too unimportant to consider. Risk increases when an objective cannot meet the SMART criteria.

Score and document each objective/SMART criteria pair (in the matrix, Figure 8.6), especially if agreement varies within the team of decision makers. Use the importance scale and enter a value from 1 to 5 in the empty box. For the MT example, there are 25 boxes (five objectives, five SMART criteria). The cumulative scores (located in the last row of the tool) indicate the most important objective. Have each team member complete this matrix and then summarize the results. This toll works both virtually and in real time. The MT example demonstrates that all objectives rate similarly and that no single objective dominates.

In conjunction with the SMART criteria tool, reevaluate the needs and determine if discrepancies exist. Incidentally, the needs analysis that was discussed previously would have exposed a major problem before reaching this stage. Minor problems or discrepancies may arise at this stage, requiring further negotiation.

In Part 2 (Figure 8.7), the objectives are "operationalized" by introducing the requirements that define the objectives. Requirements are either user/patient/customer driven or are functional (process descriptive). The word *requirements* also relates to operational parameters. At the project selection phase, these can be high-level requirements. Table 8.1 details a few high-level requirements.

However, before the project begins, develop a more explicit set of requirements. One additional challenge is to understand the relationship between patient (user) and functional requirements. Table 8.2 provides a

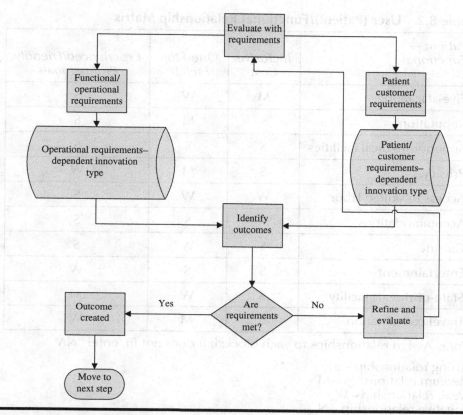

Figure 8.7   Operationalize step.

Table 8.1   High-level MT Project Requirements

Patient or Functional	Requirements	Established Parameters
Patient	Exceeds expectations	Top score on patient satisfaction survey results
Patient	Privacy and confidentiality	Highly secured medical records
Patient	Inclusive costs	All travel, lodging, food, and medical services included
Functional	Five-star accommodations	Meets five-star-hotel criteria
Functional	Response time	Minimum time to meet patient's needs
Functional	Superior medical professional experience	No. of successful procedures

Table 8.2   User (Patient)/Functional Relationship Matrix

Patient → Functional ↓	Inclusive Cost	One-Stop Facility	Experienced/Friendly Professionals
Five-star rating	M	W	S
Reputation	S	M	S
Superior medical facilities	S	S	S
Privacy	S	M	W
Access to skilled labor	W	W	S
Accommodations	S	S	S
Cuisine	S	W	S
Entertainment	S	S	W
State-of-the-art facility	S	W	M
Travel coordination	S	M	W

Note: Assign relationships to each block; if it does not fit, enter "NA".

Strong relationship—S
Medium relationship—M
Weak relationship—W
Negative relationship—N

mechanism for evaluating these relationships. Strong or medium-sized relationships require full exploration. Consider capturing the relationship and the defined requirements in Sections III and IV of the IOP instrument. A relationship exists when functional and patient/user characteristics affect one another. That is, as the functional requirement changes, it affects the user (patient) directly. The strength of these relationships directly influences the objective.

For example, consider the MT case study (Table 8.2) where functional and patient requirements are an issue. The team wants to evaluate how three patient-related success requirements relate to operational concerns. Assume that each person on the team decides to identify a relationship from his or her perspective. This matrix provides a method of examining relationships from a basic and personal perspective. Table 8.2 was designed to document an individual's perception.

Finally, the team establishes outcomes (the objective matched with its requirements). If there is a mismatch, the fate of the potential project is highly questionable. For the MT case study example, if the patient experience is not comparable to a luxury holiday (vacation) with five-star service, dedicated amenities, and accessible health-care staff, then the project outcomes may not satisfy its purpose. If the team reaches an unsatisfactory conclusion, then the project may require further refinement or be incompatible with the organization. If the assumption is that the project meets its outcomes, the team can proceed to the next step, and the project has passed a significant milestone.

CASE STUDY PERSPECTIVE

Step 3: Critical "Learnings" in regard to the case study:

- Numerous objectives have varying contributing and conflicting requirements.
- Keep focused on the high-level requirements.
- Some requirements overlap; some contribute more than others.
- A five-star service experience is critical.
- High-level requirements come from both the patient (customer) and the business (including standards, policies, and practices).
- Outcomes focus the team on what the customer (patient) will experience.
- Often the midstages of N²OVATE™ provide the most compelling information on sustained success.
- For the MT case, it is a question of narrowing down the number of objectives and high-level requirements to make the best decision.

DISCUSSION QUESTIONS

1. What, if any, MT objectives could conflict with the high-level requirements (Tables 8.1 and 8.2)?
2. Create three to five outcomes. Does the project remain viable, capable, and sustainable?

Step 4: Validate and Verify

Once the outcomes are accepted, it is time to validate and verify. Making a rash decision based solely on an outcome may eliminate potential projects while increasing risk and failure. It is best to enter this step with an

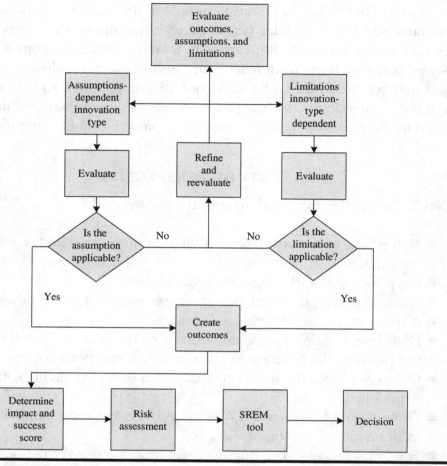

Figure 8.8 Validate step.

eye on determining if the outcome is worth the overall investment of time, resources, and effort. The beginning stages of this step require an evaluation of major assumptions and limitations (Figure 8.8). A limitation is "that item, standard, process, or decision that prevents, deters, or interferes with performance" (McLaughlin and Caraballo, 2013a, p. 102). Limitations restrict performance and the ability to maximize effort. A potential limitation, for the case study example, is the price of offering such services. Fewer patients may opt for this service level. Limitations include

1. That the patient must relocate for the procedure (potential for language problems)
2. The high cost, given the five-star service requirements

3. The lack of (or limited) access to home-based physicians
4. The time required away from home (travel time to and from Dubai)

There are many limitations, and these need to be fully considered before deciding the fate of the project.

An assumption is an intangible perception, based on available information, experience, and opinion. Future performance validates all assumptions. The more a project requires assumptions, the greater the need for viable alternatives, given the higher risk of failure. A typical assumption, for this case study, is that patients have experienced a typical hospital experience to compare to the "five-star services" potentially offered. If the team misses or incorrectly identifies critical assumptions, the delay could be devastating and/or exceedingly costly. The team needs to identify all critical assumptions for evaluative purposes. Be sure to check each limitation and assumption for validity (that the limitation or assumption is true).

Some additional assumptions of this case study include

1. That medical personnel are experienced with procedures/rehabilitation
2. That the facilities have up-to-date equipment
3. That the patient can travel (via scheduled airline) to Dubai without difficulty
4. That the patient's family will enjoy what Dubai has to offer (recreational activities)
5. That the patient meets all guidelines regarding health status

Evaluate each critical (team and management can decide which fits this criteria) assumption and limitation (see Table 8.3). Detail how the assumptions or limitations are measured (determined), even if it is an opinion or perception. Evaluate the effect (E) of each assumption or limitation and its overall importance (I) (Table 8.4). Complete this exercise either individually or in a group. Discuss any discrepancies and negotiate a final decision. Use the results to decide whether to move forward, revise, or scrap the potential project.

You would not expect every assumption or limitation to affect the objective(s) and subsequent requirements. Where the effect is strong and the importance critical, monitor the assumption or limitation. If there is a weak relationship, chances are the effect is small and the importance minimal. Be aware that an objective/requirement could be impossible to achieve consistently if the assumptions are violated or the limitations too influential.

Table 8.3 Assumptions/Limitation Evaluation Matrix

Evaluation	Measure	First-Class Service	Ability to Handle Rehabilitation of Patient	Family Member Concerns	"All-inclusive" Resort	Cost Equals Value
A—Medical experience	Years of experience	E = M I = MI	E = M I = C	E = W I = U	E = W I = U	E = W I = MI
A—Patient can travel	Miles flown	E = S I = C	E = S I = C	E = W I = MI	E = M I = MI	E = S I = C
A—Patient health status	Medical records	E = S I = MI	E = S I = C	E = W I = U	E = W I = U	E = W I = U
L—Patient must relocate	Distance from Dubai	E = M I = MI	E = S I = MI	E = S I = C	E = M I = MI	E = S I = C
L—No access to primary physician	Time differences limited interaction	E = M I = C	E = S I = C	E = M I = MI	E = W I = U	E = S I = C
L—High cost	All costs including travel, food, etc.	E = S I = C	E = M I = C	E = S I = C	E = S I = C	E = S I = C

Table 8.4 Effects and Importance Scale for A/L Evaluation Matrix

Determinants of Effect	Measures of Importance
Strong	Critical
Moderate	Moderate
Weak	Unimportant

Once the assumptions and limitations review is complete, the objectives become outcomes (which include requirements, assumptions, and limitations). Determine project outcomes by evaluating objectives, requirements, and assumptions/limitations. An outcome is a project objective that is framed within its requirements and defined by its assumptions and limitations.

Further refining outcomes begins with the process of determining the overall impact of the outcome. This will require an estimation of the chance of success and the risk of failure. Success and failure are not mutually exclusive—one aspect can succeed, another fail. This is why the team receives training to use such tools to maximize the chance of success. Suppose the team arrives at three outcomes. Table 8.5 lists these three outcomes. The innovation project team (decision makers) evaluates the outcome for its overall impact (influence) and success. Define success as the probability (chance) of achievement over a sustained defined amount of time. Define impact as the influence of a particular outcome for achieving success using the rating scales defined in Table 8.5. Evaluate the outcome using Table 8.6. Consider how the outcome influences long-term success and, given present realities, the chance that outcome will be successful. Again, enable the innovation project team (decision makers) to evaluate separately and to compare

Table 8.5 Scoring Criteria for Impact versus Success Outcome Evaluation

Scale	Impact	Success
1	Low or no impact	No chance of success
2	Minimal impact	Minimal chance of success
3	Moderate impact	Medium chance of success
4	High impact	Good chance of success
5	Superior impact	Excellent chance of success

Table 8.6 Impact versus Success Outcome Evaluation

Outcome	Overall Impact	Chance of Success
Five-star service	5	5
Inclusive	4	5
Costs seen as value	4	4

results. Expect that there will be differences in opinion and views. Be prepared to objectively negotiate any conflicts or disagreements. These tools are most helpful when little data is available. Securing a common sight picture (perceptions) among team members is tantamount to aligning and maintaining support for the project.

The results from the impact versus success outcome evaluation only reconfirm the existing outcomes. Both the influence (impact) and long-term success are dependent on these outcomes as driving forces for the project.

Evaluating the results involves either examining Table 8.6 or charting the result (Figure 8.9). Chart the results by creating two scales (success versus impact). The larger the scores (both criteria), the larger the "bubble" or oval becomes. Be creative and inventive with these concepts. The purpose is to evaluate the outcome and determine if the project is value-added.

Finally, the last remaining portion of the validate phase is to assess and verify risk. Risk accumulates as the potential for failure (due primarily to

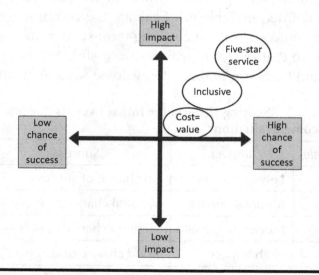

Figure 8.9 Outcome impact and success evaluation.

reduced performance) increases. Risk increases the number and impact of failures. Risk also can involve harm to individuals (safety concerns, physical and mental distress, injury, or death). The inability to meet the intended (or expected) outcome is failure.

The success–risk evaluation matrix (SREM) tool evaluates risk and success. Success, as with the outcome impact and success evaluation tool (Table 8.6), measures the achievement of the outcome over a sustained length of time. Success is required for sustained innovation, and future stages will measure and quantify this success. For nonprofit or governmental agencies, success is often measured differently than their private-sector counterparts. Where nonprofit and government organizations seek some level or amount of value-added benefit over time, private-sector and for-profit entities might seek a competitive advantage in the marketplace or a monetary ROI.

To complete this chart, consider a set of outcomes and evaluate the risk of failure and the chance of success. Defining failure is industry dependent. Outcome satisfaction (often measured as a reduction in performance) less than expected (or desired) defines failure for the MT case study. For example, if the service levels decrease, a loss of a five-star rating will seriously affect the project. This is why it is imperative to measure the service level with each patient. Any downward trend in the service level would not only increase risk but also significantly influence a satisfaction response as well as revenue, costs, and reputation.

First, define success. A "five-star service" rating involves multiple descriptors such as

1. Cleanliness (lodging, employees, facilities, etc.)
2. Functionality (how well something works)
3. Attentiveness (of personnel, friendliness, response time, etc.)
4. Item quality (bedding, towels, furniture, etc.)
5. Exceeding expectations of patients (family members)

The list is certainly longer than stated here. Next, evaluate risk (Table 8.7) for each outcome/success pair. Finally, assign a numerical value to the risk from Table 8.7.

Next, select a few measures of success and evaluate these with the SREM (Table 8.8). Classify the success probability as either high, medium, or low. Next, identify a risk unique to that success item. Choose a value from Table 8.7 that best represents the level of risk. Evaluate where on the SREM

Table 8.7 Assessing Risk (Failure)

Evaluate on Two Dimensions: Severity of Failure; Chance of Personal Harm	How Likely Is (Failure/Harm) to Occur				
	Very Likely	Likely	50/50 Chance	Unlikely	Very Unlikely
Frequent/severe failures; serious risk of harm	1	1	2	3	3
Intermittent failure; potential harm	1	2	2	3	4
Limited failure; limited chance of harm	2	2	3	4	5
Sporadic failure; minimal chance of harm	3	3	4	5	6
No failure reported; no reported case of harm	3	4	5	6	6

Table 8.8 Success/Risk Evaluation Matrix (SREM) Analysis

Success	(H, M, L) Success	Risk	Quadrants	Risk Number	Success/ Risk Pair
Functionality	M	Broken or inoperative devices	Strength	5	1
Attentiveness	H	Inconsistency among caregivers	Portal	2	2
Exceeding expectations	H	Expectations too high or services standards inconsistent	Strength	3	3

coordinate scale (Figure 8.10) it rates and the name of the quadrant that best represents the success/risk event. Identify and list this quadrant's name in Table 8.8. Next, insert an oval or some figure or character onto the SREM coordinate map to represent each success/risk pair. This will be instrumental in any risk mitigation plans that the innovation project team may introduce if the decision to pursue the project is made.

The coordinate map consists of four quadrants, two of which represent opportunity ("strengths" and "portal"); the other two categories represent a stagnant (status quo) or reducing presence (weakness). In all three evaluations of the Dubai case study, all outcomes are positive. Figure 8.11 demonstrates the visual evaluation of the success criteria attributed to the

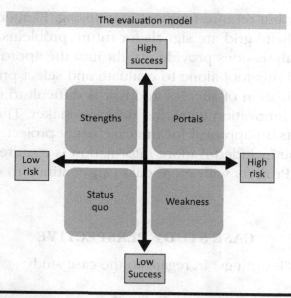

Figure 8.10   SREM coordinate map.

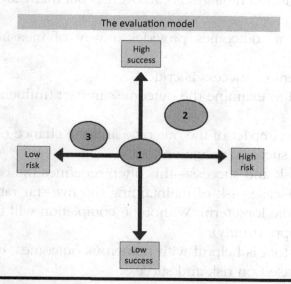

Figure 8.11   Success, risk evaluation matrix (SREM) quadrant analysis.

outcomes. All three are opportunities within the organization. Only #2 is risky, but it offers an exciting opportunity (called a portal—a doorway to a new and dramatic opportunity).

The SREM quadrant analysis (Figure 8.11) provides a visual analysis of the success/risk evaluation. This chart clearly highlights the positive aspects of the outcomes and aversion to risk. Higher risks can present a great opportunity but require frequent monitoring. Elements on the lower half of the coordinate grid are signals for future problems. Although not complete, the analysis does provide insight into the approval process. Clients have used this tool alone to evaluate and select projects. Its comprehensive combination of success and risk is difficult to dismiss and invaluable to the innovation team and decision maker. The analysis up to this point suggests an approval for the case study project. The remaining three steps can be included if more information is required before finalizing a decision. Projects with more data can continue to evaluate through Steps 5–7.

CASE STUDY PERSPECTIVE

Step 4: Critical "Learnings" in regard to the case study:

■ All the objectives seem to be critical.
■ Assumptions and limitations can overlap but many are unique to the objective.
■ Converting to outcomes provides a way of measuring sustained success.
■ Measurement of success is critical.
■ It is helpful to examine the outcome's impact (influence) in terms of success.
■ Measure the impact of the outcome and the chance of success—use the impact success evaluation tool.
■ Consider risk and success—this often redefines the outcome.
■ For the MT case, risk of maintaining the five-star rating may affect success in the long term. Without it, completion will flourish (truly a branding opportunity).
■ The SREM tool is helpful with numerous outcomes, evaluating each outcome based on risk and success.

DISCUSSION QUESTIONS

1. How does an outcome with conflicting assumptions or limitations affect overall success?
2. Choose an outcome from the MT study and apply the SREM tool (cleanliness or item quality).

Step 5: Adaptation and Alignment

Upon accepting the outcome, now referred to as the innovative outcome, the team examines the human alignment (support) to the proposed project. Examining alignment determines how well an innovation opportunity project supports the team and organizational goals and values. Alignment begins with the ability to associate the outcomes with organizational values, culture, and scope (Figure 8.12). Overall, attaining value for the organization and user is the ultimate prize. If the project not only demonstrates cost savings

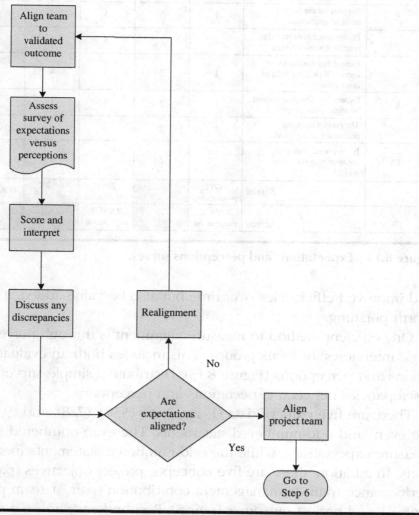

Figure 8.12   Alignment and adaptation.

Statement number	In the "My choice" column, enter the numerical value that best describes how much you agree (disagree) with the statements provided	Stongly disagree	Disagree	Neither disagree nor agree	Agree	Strongly agree	My choice
1	The project is expected to meets its objectives.	1	2	3	4	5	
2	Implementation is expected to complete on time.	1	2	3	4	5	
3	No delays are expected in meeting the timelines.	1	2	3	4	5	
4	No project is expected to be successful.	1	2	3	4	5	
5	Support for the project remains unchanged.	1	2	3	4	5	
6	Performance is expected to remain at similar levels.	1	2	3	4	5	
7	Expect that customers or users will perceive item as innovative.	1	2	3	4	5	
8	Expect that few changes will be made to the project.	1	2	3	4	5	
9	The project team has performed as expected.	1	2	3	4	5	
10	Expect management to continue support for this project.	1	2	3	4	5	
	Scores	AVG perceptions	0	AVG expectation	0	Difference	0
	Scores	RANGE perceptions	0	RANGE expectation	0		

Figure 8.13 Expectations and perceptions survey.

and improved efficiencies over time but also be value-added, it is a project worth pursuing.

One efficient method to measure alignment is through perceptual surveys, interviews, or focus groups. This includes both an evaluation of expectations and perceptions (Figure 8.13). Distribute a simple survey to measure discrepancies between expectations and perceptions.

There are five pairs of data (1, 2), (3, 4), (5, 6), (7, 8), and (9, 10) with the even- and odd-numbered statements. The even-numbered statements measure expectations, while the odd-numbered statements measure perceptions. In addition, there are five concepts: project objectives (pair 1), project performance (pair 2), management contribution (pair 3), team performance (pair 4), and project outcomes (pair 5). Respondents choose a number from one to five that expresses their agreement or disagreement with each statement and enter their selection in the "My Choice" column.

Examine the difference between the perception (odd-numbered) and expectation scores (even numbered). If an individual's perceptions exceed expectations (a positive difference), then the person is satisfied and their reality is better than expected. If an individual's expectations exceed perceptions (a negative difference), then the person is not satisfied and their reality is less than expected. These persons may not align well with the project outcome. In addition, examine each concept pair for differences in expectations and perceptions.

For example, select project objective statements (statements one and two from Figure 8.13). If an individual scores for statement one a "4" and for statement two a "2," then the difference score is "–2," with expectations greatly exceeding perceptions (reality). This indicates that the individual expects more than truly exists. This signals an alignment problem. Negative values indicate that the individual's reality does not coincide with their overall expectations. Averaging the responses gives an overall team evaluation. Check the range for inconsistencies in the response. A large range indicates mixed feelings. Aligned teams should score zero or above. A poorly aligned team with negative scores indicates disappointment with reality as compared to their original expectations. The Excel-enabled document is available upon request. Gather additional information from team member interviews.

The process of realignment helps team members to adapt to project and program realities. Recommend that all team members recommit to the project outcomes/objectives. One useful suggestion is to place the outcome/objective in a conspicuous place, so that team members can constantly realign themselves to this concept. Use it as a header or footer on all e-mails. An aligned and adaptable team produces.

Since innovation is often a "learn-as-you-go" endeavor, adaptive individuals make the best team members. Adaptive individuals are those who can easily adjust to changing realities. Team members that are resistant to change or have issues with expecting more than is possible are best removed (or reserved as subject matter experts [SMEs]). These individuals can be disruptive and will disempower the team and divert its focus from approving (disapproving) the innovation project at hand.

CASE STUDY PERSPECTIVE

Step 5: Critical "Learnings" in regard to the case study:

- Keep the decision-making team aligned.
- Use this step if a decision is not yet approved.

- The large number of objectives could cause a certain amount of mis-alignment; however, the objectives are well aligned for the MT case.
- Measure success as it provides a time line for the outcome(s).
- This step is helpful when many decision makers are required.
- A quick step to establish alignment can be used at any point in the project selection process.

DISCUSSION QUESTIONS

1. If a team were misaligned, what would you do to determine the extent of the misalignment?
2. What ways could you think of to avoid misalignment?
3. Do you see any value in using this tool throughout the selection and implementation process?

Step 6: Tabulate and Track Performance

A critical aspect of any innovation project is whether it can deliver a decent payback over time. Organizations invest in innovation for a specific reason, for example, profit, competitive advantage, or increased value or market share. Figure 8.14 describes the process for tabulating and tracking both the investment and the performance attributed to the proposed project. Since the project is still in the formative stages, it is critical to establish the performance measures that define its identity.

At this stage, we estimate the benefits and those financial, operational, and strategic measures associated with the project. For this hypothetical case study, this includes measuring the benefit, projected costs, and unique measures that define the project.

Every project must yield a benefit so that its overall value is established. For profit-driven businesses, this is ROI—that is, what is invested is a frac-tion of the benefit obtained. ROI is defined as a profitability measure that evaluates the performance of a business by dividing net profit by net worth.

Several different financial metrics use the term *ROI* and there is often confusion over the ROI calculation, even among experienced financial ana-lysts. Analysts often refer to the return on capital employed, return on total assets, return on equity, and return on net worth, as ROI. In other cases, the term sometimes refers to cumulative cash flow results over time. Some refer

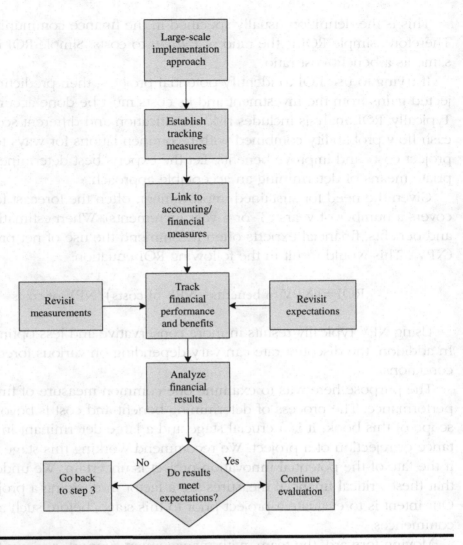

Figure 8.14   Step 6: Tabulate and track performance.

to other cash metrics as ROI, such as the average rate of return and even the internal rate of return; this is not correct.

Thus, several different ROI metrics are in common use, and the term itself does not have a single, universally understood definition. Therefore, when reviewing ROI figures or when asked to produce one, it is good practice to be sure that everyone involved defines the metric in the same way. From a project perspective:

Simple ROI = (gains from investment − costs of investment)/costs of investment (Should this be "100" or perhaps "Return − Cost of Investment × 100/Cost of Investment?")

This is the definition usually specified in the finance community. Therefore, simple ROI is the ratio of *returns* to costs. Simple ROI is not the same as a benefit/cost ratio.

If trying to use ROI to identify potential projects, then predicting projected gains from the investment and its costs must be done accurately. Typically, ROI analysis includes risk identification and different scenarios of cash flow probability combined with recommendations for ways to reduce project costs and improve benefits. Let the experts best determine an appropriate means of determining an acceptable approach.

Given the need for sustained improvement, often the forecast for ROI covers a number of years (3- or 5-year increments). When estimating costs and benefits, financial experts often recommend the use of net present value (NPV). This would result in the following ROI equation:

$$ROI = (NPV \text{ of benefits} - NPV \text{ of costs})/NPV \text{ of costs}$$

Using NPV typically results in more conservative and less optimistic ROIs. In addition, the discount rate can vary depending on various forecasted conditions.

The purpose here was to examine one common measure of financial performance. The process of determining benefit and cost is beyond the scope of this book. It is a crucial stage and a large determinant in the acceptance or rejection of a project. We recommend working this stage (step) only if the fate of the potential innovation project is uncertain. We understand that these critical financial measures are a factor in deciding a project's fate. Our intent is to evaluate a project prior to this stage, before such activity commences.

Moving forward, the team, with management support, reviews the performance measures and establishes the goals that constitute success. Additional work may be needed to clarify these measures and to establish operating guidelines and appropriate systems to capture the benefits of success.

For this step, we use the outcome(s) and establish a measure of recurring benefit (such as ROI) for predictive purposes. The efficiencies gained with the MT rehabilitative services application should outweigh any existing or future difficulties. Some reasonable payback period is part of the overall solution. Benefits should be observable within 3–6 months (an average); therefore, the accounting systems need to be robust enough to track and document this progress. If the team and management feel that true, improvement is possible and the outcome/objective attainable, then they should decide to go ahead with the project. Further financial evaluations will clarify the decisions made. These financial evaluations often take place as the implementation (operationalization) of the project begins.

CASE STUDY PERSPECTIVE

Step 6: Critical "Learnings" in regard to the case study:

- Financial analysis is critical for project continuance.
- Complete a financial analysis with a large number of outcomes.
- For the MT case study, a thorough financial analysis could be time-consuming, given the large number of outcomes. Recommend that if not approved before Step 6, an ROI evaluation be conducted.
- Estimate costs and benefits realistically—use past history as a determinant of success.
- Rely on the financial information as a key (but not the only) determiner of project approval.

DISCUSSION QUESTIONS

1. Discuss and estimate the major costs involved in the MT project—think about the broad range of costs rather than specific items.
2. Explain the value of financial analysis in project selection decisions.
3. What one cost or benefit could upend the future opportunity of this project?

Step 7: Execute and Evaluate

Finally, at this stage, leadership and management (decision makers) will decide either for or against the project (Figure 8.15). If the decision is made to pursue the project, plans can begin to implement the project. This is an excellent time to review the project outcomes and objectives and to create a plan for implementation. It is especially important to review and solidify those project measures used to identify benefit in Step 6 (tabulate and track performance). More than likely, a new team will be required to move the project forward. Decide what type of innovation works best. For the MT case study, a new application process seems a "best fit." The next chapter will detail how a project such as this is implemented for success. The key

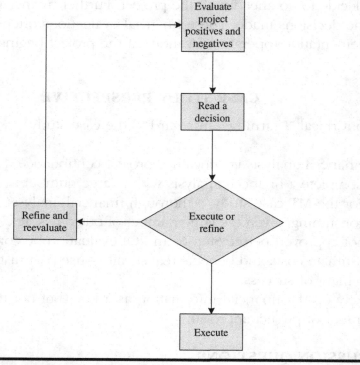

Figure 8.15   Step 7: Evaluate and execute.

to implementation for innovation efforts is correctly identifying the type of innovation (new, improved, change) required. The process uses a modified version of N²OVATE™, specially designed for the type of innovation and the client organization.

Summary

This chapter introduced an operational process to select an innovation project using a case study as an aid to better understand the N²OVATE™ process. Generally, the process takes anywhere from 4 to 12 hours to complete. A tremendous amount of information is generated concerning the project, useful for the next (implementation) phase. This chapter was an overview of the process, and those who want to investigate the methodology in more detail can contact the authors at drgregmclaughlin@ipsinnovate.com, drbillkennedy@ipsinnovate.com, or sandy@nsmg-intl.com. As with any innovation project, the process flowcharts are a place to begin. We expect some modification for each project submitted for acceptance based on business or organizational culture, nationality, and the work environment present to support innovation. These flowcharts give the reader a detailed process through which to select a project. Given the amount of knowledge gained, this entire process is worth executing each time when submitting a macro project for approval.

Discussion Questions

1. Discuss between three to five needs that your organization or business faces today. Is there any potential for any of these needs to become an innovation project?
2. Discuss the concept of risk as you understand it. How does risk become a factor in evaluating (selecting) an innovation project?
3. Discuss when, where, and how management will interface with the N²OVATE™ process.
4. Discuss the importance of individual contributions to an innovation project. Which steps rely heavily on human contribution?

Assignments

1. Discuss the process of validating a set of needs (requirements). Complete a needs analysis using the needs analysis tool.
2. Choose an MT case study objective (be sure it is measurable and unique from this chapter), apply the SMART criteria, and complete a SMART criteria evaluation tool.
3. Choose a different outcome from one presented in this chapter. Perform an SREM analysis.

Chapter 9

Managing an Innovation Opportunity Project from Concept to Reality

Introduction

On reaching a decision to execute an innovation project, a different process is required to guide the implementation. If not yet decided, identify the type of innovation best suited for the project. Each type of innovation has its own version of the N²OVATE™ process, demonstrating its agility and effectiveness. For the medical tourism (MT) case study presented in this book, a "new application" approach would work best (see McLaughlin and Kennedy, 2016, for further clarification on "new" types of innovation). New applications are unique offerings that did not exist previously in the setting proposed. That is, the emphasis on five-star rehabilitative services is a new type of innovation not previously existing in the emirate of Dubai. It is a new application on an existing process, product, or service. It is also innovative in that it serves an unsatisfied need, provides a benefit, and presents a competitive advantage.

Traditionally, the first step in the action phase of implementing an innovation project should always begin with identifying the expected benefit the project will yield (if not completed in the project selection phase). Confirm that benefit with available data (simulate if needed). Use the N²OVATE™ process to further evaluate the opportunity and use it to bring the project to fruition. Large projects can add complexity and additional variables and are obviously more difficult to manage and implement. The size and benefit of the project adds another dimension to the appropriate strategy for implementation.

We refer to large innovation projects as "macro innovations." Macro innovations typically change day-to-day operations, user behaviors, and/or the legal, social, or econometric environment. We classify projects that are smaller in scope and less disruptive as "micro innovations." The resulting size of the project radically affects the process used for implementation.

Macro Innovations

When most people consider innovation, they think about a "new" discovery, technology, or product (and in some cases, a service). Based on personal experience, people tend to think of products that revolutionized their lives or the environment when considering how to define an innovation. An important consideration regarding macro (large-scale) innovations is they can significantly alter the very culture and organization that created or championed a successful business while also achieving the goal of satisfying a perceived user (society) need (requirement). These innovations tend to receive the greatest amount of attention and operate at a strategic level in any business, agency, or organization. Our MT case study is an example of a macro innovation that will certainly spawn numerous micro projects.

Macro innovations affect a large number of individuals and change the "rules" forever. Numerous methodologies and strategies exist for macro innovations. One of the more famous strategies is "blue ocean," which is characterized and defined by "untapped market space, demand creation, and the opportunity for highly profitable growth" (Kim and Mauborgne, 2005, p. 106). Blue ocean strategies are rare as this changes the existing paradigm by creating a new product, technology, or service that never existed previously. Another well-known macro strategy is "disruptive innovation," which describes the upheaval that occurs when a new product or technology (a discovery) is introduced to the marketplace. The process for disruptive innovations leapfrogs traditional methods. More often than not, macro innovations can be disruptive, changing existing paradigms, causing markets to realign and organizations to cease or expand by adding to a new set of realities. While the innovation project teams will facilitate these projects, the business or organization's management (the decision makers) is the key to investing hard-earned cash to make these innovations a reality.

This can often result in a tremendous investment of resources (monetary, human capital, etc.) and time to achieve desired goals and objectives. That said, we maintain the position that the vast majority of innovation projects should be micro innovations, which typically affect not only the user (society/customer) but also the business or organization at the operational and tactical level.

If innovation is more dynamic than just a new invention or discovery, then more people can involve themselves in activities that produce innovative outcomes. In reality and from our perspective, innovation can occur on a daily basis. Individuals (employees/associates) direct these projects, committed to the same standards of excellence. These micro (smaller-scope) innovations do not disrupt the organization, but they can certainly have game-changing potential for life and reality in general. In micro or smaller-scope innovation projects, it is typical for organizations to assign an individual or small teams to spearhead and direct the project proceedings. Fundamentally, we feel it is prudent to consider a scalable approach based on scope, which we offer in the following discussion on micro innovation.

Micro Innovations

Micro innovations should involve the largest number of employees, suppliers, customers, and stakeholders. These innovations tend to be more relevant to the individual, given that the same individuals will see the greatest benefit. Employees will feel empowered, responsible, and engaged. Many micro innovations have led to significant long-term benefits. Micro innovation is, in fact, "incremental improvement." Incremental innovation fulfills a need by improving the performance of an item. Items could easily be policies, procedures, a process, products, or services. Performance improvements, beyond those attributed to continuous improvement, exceed expectations and thereby qualify as innovative.

Micro innovation can just as easily occur with upstream or downstream suppliers or customers on a specific item-by-item basis. Directing innovative activities that add value for users improves their perceptions and overall evaluation. This can solidify long-term working relationships and provide the agency or organization with a distinctive competitive advantage. Customers (users) trust those that look after their best interests. Focusing innovations at a customer level could provide a significant competitive advantage, especially if the user experiences these innovations on a frequent basis.

Implementing a Successful Project

Once the project receives approval, it is time to implement it. As with any innovation project, conditions and situations may change prior to implementation. Therefore, there are always periodic or recurring negotiations and evaluations that must occur to take the project from concept to reality. To understand the implementation phase, the authors will use the MT case study scenario provided in Appendix II and in Chapter 8.

A "New" Application

It is difficult for most businesses and organizations to produce unique products or services on a regular basis. Limiting factors such as time, cost, and the available resources required to pursue innovation opportunities tend to rule out these types of projects. Businesses (organizations) must search for an alternative that enables these entities to offer new products and services to maintain a technological or competitive advantage. To accomplish this goal, many organizations initiate strategic alliances with another company or organization, involving intellectual property agreements or often acquisitions of companies that are capable of filling the capability and knowledge gaps to pursue future innovation opportunities. Others innovate by introducing a new product or service application without the expense of design and development costs, time requirements, and additional resources. This "new" offering utilizes existing resources and applies a unique approach not yet available in the marketplace. The MT case study is a perfect example:

Medical Tourism is an established practice in many parts of the world. For Dubai, this is a growing and vibrant sector—and is a priority with the government. Rehabilitative services, is just a subset of the larger medical tourism offerings. What is unique is the application of a Five-Star Service encounter (that only Dubai can provide) to this offering. It is a new type of innovation (as it satisfies an outstanding need)—applied to an existing industry. This need, that has become an innovation outcome, combines existing resources with a service standard that leads to an outstanding patient experience. It meets the criteria of innovation as it changes the paradigm, resets the service level for rehabilitative services, and promises to dominant market share for the near future.

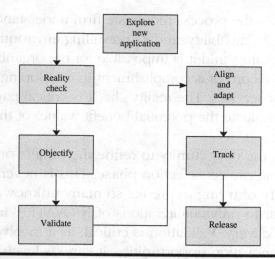

Figure 9.1   N²OVATE™ process adjusted for a new application (EROVATR).

These innovations will enable Dubai to maintain brand recognition and leadership in a highly competitive marketplace.

For new applications, we suggest a seven-step implementation process (Figure 9.1). The process highlights the need for scanning the existing competitive environment. The need (patient demand) must be strong enough to drive the application throughout its development and implementation stages. This "new" type of innovation requires detailed input, including information about the patient and user and information that expresses the need or desire for such an item, even if it does not yet exist. To meet this challenge, there is a need for focused (detailed) market research or access to customer analytics (informatics). A functioning informatics department may be the best source to determine the efficacy of this new application. In the case of Dubai, information comes from both their existing MT presence and those countries/localities that have adapted such practices.

Realize that the patient may not be able to fully describe what they want (or need) until they experience the five-star service. The project selection process (including assessment and diagnostics) is critical to understanding patient needs and expectations, but also to ensuring the capacity to deliver and maintain service quality. Much of the needed information can come from existing patients eager to discuss their experiences. All patient-facing employees must understand their responsibility in collecting information on what the patient wants, needs, or desires. Interestingly, our experience has also shown us that organizations that do not collect this candid patient (customer) feedback often miss potential innovation opportunities.

The second step in the process requires a firm understanding of the reality of the organization, its capability, and its prevailing environment. Patients may want or desire something, and it is impossible for the organization to deliver it given its previous record of accomplishment in developing new use applications for products or services. The reality check is critical part of this innovation as it stands to evaluate the potential benefit (value) of the product before implementation.

The third step is the opportunity to refine the project objective that was developed during the project selection phase. This is never a simple task given the complexity of trying to predict so many unknown factors. The fourth step is similar to previous iterations of N^{2}OVATE™ in that it validates or verifies service delivery. Validation is critical, as it involves an evaluation that looks at innovation opportunities at various levels of perception and depth. The fifth step provides guidance on implementation, that is, the rollout of the service. The key is to align employees, management, patients, and suppliers with the new application. Again, given the strong emphasis on perception, the innovation must satisfy a need and deliver superior performance while remaining competitive with other like products. The sixth step involves tracking the product, which requires both a strong internal and external set of measures or metrics (i.e., key performance indicators, key performance measurements, and critical success factors). It is not only critical to demonstrate the benefit and value of the innovation opportunity; the innovation must also demonstrate how it meets a need that has remained unsatisfied up to the point in time at which this product or service becomes available. The final step is rollout to the patient or user.

Step 1: Exploring the New Application

As mentioned previously, this step involves a great deal of gathering and analyzing information to determine the true need for the application. Figure 9.2 shows a systematic process flowchart for this step. Step 1 is critical for the Dubai case study, as there is an opportunity for many spinoff micro innovations. Exploring new applications requires an evaluation of four inputs:

1. Patient and user (family) needs (what existing needs remain unsatisfied?)
2. Existing workarounds (substitutes) with a positive impact (may become a future standard of performance or SOP)

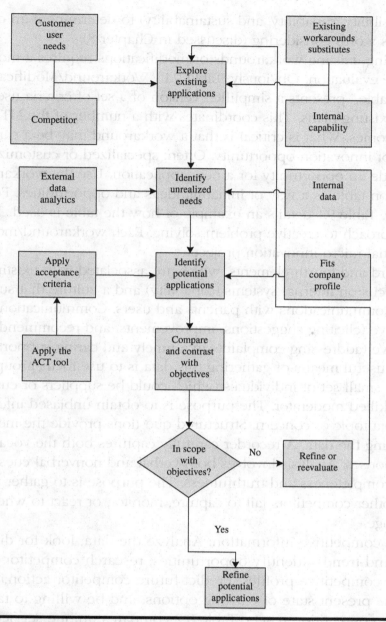

Figure 9.2   Step 1: Exploring new applications.

3. Competitive information (are the outcomes easily replicated?)
4. Strict acceptance criteria (standards of excellence) by which to judge performance

Existing and outstanding patient (user) needs should be as frequently reviewed as opportunities for new applications. We advise applying three criteria (visibility, capability, and sustainability) to determine if an outstanding need is worth considering (discussed in Chapter 8).

Reviewing existing workarounds or modifications requires a more comprehensive evaluation. Obviously, Table 9.1, "Workaround/Modification Exercise Table," presents a simplified version of a set of criteria used to evaluate existing plans. This coordinates with a number of the MT case study outcomes. What is critical is that a workaround may be a candidate for this type of innovation opportunity. Often, specialized or customized effects may provide an opportunity for a new application. Use the workaround/modification table as a way of initiating ideas and opportunities. For the MT case study, Table 9.1 details an example of how the table is used. This is a simple approach to creative problem-solving. Each workaround/modification is a potential micro innovation project.

The third and fourth elements, which are associated with existing applications, focus on internal systems (capability) and a culture that supports two-way communications with patients and users. Communications must be proactive (eliciting suggestions, improvements, and recommendations) and reactive (addressing complaints in a timely and caring/supportive manner). One useful means of gathering this data is to use focus groups. A focus group is a small set of individuals (which could be suppliers or customers) led by a skilled moderator. The purpose is to obtain unbiased information relating to a topic or concern. Structured questions provide the mechanism for collecting the data. A recorder carefully captures both the vocal and nonvocal responses. Analysis involves both verbal and nonverbal cues that help describe completeness and truthfulness. The purpose is to gather information that other competitors fail to capture, monitor, or react to when conditions change.

Gather competitive information. Analyze the data; look for distinctive patterns and trends. Identify opportunities, research competitor activities, and build competitive profiles. Predict future competitor action, assess against the present state of existing options, and be willing to take action before the competition reacts. Table 9.2 compares unique service offerings (Dubai MT case study) versus existing competitors. Construct Table 9.2 by identifying the unique attributes of the service that distinguish the innovation from its competitors. Identify the key competitors and their offerings that could challenge the unique Dubai counterparts. Rate these against the objectives (or outcomes) established for this project (detailed in Chapter 8).

Table 9.1 Workaround/Modification Exercise Table

Item	Workaround/ Modification	Benefit	Failure	Value to Organization	Substitute	Decision
Patient requests	Personal concierge	Maintains Five-star rating	If response time does not improve	Five-star service personalized	Additional staff needed	Go
Accompanying guests	Trip and entertainment concierge	Patient and guest satisfied	Guest makes little use of service	Five-star rating guest satisfaction exceeds expectations	Traditional approach guest must entertain themselves	Go

Table 9.2 Competitor Assessment to Objectives (Outcomes)

Service Offerings	Key Competitor	Objective 1	Objective 2	Objective 3	Objective 4	Objective 5
Concierge services for patients	No known alternative	3	3	3	3	3
Entertainment for families	Cannot meet Dubai standards	1				
State-of-the-art facilities	Compatible	2	2	2	2	2

Use the following scale:

3—Competitor value exceeds MT case study objectives (outcomes)
2—Competitor value equals MT case study objectives (outcomes)
1—Competitor value less than MT case study objectives (outcomes)

This simple tool will quickly highlight difficulties or potential opportunities. Do not be afraid to challenge the status quo. Understanding your competitor is more than half the battle of trying to develop a competitive advantage. Yet, many businesses relegate this analysis to a minor role.

Data analysis, whether it be simple or complex (analytics), should uncover potential opportunities for the business or organization. This section also relies on external analytics and internal data. Those organizations without this information (or the capacity to gather such information) can easily brainstorm unrealized needs or use focus groups and surveys to gather this information. Consider a method to gather these needs from patients. Figure 9.3 ("Patient/User Unrealized Needs Perceptual Survey") is an example of such a perceptual survey. Answer each statement by selecting a response that best meets your agreement or disagreement with the statement provided. Enter your choice in the "My Choice" box. Needs are defined as something wanted or desired. Often, medical requirements (medications, therapy, health status, etc.) may take a similar role as needs.

Scoring and Interpretation

To score the perceptual survey, convert all statement scores into one of three score categories:

- 1 = When the respondent scores a positive response: agree, strongly agree
- 0 = When the respondent scores a neutral response: neither disagrees nor agree
- −1 = When the respondent scores a negative response: disagree, strongly disagree

Try to develop a cohesive description of the statements that received a rating of one (1). Examine the variation between those statements that score a zero (0) and especially a negative one (−1). This indicates a more complex

Scoring and Interpretation

Unsatisfied Needs	Strongly Disagree	Disagree	Neither Disagree nor Agree	Agree	Strongly Agree	My Choice
Services, associated with my treatment always meets my needs	1	2	3	4	5	
When something I need cannot be easily met, the staff searches for alternatives	1	2	3	4	5	
Information regarding patient's needs should be accessible	1	2	3	4	5	
Patients should be able to suggest potential needs	1	2	3	4	5	
Needs are better voiced through the Internet rather than face-to face encounters	1	2	3	4	5	
When a service meets my needs, I automatically voice my appreciation	1	2	3	4	5	
I only consider returning if my needs are fully satisfied	1	2	3	4	5	
I am more comfortable purchasing a medical procedure, such as in Dubai, with which I have some experience	1	2	3	4	5	
If my need is impossible to fulfill, I would still be satisfied	1	2	3	4	5	
I base my decision to purchase based on whether my needs are satisfied	1	2	3	4	5	

Figure 9.3   Patient/user unrealized needs perceptual survey.

satisfaction/purchasing process. The purpose of the survey is to determine how needs factor in innovation satisfaction and ultimate purchase (repurchase) decisions. In addition to these statements, we suggest adding statements directly related to your product or service.

Finally, the remaining elements of this first step (Figure 9.4) center on identifying potential opportunities. Use some form of acceptance criteria

Acceptance criteria	ACT - Acceptance criteria evaluation tool					
	Less than expected	Expected	Greater than expected	Sustainable	Easy to implement	Why
Distinctiveness		×		L	S	
Trend-setting		×		L	D	
Minimal resources			×	S	S	Requires only personnel
Meets patient need or desire		×		S	M	
Competitive advantage		×		M	S	
Revenue positive		×		S	M	
Better value			×	S	S	Perceived better value
Increased market share			×	M	S	Short-term bounce
Controllable costs		×		S	S	

Instructions

Develop a set of acceptance criteria. Select a "new" application, opportunity, or feature. Evaluate the feature against each acceptance criterion and determine whether overall performance expectations would be less than expected, expected, or greater than expected.

Sustainment

Evaluate the sustainability of the feature or opportunity using the following scale:
Limited (L) = less than 1 year
Marginal (M) = 1–3 years
Superior (S) = over 3 years

Ease of implementation

Evaluate the ease of implementing such an opportunity using the following scale:
Difficult (D) = involves many departments, requires additional resources, affects many employees
Moderate (M) = involves one or two departments, minor resources needed, affects patient positively
Simple (S) = involves only one department, minimal resources, positive impact for patients

Figure 9.4 Acceptance criteria for new application opportunities.

to evaluate these opportunities. Choose criteria from a broad spectrum of evaluation and do not just focus on financial or cost benefit. Criteria must evaluate the innovation opportunity potential (i.e., sustained success that exceeds expectations). Consider criteria that evaluate established performance metrics. To create a set of opportunities, collect ideas by using a technique such as brainstorming. Brainstorming is a structured process of submitting ideas in such a way as to avoid criticism or critique. Keep a log of all ideas. This technique works well in either a virtual or a face-to-face encounter. Reduce the number of entries by using a filtering technique such as 10–5–1 voting. Each person gets 10 votes; they can vote for 10 items each with one vote; they cannot assign more than 5 votes per criteria; and they must choose a minimum of 3 criteria and assign no more than 5 votes to a single criteria. For example, suppose the team wants to examine adding a dimension to the rehabilitative services, such as acupuncture. Apply the acceptance criteria evaluation tool (such as the example shown in Figure 9.4) to this proposed added feature (opportunity). Evaluating the results indicates that the additional feature (acupuncture) would add benefit in the short term.

This tool uses the experiences and knowledge of employees to examine a product, service, or technology. It is meant to capture the ideas and thinking of a wide range of employees. Given that, individuals decide what is or is not innovative (this tool can capture criteria that are often overlooked or not considered). The more individuals that recognize the innovative characteristics of this item, the greater the opportunity to reach this audience and generate sustained success.

External influences used to judge or purchase innovations are needs, customer appeal, and overall affordability. Patients use multiple criteria before selecting a new product, service, or technology. Individuals use numerous criteria (unequally weighted) to evaluate innovation. This tool (Figure 9.4, "Acceptance Criteria for New Application Opportunities") attempts to rate a set of typical criteria a consumer would use to judge an innovation and initiate purchase. Individuals judge the criteria by evaluating whether the criteria equal, fall short of, or exceed expectations. Since each person creates his or her own expectations, the tool captures the amount of influence the consumer will use in their purchase and innovation assessment decision. The authors predict that a strong relationship between expectations and the amount of influence exerted adequately defines how a person will decide to purchase or not. The scoring attempts to capture this changing perspective. Rather than capturing an average score, examine the number of items in the "expected" and "greater than expected" columns. These criteria drive consumer behaviors such as purchasing and satisfaction.

The last elements of Step 1 compare and contrast these ideas (opportunities) among a set of objectives or outcomes. Usually the previous version's established objectives will work for the new version of the product, service, or technology. These are neither tactical nor operational measures but strategic measures used in decision-making. If these measures are positive, then management may implement this opportunity. If not, then the opportunity may require further evaluation, refinement, and modification.

Step 2: Reality Check

If the "new" application meets and completes Step 1, then move on to Step 2, which is called the "reality check" phase (Figure 9.5). This phase is used to verify what we know about the new application.

CASE STUDY PERSPECTIVE

Step 1: Critical "Learnings" as regards the case study:

■ Before implementing the new service, be sure all critical needs are satisfied.
■ Use data to help formulate decisions—be sure to obtain both external and internal data.
■ The N²OVATE™ has evolved into the EROVATR process for "new" applications.
■ Remember to complete a competitive assessment.
■ Collect perceptual data (surveys, focus groups) to validate patient needs.
■ For new opportunities identified during this process, ensure these meet developed acceptance criteria.
■ Acceptance criteria measure various objectives (outcomes) in terms of what the patient expects.
■ The way to measure real-time patient expectations is to evaluate these expectations versus critical patient acceptance criteria using the acceptance criteria tool (ACT).
■ For the MT case, examine the multiple opportunities that will be cost-effective and add competitive value.

DISCUSSION QUESTIONS

1. To maintain a competitive advantage, what suggestions (or potential opportunities) would you offer the Dubai Health Authority?
2. What additional acceptance criteria would you suggest for evaluating new services that must meet the stringent quality control imposed by the Dubai Health Authority?

ASSIGNMENTS

Identify an opportunity and apply the acceptance criteria evaluation tool (Figure 9.4). Find a blank form at the IPS DropBox (copy and paste the URL into your browser) https://www.dropbox.com/sh/ew48bypr78ge6tk/AABeGkLPAonWcQwJCX0grDdJa?dl=0.

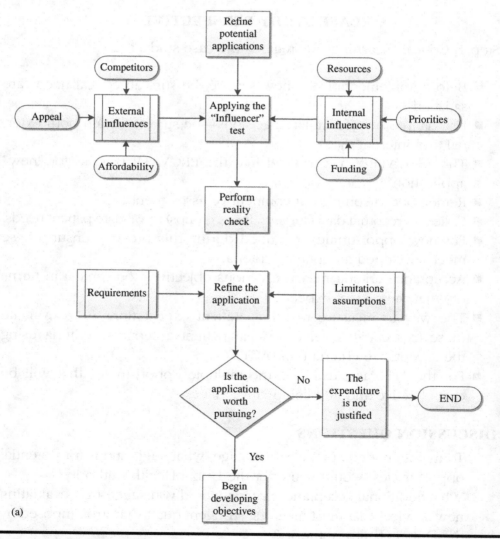

(a)

Figure 9.5 Step 2: Reality check.

Prior to reality checking the innovation opportunity, the first evaluation begins by understanding how this new application will influence all elements of the business or operation. For the case study, determine the influence that offering five-star rehabilitation services will have on the industry. From Figure 9.4, it can be seen that both internal and external influences affect the new application. Internal influences include (but are not limited to) funding, resources, and existing priorities. External influences include competitor practices, overall appeal, and affordability. The authors developed a new tool to help in assessing the amount and degree of influence. Interchange the word influence with the word "impact," as many influence elements affect the decision whether to proceed or not. This tool has numerous uses, not just at this stage but anytime the number of influencers may modify a decision, or require the ability to "think" in more than the two dimensions.

Influence Matrix

The team can begin with the external or internal influences. Rather than looking at these in a linear fashion, consider both a linear and an interactive approach. To begin, consider the internal influences of resources, funding, and priorities on the outcome. Consider the one-dimensional influence separately and then begin to consider two of the influencers together as a contributor. Does priority influence the funding or resources allocation? If this interaction is present, which it is, how does it affect availability? Answer these questions and you can begin to understand the degree of interrelatedness and complexity needed before reaching a final decision. Think of these influencers not individually but in the context of how they interact with one another (Figure 9.4).

To begin, operationally define attributes (characteristics) that patients (purchasers) will use to evaluate the service. Consider the following general definitions:

Resource availability—resources available without major external support
Priorities—a measure of value and frequency
Funding—determines financial profile for funding the project
Competitors—activity directly related to products offerings or replacements (substitutes)
Availability—degree of difference between the product (service) the application replaces or updates

Appeal—perception (or novelty) of "newness" by the patient or user

Using this tool (Figure 9.6), the team identified key "influencers" that could or would affect the decision; the four influencers are reputation, cost, the 2015 Dubai Vision, and uniqueness. Table 9.3 lists the influencing matrix evaluations with scoring defined in Figure 9.4. The largest score suggests

Influence matrix - services							
Influence component	Resources	Funding	Priority	Competitors	Affordability	Appeal	Total score
							0
							0
							0
							0
							0
							0
							0
							0
							0
							0

Instructions: Choose a influencer element; determine how much influence the element will have on purchase behavior. The greater the influence, the higher the score. A score of "1" (parity) suggests that its influence will be essentially the same as the product it is replacing. Lower scores—less influence; higher scores—more influence.

Definitions

Resource availability—resources available without major external support
Priorities—a measure of value and frequency
Funding—determines financial profile for funding the project
Competitors—activity directly related to products offerings or replacements (substitutes)
Availability—the degree of difference between the product (service) the application replaces or updates
Appeal—perception (or novelty) of "newness" by the patient of user

Scoring

Resource availability scoring:	Low - .25, .5, .75; Medium - 1.0, 1.25; High - 1.50. 1.75. 2.0
Funding scoring:	Low - .25, .5, .75; Medium - 1.0, 1.25; High - 1.50. 1.75. 2.0
Priority scoring:	Low - .25, .5, .75; Medium - 1.0, 1.25; High - 1.50. 1.75. 2.0
Competitor savvy scoring:	Low - .25, .5, .75; Medium - 1.0, 1.25; High - 1.50. 1.75. 2.0
Affordability scoring:	Low - .25, .5, .75; Medium - 1.0, 1.25; High - 1.50. 1.75. 2.0
Customer appeal scoring:	Low - .25, .5, .75; Medium - 1.0, 1.25; High - 1.50. 1.75. 2.0

Figure 9.6   Influence matrix tool.

Table 9.3 Influence Matrix: Case Study

Influence Component	Resources	Funding	Priority	Competitors	Affordability	Appeal	Total Score
Reputation	1	1	1.5	2	1	2	6
Cost	2	2	1	1.5	1	2	12
Dubai Vision-2015	1	2	2	1	2	2	16
Uniqueness	2	2	1	2	2	2	32

the influence element that greatly affects how patients will choose this provider—in essence, the criterion that most influences a patient's decision to purchase the service.

Figure 9.6 suggests that "uniqueness" may be the quality that patients use to perceive and evaluate the service to determine whether to initiate a purchase. Influence characteristics may change after the first purchase. For the case study, patients may shift their focus to more internally focused concerns.

The results, although simulated, say that uniqueness and the Dubai Vision 2021 (2015) are the driving influencing factors. These factors (elements or components) represent the loci of attention for the application to be successful. Implementing this tool within the marketing and sales functions may provide a unique set of insights into the patient or user's desires or feelings. Similarly, using this tool with suppliers may provide a unique vantage point from which to better understand their perspectives and approaches. This tool applies whenever factors or elements influence the result or decision-making process.

The influence matrix is the last of the reality checks that started with Step 1. Once completed, the team begins to review requirements, assumptions, and limitations. This is not identical to the requirements developed in the project selection stage (which examined the overall characteristics of the opportunity). These requirements, limitations, and assumptions have a distinctive operational emphasis that is used to refine the application. For example, buying a suit is the first stage, fitting the suit the second, wearing the suit the third. At this point, a decision concerning the viability of the project is forthcoming. Finally, is the project worth continuing? The information collected and the performance observed should predict an outcome from the step. An application worth pursuing is one that generated benefits despite the general business environment.

Step 3: New Applications

Step 3 continues the process of evaluation, this time with the emphasis on whether the project remains a viable option. Recall that in the project selection phase, the team and management choose objectives for the project. The team validates those objectives, and they become a focal point for the project as it proceeds to implementation.

CASE STUDY PERSPECTIVE

Step 2: Critical "Learnings" as regards the case study:

- Decide what are the critical "influencers" that will affect a purchase decision.
- Consider internal and external sources.
- The N²OVATE has evolved into the EROVATR process for "new" service applications.
- An influence diagram is a must in a situation with multiple competitors, given the interrelationships among influence criteria.
- Consider patient expectations (beliefs) to be as critical as patient satisfaction.
- Acceptance and influence share much in common, as both measure patient (consumer) reactions to possible purchase criteria.
- For new opportunities identified during this process, ensure that these opportunities meet developed acceptance criteria.
- A reality check is needed before deciding to proceed.
- For the MT case, the critical influence element is "uniqueness," which suggests that for this service and service level, consumers (patients) would want a unique experience.

DISCUSSION QUESTIONS

1. To maintain a competitive advantage, what suggestions (or potential opportunities) would you offer the Dubai Health Authority?
2. What additional acceptance criteria would you suggest for evaluating new services that must meet the stringent quality control imposed by the Dubai Health Authority?

ASSIGNMENTS

Create a set of criteria based on a hypothetical application. Associate scoring of the influence factors to correspond with the tool's objectives. Identify which element scores the highest and why it is critical for success.

During the implementation phase, the objectives (outcomes) again come under scrutiny. There is a constant need for proactive review and reevaluation, as visualized in Figure 9.7. Step 3 reviews objectives and expectations but also aligns to form project outcomes. The alignment between outcomes and objectives is direct; outcomes include a combination of requirements and assumptions/limitations. If outcomes are not developed, then use the existing project objectives. For the case study, use either the objectives or the outcomes.

Meeting or exceeding the outcomes (objectives) defines the measure of success for a project. Over time, objectives (requirements) may change to reflect new knowledge or a change in the business environment. Therefore, it is critical to understand why these discrepancies exist and what remedies are possible to bring these new objectives into alignment. Construct the objective (outcome) discrepancy evaluation tool (Table 9.4) to determine the causes and potential remedies for aligning old and new objectives (outcomes). Begin with the existing outcomes (objectives) and evaluate these with the modified or new outcome. Describe the discrepancy that exists and

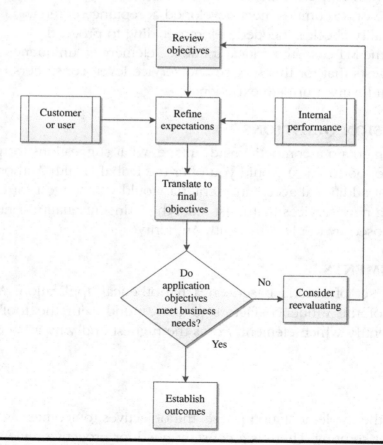

Figure 9.7   Step 3: Objectify.

Table 9.4   Objective Discrepancy Evaluation

Original Objective	Replacement or New Objective	Discrepancy Found; Identify the Causes	Remedy

identify the reasons for the misalignment. Determine a remedy (or solution) that brings the new outcome into alignment with the requirements and the assumptions and limitations of the existing objective. If no discrepancy exists, as in the MT case, then skip the tool.

Considering why the discrepancies exist reduces the risk of misalignment and project failure. The purpose of this step is to reach agreement on the outcomes as the project implementation continues. Failure to address these issues could result in destructive behaviors if disagreements exists and are not resolved. Moving forward requires an examination of expectations as well. Remember that individuals use expectations to develop their beliefs and attitudes, which become long-term predictors of behavior. Expectations represent beliefs and dictate how and why an individual acts or behaves. These differ from measures of satisfaction, which evaluate how well a service or product performed. Project expectations (Figure 9.8) are important in assessing overall commitment and agreement among those involved with implementation. Complete the project expectations survey to assess individual expectations.

Assign a numerical value to each of the five survey responses, placing the value in the "My choice" column. Average these over the 10 statements. Keep track of the range of the responses per individual. Interpret the results as follows:

■ Average = 5.0 or better: positive expectations (formed a positive outlook)
■ Average = 2.8–3.8: medium (neutral) expectations (requires some form of alignment)
■ Average = 0–2.6: low expectations (could lead to negative consequences)

A low value indicates disagreement between project expectations and personal expectations regarding the outcomes. A positive value indicates both agreement and satisfaction with the project outcomes.

Statement number	Enter the numerical value (1–5) in the My choice column that best describes how you agree (disagree) with the statements provided	Strongly disagree	Disagree	Neither disagree nor agree	Agree	Strongly agree	My choice
1	The project is expected to meets its objectives.	1	2	3	4	5	
2	Implementation is expected to complete on time.	1	2	3	4	5	
3	No delays are expected in meeting the timelines.	1	2	3	4	5	
4	The project is expected to be successful.	1	2	3	4	5	
5	Support for the project remains unchanged.	1	2	3	4	5	
6	Performance is expected to remain at similar levels.	1	2	3	4	5	
7	Expect that customers or users will perceive item as innovative.	1	2	3	4	5	
8	Expect that few changes will be made to the project.	1	2	3	4	5	
9	The project team has performed as expected.	1	2	3	4	5	
10	Expect management to continue support for this project.	1	2	3	4	5	
Total		Scores	AVG perceptions	0	AVG expectations	0	Difference	0
Total		Scores	Range perceptions	0	Range expectation	0		

Examine the difference between the perception (odd numbered) and expectation scores (even numbered). If perceptions exceed expectations (a positive difference), then the person is satisfied and the reality is better than expected. If the expectations exceed perceptions (a negative difference) then the person is not satisfied and the reality is less than expected. These persons will not align well with the project.

Figure 9.8   Project expectations survey.

If there is a large amount of difference between the averages, this suggests that inconsistencies exist between respondents. This could be as simple as those who "touch" and those who "manage" the process. This requires some form of alignment to bring both sides to a place (space) in which they can come to an agreement.

Finally, use the information recently captured in the previous exercises to refine outcomes and expectations. Outcomes (objectives) and expectations support the business case for this project. These are measures not typically associated with project management, and yet individual differences can lead to infighting, delays, replacements, and even cancellations.

Remember that the human element is critical in innovation project management.

CASE STUDY PERSPECTIVE

Step 3: Critical "Learnings" as regards the case study:

- Revisit the outcomes originally established.
- Frame the outcomes as something the team can review at the start of each team meeting.
- Keeping the team focused on the objectives (outcomes) is critical for success.
- Consider team member expectations (beliefs) as critical for project continuity.
- This step is truly for those working on projects in real time; we assume that the teams implementing the Dubai project meet these requirements.

DISCUSSION QUESTIONS

1. Identify a reason for assessing outcomes. If an outcome that measures service level changes (five-star service changes to six-star service), will the requirements and limitations/assumptions remain the same? Explain.
2. Describe your expectations (beliefs) regarding the case study. Would you expect these to align with other students' expectations? What is the consequence if expectations differ substantially?
3. Is there a need for revision or an assignment of new outcomes?

ASSIGNMENTS

1. Use the expectations survey and finesse the language to evaluate an ongoing project within your business or organization. What type of results would you expect?

This step considers the team dynamic and the role it plays in overall project success. Failure to address these concerns may adversely affect the overall outcome and have a negative influence on sustained success. Assuming that agreement on the goals (set by the team) and outcomes (set by management) is always positive or at best neutral can easily compromise the integrity of the team and its ability to achieve success. After aligning outcomes (objectives) and expectations, move on to Step 4.

Step 4: Validation

Validation (Figure 9.9) begins with a formalization of outcomes (objectives) and elements that define the new application. For the MT–Dubai example, the five outcomes (Chapter 8) must coincide with the application (rehabilitative service patients). If the outcomes and key components of the application are compatible, then the process can move forward.

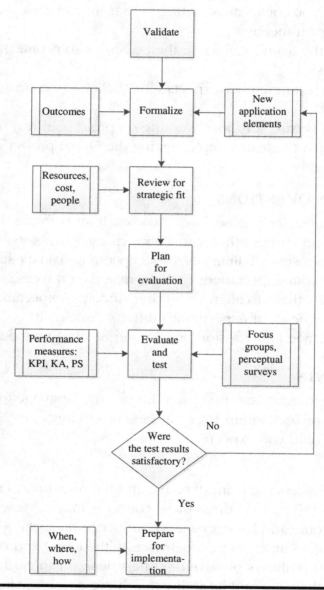

Figure 9.9   Step 4: Validation.

Validation is a similar phase for all project implementations, no matter what the type of innovation. It is the final step before full implementation begins. This step begins by matching outcomes to application elements and ensuring these coincide and reinforce one another. Formalization involves a review of the outcomes for relevancy and applicability. To meet these criteria, the outcome must include

- A consensus (the outcome continues to be relevant and predictive) among management, stakeholders, and consumers
- Verification via empirical evidence (both from descriptive and inferential statistics)
- A historical precedent (i.e., past similar projects used identical or similar outcomes)
- Success criteria that are competitively driven (using standard or accepted performance information) and regularly utilized by competitors

Often an outcome meets three to four of these criteria; however, empirical evidence should be the top choice since it is bias free. Empirically driven tools include

- Run charts (a description can be found in *ENOVALE: Unlocking Sustained Innovation Project Success*, McLaughlin and Caraballo, 2013b)
- Descriptive (exploratory) analysis
  - Exploratory data analysis (EDA) is an approach/philosophy for data analysis that employs a variety of techniques (mostly graphical) to maximize insight, uncover underlying data patterns, detect outliers and anomalies, test assumptions, and develop operational settings. (http://www.itl.nist.gov/div898/handbook/eda/section1/eda11.htm)
- Control charts described in *Innovation Project Management Handbook* (McLaughlin and Kennedy, 2016)
- Inferential statistics (statistical analysis)
- Risk analysis (Suggest @Risk as an excellent addition to Microsoft Excel)
- Pattern and trend analysis in *ENOVALE: Unlocking Sustained Innovation Project Success* (McLaughlin and Caraballo, 2013b)

Keep the empirical analysis simple but descriptive. Include such key measures as

KPI: key performance indicators (response time, recovery time, number and length of health-care professional visits, patient coverage, recuperation times, etc.)

KA: key attributes (service rating, room size and décor, health-care professional experience, meal quality, comfort index, etc.)

PS: patient satisfaction, patient expectation (return rate, referral rates, etc.)

For each measure, identify a standard to judge performance. For example, patient satisfaction scores should average at 90% and above. If the rate falls, then take action.

These measures serve as a predictor of future performance and success; they also serve as a mechanism to detect and act on change. Create a dashboard for every critical KPI, KA, and PS measure. A dashboard is an easy to comprehend graphical chart, graph, or template that tracks key performance criteria (KPI, KA, PS) over time. Some examples* are shown in Figure 9.10.

This shows recuperation times for Dubai patients (gray boxes) and industry average (circles). Notice the advantage that Dubai delivers over its competitors. Figure 9.11 displays the actual scores with an average of 97%. Figure 9.12 displays a control chart of patient respond times with an average of 8 minutes from

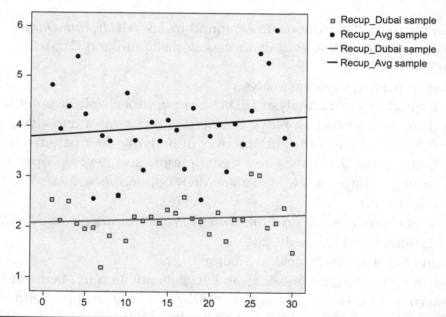

Figure 9.10   KPI (Recuperation time: Dubai versus industry average).

---

* Hypothetical data used.

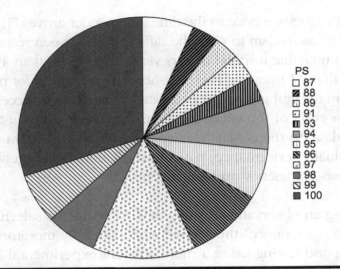

Figure 9.11   Patient satisfaction (PS) percentage approval scores.

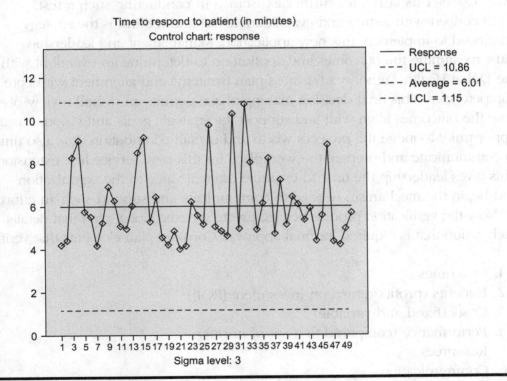

Figure 9.12   Respond times—30-day sample.

when a patient requests service to the time a responder arrives. The control chart provides a mechanism to view the differences between respond times. It is interesting to note that respond time never occurs in less than 4 minutes and never in more than 11 minutes. These dashboards are critical for maintaining performance, an integral ingredient for sustained innovation success.

The "test" portion of the validation phase involves "proving the concept." By collecting data on the actual "service experience," the team (management) can evaluate performance, patient satisfaction, and potential alternatives that increase efficiency and effectiveness.

1. Conducting an observational study or a "dry run" by selecting 5–10 patients to "experience" the service while carefully monitoring the results
2. Designing and testing using a more efficient experimental approach to evaluate all components of the service "experience"
3. Simulating the entire five-star "experience" to evaluate its capacity and its ability to perform

Designing and planning for such an evaluation is an entire topic on its own. Contact us at IPS for further assistance in conducting such a test.

In concert with testing and evaluation, revisit and rethink is the strategy employed to implement this new application. Management and leadership must reexamine the outcomes and application to determine an overall fit with the Dubai Health Authority's business plan (strategy) and alignment with core competencies. This final decision-making phase permits an overall review of how the outcomes align with and support the strategic goals and vision. It is an opportunity to judge the project's worth and overall contribution. It is also time to communicate and prepare the workplace for this new service line extension. This gives leadership the time to examine the real value to the organization and begin the mechanism needed to communicate and support such an effort.

Now the verification process begins. Create an executional plan that details each action that is required for final approval. Consider plan elements that verify

1. Outcomes
2. Benefits (profits/return on investment [ROI])
3. Costs (fixed and variable)
4. Performance (compared to a set of norms)
5. Resources
6. Communications
7. Competitive response

Begin the final evaluation process. Use a variety of methods to collect and validate the data. Use various techniques described in this book combined with techniques that capture perceptions, beliefs, and attitudes (interviews and surveys). Determine if differences exist and how best to evaluate these differences. If the results meet criteria and test to be satisfactory, then operationalize the project. If not, conduct "5 Why" sessions (asking "why" numerous times until a specific set or single reason or cause [could be more than 1] is identified). This is the time to address and fix problems rather than after the launch. If a project reaches this stage, the chance of disapproval should be slim. Regardless of outcome, document your activities and file for future reference in case the innovation opportunity decision is not favorable or the project is delayed.

CASE STUDY PERSPECTIVE

Step 4: Critical "Learnings" as regards the case study:

- MT case study outcomes remain the same as the decision to proceed materializes.
- Validation and verification require data, analysis, and a final decision.
- Collect data to validate the "service experience" using descriptive methods, exploratory data analysis, and statistical inference.
- Dashboards are an excellent means of monitoring performance and evaluating competitive advantage.
- Designing a test to verify the "service experience" is critical.
- Ensure the organization's strategy and culture will support the new application.

DISCUSSION QUESTIONS

1. Identify and discuss additional KPI, KA, PS measures that support the Dubai MT case study.
2. What type of data would you need to evaluate the "service experience" before deciding to implement?

ASSIGNMENTS

1. Develop a test method to evaluate and verify the MT case study.
2. Explain how to evaluate and test each outcome.

Step 5: Alignment

During Step 5 (Figure 9.13), full operationalization is now in progress. Alignment refers to the process of "getting everyone on the same page" to roll out the innovation. This step is similar to the one described in Chapter 8 for the project selection process. The objectives associated with alignment focus on

1. Communications (the message)—both externally and internally
2. Internal operations (including space allocation, resources/materials, facilitation, process, planning, etc.)
3. Policy and strategy concerns

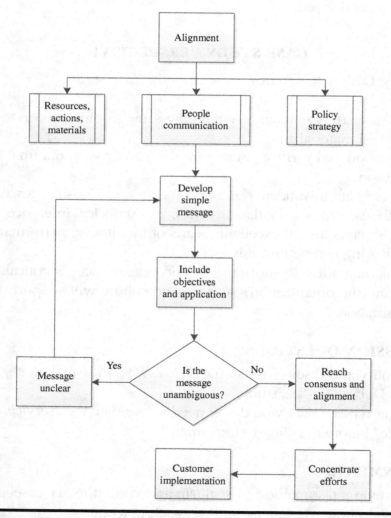

Figure 9.13   Step 5: Alignment.

Communications are the fulcrum for success. Communicating how the application meets an unsatisfied need, how it adds value, and how it outperforms similar products, services, and technology are all critical from both an innovation and sustained success perspective. You want your customers or users to readily appreciate the application's innovative capabilities, identify how it exceeds their expectations, and see how it will drive them to purchase.

Finally, there is the message that must reach the consumer (patient). The message must be unambiguous (clear), accurate, and timely. The message is more than advertising, more than media, more than word-of-mouth; it is direct and uncomplicated—meeting an unsatisfied need (requirement) with value to the patient and the patient's family. To deliver the message requires a marketing approach that highlights the value and benefits that the innovation will deliver; it must appeal to the consumer segment that is most interested in this service.

Step 6: Tracking

It may seem redundant to continue discussing tracking and monitoring various performance and financial metrics, but the reality is that these measures directly relate to success. Formalize the measurements into performance indicators that relay real-time information on evaluating outcomes. A functioning measurement system is both real time and forward looking. It is sustainable and repeatable, and it can judge the existing process and provide information on trends and developing patterns. The process (Figure 9.14) provides the empirical feedback and actionable information necessary for managers to make critical decisions.

CASE STUDY PERSPECTIVE

Step 5: Critical "Learnings" as regards the case study:

- Alignment requires a clear unambiguous message (both externally and internally) to ensure that "everyone is on the same page."
- Internal communications are as critical as external.
- The message must be clearly understood by all who participate.
- Strategies and policies must support the message.
- Use a marketing approach to "spread the word."

DISCUSSION QUESTIONS

1. Explain the reasons for a clear and unambiguous message.
2. Identify some of the words and phrases that the message should contain.

ASSIGNMENTS

Design a message that will inform customers of a new application-oriented type of innovation. Pick an existing product or one you are familiar with and determine its appeal to customers and users.

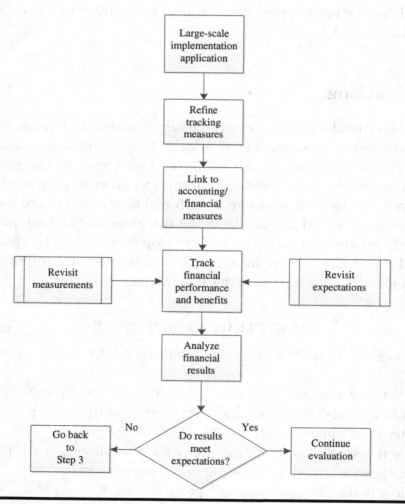

Figure 9.14   Step 6: Tracking.

This step begins by refining (or establishing) tracking metrics for the new approach. For the Dubai MT example, it would be the measure of the five-star service, satisfaction levels, process levels (respond time, rehab time, food quality, etc.), and financial measures (ROI, revenue, costs, etc.). Refining these measures may be as simple as tracking services, incorporating preferences, and maintaining a profitable position. The key takeaway is to examine the present system and look for additional opportunities.

These metrics must link to the companies or organizations' accounting and financial systems capable of tracking the new service. Antiquated systems may provide only "after the fact" or less-detailed information required to accurately measure the innovation implementation. At this stage, during the evaluation, consider the quality of the metrics and their ability to provide accurate and reliable information. Perform the same review on expectations and perceptions of profit and performance. Determine if there is a gap between what is expected (promised) and the reality of what is possible given the marketplace and existing economic and business conditions. Gaps here indicate potential problems when results do not meet expectations.

Finally, refer back to the tracking and performance discussion in Chapter 8. The more the organization tracks performance the easier it will be to address problems (they will be identified quicker) and provide a solution to these problems. Combined with Step 5, after testing and evaluating the service, it should be obvious if the service will meet or exceed its stated outcomes.

Step 7: Release

Finally, the remaining step is consistent throughout all project implementations. The purpose is to evaluate and monitor (see Figure 9.15) for control purposes items such as tolerances, specifications, guidelines, and directives are defined and refined. The emphasis now is control and reaction.

Control is required when the process varies or drops below expected values; reaction is the steps taken to bring the process back to acceptable performance levels. This will include back-up plans and contingency plans to handle developing problems so as not to disturb longer-term sales patterns. This monitoring should also provide valuable information on process changes that could lead to an enhanced service experience. Releasing the process opens the portal for more innovation as micro projects can improve elements of the process on a daily, weekly, or monthly basis. Use this step to monitor and adjust the "experience" as needed.

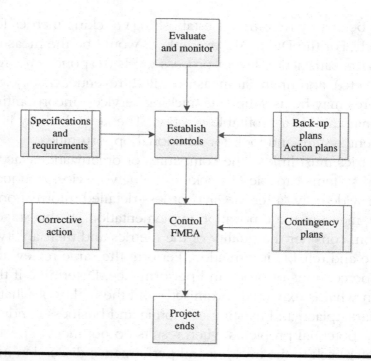

Figure 9.15   Step 7: Release.

In summary, this step is critical for sustaining and maintaining long-term performance. Because of its long-term perspective, it is common for management and leadership to overlook the importance of this step (particularly when developing a new service application) or undervalue its necessity. We recommend that managers or leaders be required to update their skills. As a reminder, applying sufficient time and resources will ensure the viability of this step. Capable managers enable the organization to react proactively to circumstances that could derail the application and lead to its early demise.

Summary

This chapter describes the process of introducing a "new" application that meets the criteria of being innovative. New applications provide a business or organization with a strategy that keeps that business at the forefront of innovation, providing ample competitive advantage. The process of creating, developing, and implementing is much shorter than that associated with a new discovery or invention. Although a reduction in timing is possible, a more likely scenario is that profits and ROI may greatly exceed expectations. Developing this strategy is key to remaining both competitive and a leader in the field. Remember that competitors will copy success, so keep innovating on a macro scale.

CASE STUDY PERSPECTIVE

Steps 6 and 7: Critical "Learnings" as regards the case study:

- Track performance to evaluate service levels and operations.
- Remember that service expectations may change rapidly when unexpected events occur.
- Only one "bad experience" can radically affect a patient's perception of the process and outcome.
- For the MT case study, measure critical service process parameters in real time.
- Release the service after effective monitoring and control plans are in place.

DISCUSSION QUESTIONS

1. Explain the importance of tracking "real-time" measures for control and improvement purposes.
2. When is the best time to release a product, service, or technology? Why?

ASSIGNMENTS

Devise a control plan that permits alternative approaches when a process moves off its intended outcomes.

Discussions

1. List the advantages and disadvantages of this approach. When would patients reject innovation as a desirable trait?
2. What outcomes (value, performance, affordability) would you expect that patients would desire before purchasing a new application, such as MT? List the outcomes in order of importance.

Assignments

1. Propose a new application for the MT case study. Use the seven steps to outline your plan. Estimate a general time line for completion (based on best-guess estimates). Perform a "reality check" (Step 2) on a new application (an add-on to the existing Dubai MT efforts). Would the application pass the reality test? Identify any missing components or elements that would bring this new application into compliance.

References

Al Hashimy, R. (2012). UAE starts World Expo campaign. Emirates 24/7 News. com. Retrieved from http://www.emirates247.com/news/emirates/uae-starts-world-expo-campaign-2012-02-28-1.445641.

Al Maktoum M. bin Rashid. (2006). *My Vision: Challenges in the Race for Excellence*. Dubai: Motivate Publishing, Emirates Printing Press.

Al Tamimi, J. (2015). Dubai makes big leap en route to becoming medical tourism hub. Retrieved 1 October 2015 from http://gulfnews.com/business/economy/dubai-makes-big-leap-en-route-to-becoming-medical-tourism-hub-1.1579606.

Al Tayer, S. M. (2015). DEWA calls for EOI for 800MW phase three of the Mohammed bin Rashid Al Maktoum Solar Park. UAEinteract.com. Retrieved from http://www.uaeinteract.com/docs/DEWA_calls_for_EOI_for_800MW_Phase_three_of_the_Mohammed_bin_Rashid_Al_Maktoum_Solar_Park/71158.htm.

Anonymous. (2015). Dubai medical tourism program. Dubai Health Authority. Retrieved 24 September 2015 from https://www.dha.gov.ae/EN/SectorsDirectorates/Directorates/HealthRegulation/Medical-Tourism-Office/Pages/default.aspx.

Aslakson, R. A., Schuster, A. L. R., Miller, J., Weiss, M., Volandes, A. E., and Bridges, J. F. P. (2014). An environmental scan of advance care planning decision aids for patients undergoing major surgery: A study protocol. *The Patient*, 7(2), 207–217.

Aspen Group. (2013). The Aspen Institute Society of Fellows. Retrieved 1 February 2013 from http://www.aspeninstitute.org/society-fellows/history.

Baregheh, A., Rowley, J., and Sambrook, S. (2009). Towards a multidisciplinary definition of innovation. *Management Decision*, 47(8), 1323–1339.

Barker, J. A. (1989). *The Business of Paradigms*. Burnsville, MN: Charthouse International Learning Corporation.

Berson, Y., Oreg, S., and Dvir, T. (2007). CEO values, organizational culture and firm outcomes. *Journal of Organizational Behavior*, 29(5), 615–633, 2008.

Bevanda, V. and Turk, M. (2011). Exploring semantic infrastructure development for open innovation. *Proceedings of the International Scientific Conference*, Pula, Juraj Dobrila University of Pula, pp. 363–386.

233

Bhatia, N. (2015). Mohammed bin Rashid Al Maktoum Solar Park. Constructionweek.com. Retrieved from http://www.constructionweekonline. com/article-34564-uae-dewa-inks-32m-deal-for-dubai-water-networks/.

Birkinshaw, J. (2011). The five myths of innovation. *Sloan Management Review*, 52(2), 43–50.

Bitar, Z. (2014). Dubai Expo 2020 to produce Dh4 trillion foreign trade. Gulfnews. com. Retrieved from http://gulfnews.com/business/sectors/investment/ dubai-expo-2020-to-produce-dh4-trillion-foreign-trade-1.1317358.

Bowman, J. (2012). Solar 101. *The Motley Fool*. Retrieved on 6 February 2012 from http://www.fool.com/investing/general/2012/02/06/solar-101.aspx.

Buisson, B. and Silberzahn, P. (2010). Blue ocean or fast-second innovation? A four breakthrough model to explain successful market domination. *International Journal of Innovation Management*, 14(3), 359–378.

Bureau International des Expositions (BIE). (2016). Retrieved from http://www. bie-paris.org.

Burns, A. S., Yee, J., Flett, H. M., Guy, K., and Cournoyea, N. (2013). Impact of benchmarking and clinical decision making tools on rehabilitation length of stay following spinal cord injury. *Spinal Cord*, 51(2), 165–169.

Caraballo, E. and McLaughlin, G. (2012). Perceptions of innovation: A multi-dimensional construct. *Journal of Business & Economics Research*, 10(10), 1–16.

Carruth, P. J. and Carruth, A. K. (2010). The financial and cost accounting implications of medical tourism. *The International Business & Economics Research Journal*, 9(8), 135–140.

Chou, S. Y., Kiser, A. I., T., and Rodriguez, E. L. (2012). An expectation confirmation perspective of medical tourism. *Journal of Service Science Research*, 4(2), 299–318.

Christensen, C. M. (1997). *The Innovator's Dilemma. When New Technologies Cause Great Firms to Fail*. Boston, MA: Harvard Business School Press, pp. 27–32.

Clausen, T., Pohjola, M., Sapprasert, K., and Verspagen, B. (2012). Innovation strategies as a source of persistent innovation. *Industrial and Corporate Change*, 21(3), 553–585.

Covey, S. R. (1991). *Principle-Centered Leadership*. New York: Simon & Shuster.

Cunic, D., Lacombe, S., Mohajer, K., Grant, H., and Wood, G. (2014). Can the Blaylock risk assessment screening score (BRASS) predict length of hospital stay and need for comprehensive discharge planning for patients following hip and knee replacement surgery? Predicting arthroplasty planning and stay using the BRASS. *Canadian Journal of Surgery*, 57(6), 391–397.

Cwynar, R., Albert, N. M., Butler, R., and Hall, C. (2009). Factors associated with long hospital length of stay in patients receiving warfarin after cardiac surgery. *Journal of Cardiovascular Nursing*, 24(6):465–474.

De Mooij, M. and Hofstede, G. (2010). The Hofstede model. *International Journal of Advertising*, 29(1), 85–110.

Demiccio, (2015).

Deming, W. E. (1993). *The New Economics*. Cambridge, MA: MIT Press, p. 135.

Detrie, M. (2009). Dubai has eye on medical tourism. *The National Newspaper*. Retrieved from https://web.archive.org/web/20091124064723/ http://www.thenational.ae/apps/pbcs.dll/article?AID=/20091116/ NATIONAL/711159830/1010.

Dickinson, E. (2016). Sheikh Mohammed most "liked" GCC leader on Facebook. Gulfbusiness.com. Retrieved from http://www.gulfbusiness.com/articles/ sheikh-mohammed-most-liked-gcc-leader-on-facebook/.

Dubai Petroleum Company. (2016). Early offshore oil field storage tank. Retrieved from http://www.dubaipetroleum.ae/about.php.

Dubaidesigndistrict (d3). (2016). Smart City. Dubaidesigndistrict.com. Retrieved from http://www.dubaidesigndistrict.com/innovation/smart-city-2/.

Dwyer, A. J., Thomas, W., Humphry, S., and Porter, P. (2014). Enhanced recovery programme for total knee replacement to reduce the length of hospital stay. *Journal of Orthopaedic Surgery*, 22(2), 150–154.

El Shammaa, D. (2009). Health cover is mandatory. Gulfnews.com. Retrieved from http://gulfnews.com/news/uae/health/health-cover-is-mandatory-1.43089.

Ellingson, J. (2009). Managing risk with a cultural perspective. *Risk Management*, 56 (10), 50–53.

Emirates News Agency. (2014). Hosting of Expo 2020 unprecedented achievement for the region. WAM.ae. Retrieved from http://www.wam.ae/en/news/eco-nomics/1395242927600.html.

Evans, C. and Wright, W. (2009). The "How to..." series. *Manager: British Journal of Administrative Management*, (65), 10–11.

Freire, N. A. (2012). The emergent medical tourism: Advantages and disadvantages of the medical treatments abroad. *International Business Research*, 5(2), 41–50.

Gao, Y., Johnston, R. C., and Karam, M. (2010). Pediatric sports-related lower extremity fractures: Hospital length of stay and charges: What is the role of the primary payer? *The Iowa Orthopaedic Journal*, 30, 115.

Ghazinoory, S., Abdi, M., and Azadegan-Mehr, M. (2011). SWOT methodology: A state-of-the-art review for the past, a framework for the future. *Journal of Business Economics and Management*, 12(1), 24–48.

Guiry, M., Scott, J., and Vequist, D. (2011). Experienced and potential medical tourists' service quality expectations. *International Journal of Health Care Quality Assurance*, 29(5), 433–446.

Gulf News. (2015). Government of Dubai Media Office. HRH Sheikh Mohammed bin Rashid Al Maktoum innovation week inauguration speech. Retrieved from http://www.mediaoffice.ae/en/media-center/news/18/1/2016/mohammed-bin-rashid-mohamed-bin-zayed-attend-9th-world-future-energy-summit.aspx.

Horowitz, M. D. and Rosensweig, J. A. (2007). Medical tourism: Health care in the global economy. *Physician Executive*, 33(6), 24–6, 28–30.

Horowitz, M. D., Rosensweig, J. A., and Jones, C. A. (2007). Medical tourism: Globalization of health care marketplace. *MedGenMed*, 9(4), 33.

Ing, D. (2013). Rethinking systems thinking: Learning and coevolving with the world. *Systems Research & Behavioral Science*, 30(5), 527–547.

Isaksen, S. G. and Ekvall, G. (2010). Managing for innovation: The two faces of tension in creative climates. *Social Science Research Network*, 19(2), 73–88.

Issac, J. (2015). DEC launches Dubai Global innovation center. Khaleej. com. Retrieved from http://www.khaleejtimes.com/business/technology/dec-launches-dubai-global-innovation-centre.

Kennedy, W. R. (2014). Individual (personal) perspectives on innovation: Federal knowledge management working group. ProQuest, UMI Dissertation Publishing. UMI Publication Number: 3611870.

Khaleej Times. (2014). UAE: A bright economic outlook. Khaleej.com. Retrieved from http://www.dubaitrade.ae/media-centre/uae-news/2165-uae-a-bright-economic-outlook.

Kim, W. C. and Mauborgne, R. (2005). *Blue Ocean Strategy: How to Create Uncontested Market Space and Make Competition Irrelevant*. Boston, MA: Harvard Business Review Press.

Koster, K. (2009). Spurred by economy, medical tourism poised for breakout in '09. *Employee Benefit News*, 23(2), 38.

Kuhn, T. (1962). *The Structure of Scientific Revolutions*. Chicago, IL: University of Chicago Press.

Lorenz, E. N. (1963). Deterministic non-periodic flow. *Journal of the Atmospheric Sciences*, 20(2), 130–141.

Masters, C. (2007). How Boeing got going. *Time*, 170(11), 1–6.

Maung, N. L. Y. and Walsh, J. (2014). Decision factors in medical tourism: Evidence from Burmese visitors to a hospital in Bangkok. *Journal of Economics and Behavioral Studies*, 6(2), 84–94.

McLaughlin, G. and Caraballo, E. (2013a). *Chance or Choice: Unlocking Innovation Process*. Boca Raton, FL: CRC Press.

McLaughlin, G. and Caraballo, E. (2013b). *ENOVALE: How to Unlock Sustained Innovation Project Success*. Boca Raton, FL: Productivity Press.

McLaughlin, G. and Kennedy, W. R. (2015). *A Guide to Innovation Processes and Solutions for Government*. Boca Raton, FL: Productivity Press.

McLaughlin, G. and Kennedy, W. R. (2016). *Innovation Project Management Handbook*. Boca Raton, FL: Productivity Press.

Melodena, S. B. (2008). Dubai: A star in the East. *Journal of Place Management and Development*, 1(1), 62–91.

Movellan, J. (2011). Where is trade dispute leading US PV market? Solarbuzz.com. Retrieved 16 February 2102 from http://www.solarbuzz.com/where-trade-dispute-leading-us-pv-market.

Musa, J. D. (1993). Operational profiles in software reliability engineering. *IEEE Software Magazine*, 10(2), 14–32.

Mutzabaugh, B. (2015). Dubai jumps Heathrow as "world's busiest international airport." USAToday.com. Retrieved from http://www.usatoday.com/story/todayinthesky/2015/01/28/dubai-jumps-heathrow-as-worlds-busiest-international-airport/22460371/.

Nakra, P. (2011). Could medical tourism aid health-care delivery? *The Futurist*, 45(2), 23–24.

Ohayon, M. (2014). Preliminary world airport traffic and rankings (2013): High growth Dubai moves up to 7th busiest airport. Retrieved from http://charmeck.org/city/charlotte/Airport/News/Documents/Release-ACIRankings2013Preliminary.pdf.

Phelps, C. C. (2010). A longitudinal study of the influence of alliance network structure and composition on firm exploratory innovation. *Academy of Management Journal*, 53(4), 890–913.

Poškienė, A. (2006). Organizational culture and innovations. *Engineering Economics*, 46(1), 45–50.

Prather, C. (2010). *Manager's Guide to Fostering Innovation and Creativity in Teams*. New York: McGraw-Hill.

Raynor, M. E. (2011). Disruption theory as a predictor of innovation success/failure. *Strategy & Leadership*, 39(4), 27–30.

Return on investment (ROI). (2016). Small Business Encyclopedia, Retrieved 22 September 2015 from http://www.entrepreneur.com/encyclopedia/return-on-investment-roi.

Risk Management. (2009). New ISO standard for effective management of risk. International Organization for Standardization.org. Retrieved November 11, 2015, from http://www.iso.org/iso/pressrelease.htm?refid=Ref1266.

Rogers, E. M. (2003). *Diffusion of Innovations*. New York: Free Press.

Saberi, M. (2014). How robust is Dubai health care system? Gulfnews.com. Retrieved from http://m.gulfnews.com/news/uae/health/how-robust-is-dubai-health-care-system-1.1316924.

Sahoo, S. (2014). Dubai to roll out medical tourism packages. *The National*. Retrieved 11 September 2015 from http://www.thenational.ae/business/industry-insights/tourism/dubai-to-roll-out-medical-tourism-packages.

Sahoo, S. (2015). Dubai moves forward with hospital rankings amid medical tourism drive. Retrieved 10 October 2015 from http://www.thenational.ae/business/economy/dubai-moves-forward-with-hospital-rankings-amid-medical-tourism-drive.

Saini, A. and Martin, K. (2009). Strategic risk-taking propensity: The role of ethical climate and marketing output control. *Journal of Business Ethics*, 90(4), 593–606.

Schröder, A. and Hölzle, K. (2010). Virtual communities for innovation: Influence factors and impact on company innovation. *Creativity and Innovation Management*, 19(3), 257–268.

Sheikh Mohammed bin Rashid Al Maktoum. (2016). United Arab Emirates Protocol Department. Retrieved from http://protocol.dubai.ae/Media-Center/Official-Placement-of-Photos#prettyPhoto.

Sheikh Rashid bin Saeed Al Maktoum. (1962). United Arab Emirates Protocol Department. Retrieved from http://protocol.dubai.ae/Media-Center/Official-Placement-of-Photos#prettyPhoto.

Sheikh Zayed bin Sultan Al Nahyan. (2016). United Arab Emirates Protocol Department. Retrieved from http://protocol.dubai.ae/Media-Center/Official-Placement-of-Photos#prettyPhoto.

Teece, D. J, Pisano, G., and Shuen, A. (1997). Dynamic capabilities and strategic management. *Strategic Management Journal, 18*(7), 509–533.

Todd, M. K. (2015). All roads lead to Rome for medical tourism. *Medical Tourism Strategy*. Retrieved from http://medicaltourismstrategy.com/tutte-le-strade-portano-a-roma-per-il-turismo-medico/.

Todorvic, M., Mitrovic, Z., and Bjelica, D. L. (2013). Measuring project success in project-oriented organizations. *Journal for Theory and Practice Management,* 18(68), 41–48.

Vavra, J., Munzarova, S., Bednarikova, M., and Ehlova, Z. (2011). Sustainable aspects of innovations. *Economics & Management*, 16, 621–627.

Woods, L. (2014). Research and markets: Dubai Expo 2020 projects report. Reuters.com. Retrieved from http://www.reuters.com/article/2014/02/28/research-and-markets-idUSnBw285394a+100+BSW20140228.

Zhuang, L. (1995). Bridging the gap between technology and business strategy: A pilot study on the innovation process. *Management Decision*, 33(8), 13–19.

Zhuang, L., Williamson, D., and Carter, M. (1999). Innovate or liquidate: Are all organizations convinced? A two-phased study into the innovation process. *Management Decisions*, 37(1), 57–71.

Zollo, M. and Winter, S. (2002). Deliberate learning and the evolution of dynamic capabilities. *Organization Science*, 13(3), 339–351.

Appendix I: Dubai Medical Tourism—A Case Study

Introduction

To enhance the learning experience, we are providing this case study. The case study provides a real-world description of an existing health-care innovation opportunity. The case study examines whether a new enhancement to an existing medical tourism (MT) operation in Dubai, the United Arab Emirates (UAE), is worth implementing.

Medical tourism is a term that describes consumers as "patients seeking a more affordable health-care outside their own countries" (Nakra, 2011, p. 23). Patients travel to receive medical treatment that they cannot get or do not want to access in their home countries. In many cases, patients are seeking a lower-cost alternative, premier service, or privacy.

This case study provides background information, comparisons with like operations outside Dubai, and the reasoning behind Dubai's emphasis on a quality, innovative experience. The case study provides foundational information and serves as a prerequisite for the innovation course.

Background

Dubai is one of seven emirates (Abu Dhabi, Sharjah, Ajman, Umm al-Quwain, Fujairah, and Ras al-Khaimah), that make up the UAE. The acknowledged epicenter of wealth and innovation in the UAE, Dubai is strategically located between East and West. This favorable geographic position has become the nexus of an ambitious vision developed by the vice president, prime minister and ruler of Dubai, His Highness (HRH) Sheikh

Mohammed bin Rashid Al Maktoum. Leveraging the vision of his father, Sheikh Rashid, Sheikh Mohammed envisioned what could best be described as a "develop for survival" approach to replace the country's oil revenues, which are estimated to drop significantly over the next 10–30 years. Central to Sheikh Mohammed's strategic vision is for Dubai to become the international community's leading financial services provider, the world's largest international transportation and redistribution hub, and ultimately the globe's top MT destination spot. In April 2014, Sheikh Mohammed stated four objectives that Dubai should accomplish in this regard:

1. To be the fastest growing MT destination globally
2. To be rated the top MT destination in the region
3. To develop a health-care industry to compete with the best in the world
4. To contribute to the economic development of the emirate of Dubai (Dubai Health Authority, 2015)

The number of medical tourists expected to travel to Dubai will easily reach half a million in 2015, nearly doubling the figure achieved in the first six months, according to a government official. The forecast looks at tourists staying in 2900 health-care facilities. Dubai attracted 260,000 medical tourists in the first half of 2015, up 12 percent on the same period in 2014, and generated 1 billion AED in revenue during the period. The largest percentage of medical tourists originate from Asia, which accounts for 33 percent of the total, followed by visitors from Europe with 27 percent and 23 percent from Gulf Cooperation Council (GCC) members and other Arab countries. Dubai aims to grow the number of medical tourists by around 12 percent annually to reach "more than 500,000" and generate AED2.6 billion in revenue by 2020. Dubai had set a target in 2015 to welcome 500,000 medical tourists by 2020, but it will now exceed this target by 12–13 percent. The emirate aims to achieve its 2020 target by continuing to promote Dubai as an MT destination to markets like the GCC, Africa, Asia and the United Kingdom and by offering MT packages. For this case study, we will focus only on a segment of the MT industry.

Medical Tourism

Much like Costa Rica and Thailand, Dubai has launched an aggressive effort to improve the quality, affordability, and timeliness of care in both the government and private health-care sectors. Central to the medical industry transformation and reform are the government's establishment of the Dubai Health Authority (DHA) and the Dubai Health City Authority (DHCA). The government chartered the DHA and DHCA to oversee and develop new initiatives and programs such as

1. Unification of health-care policies, improving access to quality and affordable care while reducing the reliance on out-of-country treatment
2. Unification of private and public sectors
3. Development of a premier medical academic institution
4. Substantial investment in modernizing hospitals
5. Establishment of mandatory health insurance
6. Adoption of specialty clinics based on the boutique or concierge business models, which attract a spectrum of complimentary market segments such as pharmaceutical manufacturers and pharmacies, research laboratories, wellness clinics, and so on

Further, Dubai's specialty clinics draw regional clients from GCC members seeking cardiac, spinal, dental, and plastic surgery procedures (Detrie, 2009). In sum, the efforts to date have Dubai on the cusp of emerging as one of the international community's top MT destinations.

MT has become a new tourist niche (Horowitz et al., 2007) representing 2 percent of the world's tourism spending and 4 percent of the hospital admissions in the world (2012 statistics). The industry is a $79 billion business (Chou et al., 2012) with 20 million medical tourists. It has a projected 20 percent annual growth rate (Horowitz and Rosensweig, 2007). By outsourcing medical services to less developed countries, MT has become an acceptable alternative to high-priced medical services in well-developed countries (Carruth and Carruth, 2010). By 2017, approximately 23 million Americans will travel abroad for such services.

Rather than just a business, MT has become a phenomenon, and it is growing at over 20 percent year over year. Marketplace forces, such as globalization and the reorganization of public and private health systems, drive this phenomenon, which occurs outside the view and control of the organized health-care system (Freire, 2012, p. 41). MT presents important concerns and continuing challenges as well as potential opportunities (Freire, 2012, p. 41). This trend will have an increasing impact on the health-care landscape in industrialized and developing countries around the world (Freire, 2012, p. 41). Unlike health tourism (HT), which focuses on individual "well-being" (thermal baths, thalassotherapy, and stress reduction), MT focuses on the person who plans a medical or surgical procedure, either alone or with his or her regular doctor. In contrast, HT services are proce-dures that a person could receive from a spa treatment.

One reason for the increase in MT is the high cost of medical services (contrast the $50,000 cost of knee replacement surgery in the United States with a cost of $10,000 in Costa Rica) (Koster, 2009). Another driver of MT is the lack of service quality and overall services expectation (e.g., sharing a sterile hospital room with stranger). For example, some individuals seek privacy while others seek better services. Finally, others want to enjoy their hospital stay in exotic locations and in luxurious surroundings (Carruth and Carruth, 2010, p. 136). An example is the MT business model employed in Dubai, which emphasizes the "vacation package" approach. A member of a family of four (husband, wife, and two children) has scheduled a hip-replacement procedure. They have purchased a package deal that includes air travel, hotel accommodation in a high-end luxury establishment (meals included), tickets to theme parks and museums, access to health spas and gym, and so on. This essentially gives the patient time to recover while meeting the family's need for entertainment and relaxation. (For a better understanding of MT, check the resources on the website http://www.medi-caltourismassociation.com [Figure A1.1].)

With health-care costs increasing, a comparison of spending for selected procedures demonstrates that costs in the United States far exceed those in other countries for doctors to perform relatively common procedures. Table A1.1 lists some cost comparisons that do not necessarily include air-fare, lodgings, food, and other expenses. The tendency of MT is to quote a complete package, rather than just the cost of the procedure.

There is a compelling need for all parties involved in health care to become familiar with MT and to understand the economic, social, political, and medical forces that are driving and shaping this phenomenon (Horowitz et al., 2007).

One concern has been the quality and experience of hospital personnel. To address this issue, a subsidiary of the Joint Commission International now

Figure A1.1   Medical Tourism Association website http://www.medicaltourismasso-ciation.com.

Table A1.1 Medical Procedures Cost Comparisons

Procedure	Performed in the United States	Performed outside the United States
Heart bypass	$144 K (2010 dollars)	Thailand—$24 K India—$8.5 K
Lap band surgery	$30 K (2010 dollars)	Jordan—$5 K
Dental treatments	$1000–$500 ($2012 dollars)	Costa Rica, Mexico, India, Hungary, Tunisia, Thailand $250—$125
Hip/knee operations	$43 K $40 K	India, Malaysia—$11 K Singapore, Thailand—$12 K
Hysterectomy	$20 K	India, Malaysia—$2.5 K Singapore, Thailand—$3.5 K

Source: Carruth, P. J. and Carruth, A. K., *The International Business & Economics Research Journal*, 9(8), 135–140, 2010; Freire, N. A., *International Business Research*, 5(2), 41–50, 2012.

certifies facilities in over 24 countries (Carruth and Carruth, 2010, p. 138), including those countries with extensive MT facilities. The Joint Commission is the best-recognized quality standards certification organization in the medical services sector. Patient safety is also an issue; to address this, the Medical Tourism Association (MTA) has established its own quality project, the Quality of Care Project, which evaluates medical facilities (hospitals) worldwide (Carruth and Carruth, 2010). In addition, MT facilities must operate under a set of strict guidelines, including implementing best practices, conducting business with integrity and on mission, and developing a dedicated and energetic team of administrators, support staff, nurses, and physician leaders with excellent leadership skills (Todd, 2015). To ensure the highest quality, the DHA is planning to rank all medical facilities by 2017 (Sahoo, 2015).

One benefit that MT providers have offered are luxurious facilities, improved levels of service quality, and a better overall experience than traditional providers of health care have offered in the past. Research conducted by Chou et al. (2012) demonstrated that not only did levels of expectation increase with MT but the experience also greatly influenced levels of satisfaction, which measure the differences between expectations and perceptions of service quality performance. These researchers found that a person's expectation of performance greatly affected his or her evaluation of service satisfaction. This means that the person who expected more from the experience was more satisfied (Chou et al., 2012). This expectation of confirmation is a relatively new theory that seems to explain the overall outcome of MT better than more traditional satisfaction theories. Many MT providers have invested in five-star facilities, gourmet dining, and entertainment facilities for family members who are accompanying the patient undergoing a particular medical procedure. The opportunity abounds to offer these services as a package deal that includes meals, lodging, and airfare.

There is also a dark side to MT, since it excludes patients who cannot afford to pay for the procedure they are requesting to be performed (Maung and Walsh, 2014). Although costs may run much lower than those for services performed in well-developed countries, those patients in less developed countries would still need a great deal of cash to be able to make use of the service. This is a side of MT that is often not discussed or even considered by those seeking such services.

To be successful in any country, leaders of the facilities (and government proponents) must have a "grasp of operating costs and how they used this data to fine tune pricing of their services, taking into account their integrated health delivery system, value proposition, preliminary target market identification, and the building blocks for their health tourism products" (Todd, 2015, p. 1). For continued success, leadership must develop a high level of clinical integration, health-care engineering and technology, and impressive physician credentials to bring to market a differentiated and unique MT product (Todd, 2015, p. 1).

Given this information, the UAE, and specifically the city of Dubai, has decided to invest heavily in MT, especially targeting the high-end customer/ patient. Keep in mind that Dubai has the world's largest airport, which is served by all major international airlines and a growing national airline called the Emirates. Figure A1.2 emphasizes the growing dependence of Dubai on the services and travel (transit) sectors as well as on MT. The DHA is working with the Department of Tourism and Marketing to "lock in" prices and is working with the General Directorate of Residency and Foreigners Affairs to simplify the process for obtaining a visa (Saberi, 2014).

The competition for these patients in this unique market segment is fierce. These patients are the wealthiest individuals in their countries and hold an upper-class standing. One approach to attract these patients is to highlight Dubai as a modern city with the latest technology and the most experienced physicians using a brand destination strategy (Melodena, 2008). Another strategy is to link the entertainment attractions, five-star service, and the MT industry, identifying Dubai as the "high-end" leader in this niche. A third strategy is to include the cost of rehabilitative services offering the same amenities (Figure A1.3).

Figure A1.2   Dubai city landscape (2015).

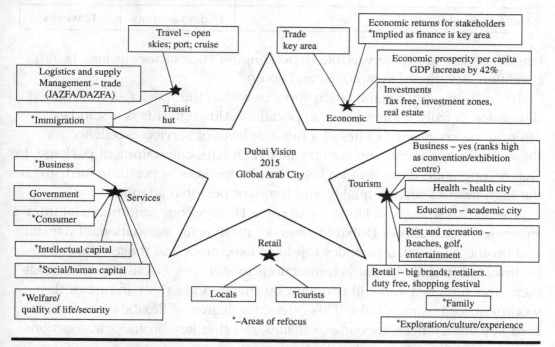

Figure A1.3   Dubai vision: Emphasis growing on medical tourism. (Adapted from Melodena, S. B., *Journal of Place Management and Development*, 1(1), 62–91, 2008.)

Rehabilitative Services

Rehabilitative services vary with each surgical procedure. Rehabilitation requires additional days in hospital or a medical facility. Table A1.2 provides some idea of a patient's length of stay for various surgical procedures. These

Table A1.2   Various Surgical Procedures and Length of Stay for Rehabilitation

Surgical Procedure	Hospital Stay	Rehabilitation
Arthroscopic surgery of the knee, shoulder, and hip	6 days (average)	5–7 days
Total hip replacement surgery	3–5 days	3–5 days
Total knee replacement surgery	3–5 days	3–5 days
Total shoulder replacement surgery	1 day	2–3 weeks
Stress fractures (dependent on type)	2–3 days	70–95 days
Spinal surgeries (lumbar, cervical, compression fractures, spinal fusion, spinal stenosis, and more)	3–20 days	5–20 + days
Cardiac rehabilitation	17 days average	12 weeks

lengths of stay are quite variable depending on such factors as age, health condition, severity of symptoms, and so on.

By including full rehabilitation services within the "package," this added dimension is truly an innovative application. Although this is a standard offering, no country has offered a five-star level of service excellence for these services, nor can any country match Dubai's entertainment package. In fact, recuperation times will be less than competitors (a presumption), given the high level of service quality and frequent personal attention.

The fourth strategy is Dubai's extensive IT, FreeZone, and financial infrastructure, which allows Dubai to promote itself as an international financial and business base that provides top-level executives and those required to be involved in daily business transactions to still seek elective medical treatment and surgeries and still maintain business conductivity in one of the world's major business hubs. This offers the degree of flexibility necessary to hold key conferences, meetings, off-sites, or other key business transactions while recovering or at a rehabilitation stage.

Summary

Expanding MT services meets the Vision 2020 goals for innovation in Dubai. One such service potential offering is rehabilitative services. Given Dubai's experience and reputation to date, such a new venture has both promise and potential. The DHA must decide whether to accept or reject such a proposal. Using the breakthrough innovations concepts and tools should provide sufficient information on the basis of which to accept or reject the project before conducting a full financial analysis.

CASE STUDY QUESTIONS (SUPPORT YOUR ANSWERS BY CITING THE LITERATURE):

1. What marketing strategies would your team propose to attract patients to this destination?
2. Given Dubai's first-class status, how would this attract patients and their family members? (Discuss how the amenities would attract patients.)
3. How would you position rehabilitative services as an innovation?
4. Can a "late comer" to this industry still be successful?
5. What would attract a patient (consumer) to Dubai, and what would deter a patient?
6. What strategies will be necessary to sustain growth?

Appendix II: Work Environment Survey

Examine the difference between the "perception" (odd numbered) and "expectation" (even numbered) scores. If perceptions exceed expectations (a positive difference), then the person is satisfied and the reality is better than expected. If expectations exceed perceptions (a negative difference), then the person is not satisfied and the reality is less than expected. These persons will not align well with the project.

Table A2.1 Perception and Expectation Score Chart

Statement number	In the "My choice" column, enter the numerical value (1–5) that best describes how much you agree (disagree) with the statements provided	Strongly disagree	Disagree	Neither disagree nor agree	Agree	Strongly agree	My choice
1	The project is expected to meet its objectives.	1	2	3	4	5	
2	Implementation is expected to complete on time.	1	2	3	4	5	
3	No delays are expected in meeting the time lines.	1	2	3	4	5	
4	The project is expected to be successful.	1	2	3	4	5	
5	Support for the project remains unchanged.	1	2	3	4	5	
6	Performance is expected to remain at similar levels.	1	2	3	4	5	
7	Expect that customers or users will perceive item as innovative.	1	2	3	4	5	
8	Expect that few changes will be made to the project.	1	2	3	4	5	
9	The project team has performed as expected.	1	2	3	4	5	
10	Expect management to continue support for this project.	1	2	3	4	5	
	Scores	AYG perceptions	0	AYG expectation	0	Difference	0
	Scores	Range perceptions	0	Range expectation	0		

Statement number	Instructions: Select the number that best describes how much you agree with each statement and record that number in the "My choice" column	Strongly disagree	Disagree	Neither disagree nor agree	Agree	Strongly agree	My choice
1	The work environment supports creativity.	1	2	3	4	5	
2	I have confidence in my own abilities to solve problems.	1	2	3	4	5	
3	My workplace provides me with challenges.	1	2	3	4	5	
4	The workplace enables me to be creative.	1	2	3	4	5	
5	The work environment is open to new ideas.	1	2	3	4	5	
6	There is a sense of cooperation among employees.	1	2	3	4	5	
7	Management rewards improvements.	1	2	3	4	5	
8	Work demands are not overburdening.	1	2	3	4	5	
9	My workplace encourages change.	1	2	3	4	5	
10	Trust is valued in my workplace.	1	2	3	4	5	
Total	Average scores	DIM 1	#DIV/0!	DIM 2	#DIV/0!	DIM 3	#DIV/0!
Total	Range scores	DIM 1	0	DIM 2	0	DIM 3	0

Calculation

Category 1 score = confidence, challenges, and trust-statements (2+3+6+10)/4; Range = max-min

Category 2 score = creativity-statements (1+4+5)/3; Range = max-min

Category 3 score = perception of work environment-statements (7+8+9)/3; Range = max-min

Interpretation

Choose the component (item) with the largest average score. The higher the score, the more the individual values a particular "value" of innovation. Large ranges (greater than 1.5) indicate inconsistency and therefore reduce reliance on a particular value.

Figure A2.1   Work environment survey.

Statement number	Instructions: Select the number that best describes how much you agree, placing that number in the "My choice" column	No value	Of little value	Has some value	Valued	Of great value	My choice
1	The innovation comes from within the organization	1	2	3	4	5	
2	How many people it involves	1	2	3	4	5	
3	How much it costs	1	2	3	4	5	
4	How long it takes	1	2	3	4	5	
5	How much profit it makes	1	2	3	4	5	
6	Maintaining competitive advantage over time	1	2	3	4	5	
7	The sustainability of the benefit	1	2	3	4	5	
8	The time to implement the innovation is short	1	2	3	4	5	
9	The value the innovation offers to the organization	1	2	3	4	5	
10	The innovation uses internal talent	1	2	3	4	5	
Total	**Average scores**	DIM 1	#DIV/0!	DIM 2	#DIV/0!	DIM 3	#DIV/0!
Total	**Range scores**	DIM 2	0	DIM 3	0	DIM 4	0

In the "My choice" column, enter a number that represents your perception. Use the following formula to construct an average and range value.

Costs, Profits: Average (Statements 3+5+6+9)/4; Range = max-min
People: Average (Statements 1+2+10)/3; Range = max-min
Time : Average (Statements 4+7+8)/3; Range = max-min

Interpretation
The largest average value (with a range less than 1.5), indicates the innovation type the individual. Large ranges indicate inconsistency.

Figure A2.2 Value of innovation survey.

Statement number	Instructions: Check the box that best matches your understanding of how innovation is defined by each statement	Undefined	Poorly defined	Marginally defined	Defined	Well defined	My choice
1	A new discovery	1	2	3	4	5	
2	New or novel (unique) products and services	1	2	3	4	5	
3	Making something better	1	2	3	4	5	
4	Replacing what does not seem to work	1	2	3	4	5	
5	Improving products and services over time	1	2	3	4	5	
6	Improving something to make it better	1	2	3	4	5	
7	Changing what does not work	1	2	3	4	5	
8	A new invention or patent	1	2	3	4	5	
9	Improving on something that already exists	1	2	3	4	5	
10	Changing for the better	1	2	3	4	5	
Total	Scores	New	#DIV/0! Improved	#DIV/0!	Change	#DIV/0!	
Total	Scores	New	Improved 0		Change 0	0	

Interpretation

Enter a number in the "My choice" column that represents your perception. Use the following formula to construct an average and range value.

New: Average (Statements 1+2+8)/3; Range = max-min
Improve: Average (Statements 3+5+6+9)/4; Range = max-min
Change: Average (Statements 4+7+10)/3; Range = max-min

The largest average value (with a range less than 1.5), indicates the innovation type the individual. Large ranges indicate inconsistency.

Figure A2.3   Perceptions of innovation.

SMART criteria evaluation weighting					
Instructions: Score each objective as to its SMART format. Use a simple five-point Likert scale to rate importance	Specific	Measurable	Attainable	Relevant	Timely
First class services					
Capacity for handling various rehabilitative procedures					
Ability to accommodate family members					
All inclusive "resort-type" setting					
Cost must have demonstrated value					
Score	0	0	0	0	0

Importance scale
1. Very unimportant
2. Unimportant
3. Neither unimportant nor important
4. Important
5. Very important

Figure A2.4 SMART criteria evaluation.

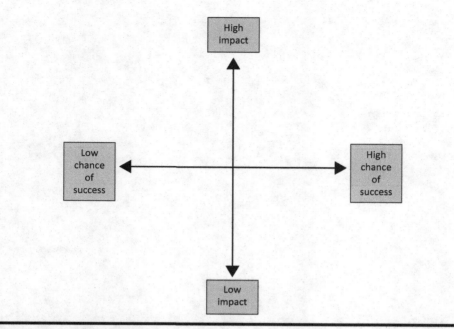

Figure A2.5   Outcome evaluation.

Evaluation	Measure	Objective 1	Objective 2	Objective 3	Objective 4	Objective 5

Figure A2.6   Assumptions/limitations evaluation matrix.

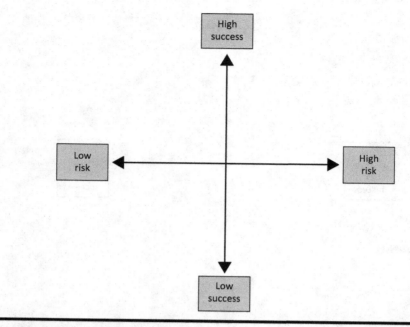

Figure A2.7   Outcome evaluation model.

Index

Printed in the United States
by Baker & Taylor Publisher Services